BOXED OUT OF THE NBA

BOXED OUT OF THE NBA

REMEMBERING THE EASTERN PROFESSIONAL BASKETBALL LEAGUE

Syl Sobel
Jay Rosenstein

Foreword by Bob Ryan

ROWMAN & LITTLEFIELD
Lanham • Boulder • New York • London

Published by Rowman & Littlefield
An imprint of The Rowman & Littlefield Publishing Group, Inc.
4501 Forbes Boulevard, Suite 200, Lanham, Maryland 20706
www.rowman.com

6 Tinworth Street, London, SE11 5AL, United Kingdom

British Library Cataloguing in Publication Information Available

Library of Congress Cataloging-in-Publication Data

Names: Sobel, Syl, author. | Rosenstein, Jay, 1955– author.
Title: Boxed out of the NBA : remembering the Eastern Professional Basketball
    League / Syl Sobel and Jay Rosenstein ; foreword by Bob Ryan.
Description: Lanham : Rowman & Littlefield, [2021] | Includes bibliographical
    references and index. | Summary: "This book tells the story of the Eastern
    Professional Basketball League. Formed in the 1940s, it was a pro basketball
    institution for over 30 years, featuring top players who just couldn't make the
    NBA-because of scandals, because they weren't quite good enough, or because of
    unofficial quotas on black players."—Provided by publisher.
Identifiers: LCCN 2020042768 (print) | LCCN 2020042769 (ebook) | ISBN
    9781538145029 (cloth) | ISBN 9781538145036 (epub)
Subjects: LCSH: Eastern Professional Basketball League—History.
Classification: LCC GV885.515.E37 S63 2021 (print) | LCC GV885.515.E37
    (ebook) | DDC 796.323/640974—dc23
LC record available at https://lccn.loc.gov/2020042768
LC ebook record available at https://lccn.loc.gov/2020042769

CONTENTS

FOREWORD

The final score was 121–103. I don't have to look it up.

I don't know the date off the top of my head, but I sure remember the score. That was the score when the Trenton Colonials defeated the Williamsport Billies in the first Eastern Basketball League game played in Trenton, New Jersey, after the Easton Madisons had relocated midseason in January of 1961. I was just about 15 years old and a basketball fanatic who played at the Lawrenceville School right up the road from the Notre Dame High School site of that game, and who was a huge fan of Nick "the Quick" Werkman, a Trenton native who was on his way to averaging 33 points a game for Seton Hall. I had a particular affinity for inventive inside players of any size, men who squeezed up shots from any and all angles, often with their backs to the basket. Half of the 6′3″ Nick the Quick's baskets came when he wasn't even looking at the hoop.

So it was when I laid eyes on Wally Choice that it was a basketball bromance of the highest degree. Wally Choice was Nick Werkman fully grown, a 6′5″ bruiser out of Indiana University who wormed and squirmed and simply willed the ball into the basket or, failing that, himself to the charity stripe. I will take the memory of his first box score in a Trenton Colonials uniform to my grave: 10 field goals, 20 free throws, 40 points. My kind of guy. I likewise remember that teammate Charlie Ross put up a 16–4–36 line. I've always been a box score freak.

The Trenton Colonials were a gift we hadn't even asked for. Local high school basketball was a major sporting concern in the Trenton area. Trenton Catholic had won a New Jersey Parochial A championship and the prestigious ESCIT Tourney in Newport, Rhode Island, back in 1957, and Trenton High was coming off a New Jersey Group IV state title. Notre Dame itself was on the move. We were doing fine.

But now we had been introduced to the Eastern League, a weekend conglomeration of middling eastern city franchises such as Wilkes-Barre, Sunbury, Allentown, Scranton, Hazleton, and, yes, Williamsport, Pennsylvania, plus Camden, New Jersey. And now we were a part of it.

I had new names to learn: Roman Turmon, Stacey Arceneaux, Frankie Keitt, Julius McCoy, Boo Ellis, Sonny Hill, Tom Hemans, Sherman White, the infamous guard Richie Gaines (complete with a menacing Fu Manchu), and oh, so many more, including my new hometown guys, an interesting bunch that included New York City playground legend Jumping Jackie Jackson, who legend said could pick a quarter off the top of the backboard and who made one pregame dunk I have *never* seen repeated. And who was 6'5".

What the Eastern League was happened to be the great-great-great-grandfather of today's NBA G League. It begat the Eastern Basketball Association, which begat the Continental Basketball Association, which begat the NBA D League, and which is now the NBA G League. There were no planes and not too many buses, either. You were one of the best basketball players on the planet outside the 80, 90, or 100 (as the league expanded) fortunate enough to be in the NBA itself. You drove from city to city. Sounds like Jules Verne–style science fiction now, but it was reality then.

Things could get a bit, shall we say, spirited. It often wasn't a matter of "if" the fight would start, but "when."

"If there were 27 games," recalled George Blaney, a future college coach of note, and a three-point maestro in his EBL days, "there were probably fights in 19 of them. And I mean brawls, people coming out of the stands."

Someone had to adjudicate all this, of course, and to be an EBL official was akin to being a prison guard at a state prison with lax security measures. One of those officials was future Naismith Memorial Basketball Hall of Famer Dick Bavetta, who by 1977 had risen from a young pup ref to become the league's supervisor of officials. A young EBL referee might not have gotten rich, but he gained invaluable experience in terms of how to handle a game. Take the night his efforts were not well appreciated by the fans in Sunbury. He was able to sneak out of his dressing room, and on his way out of the driveway he asked a policeman just exactly what was the commotion he was hearing. "The Mercuries lost tonight, but we're waiting for the referee," the cop said. "He won't make it back to New York."

Bavetta's day job in those days was on Wall Street. While his cohorts might have been rehashing their weekend dinner parties, Bavetta had other tales to tell.

"When it came to my turn," he said with a laugh, "I'd tell them about my police escort out of Scranton or the fan attacking me in the parking lot in Trenton."

The referees weren't the only ones not getting rich. "Between $50 and a $150 a game," recalled Blaney. Among those happy to receive that modest stipend was a 6'5" forward for the Scranton Miners named Carl Belz. He had been an all-Ivy player at Princeton, described later by Dave Gavitt as "a poor man's Billy Cunningham" and good enough to put up 14 points, 9 rebounds numbers for the Miners. "I got $50 a game," he once explained, "and rushed home to cash the check immediately." For his part, Blaney said he was paid in cash. You don't always need an Ivy League education to do the smart thing.

Carl Belz occupies a unique spot in EBL annals. Name another EBL ex-player who went on to become the director of a major art museum, the Rose Art Museum on the campus of Brandeis University.

But Carl Belz prized his EBL experience. He was, after all, a basketball player. "I used to drive to the games with Larry Hennessey, a Villanova All-American," Belz explained. "We'd talk basketball all the way up. I learned more basketball that year than in the rest of my career put together."

I would spend many a Saturday or Sunday night watching those Colonials, who once even hired my idol, Nick the Quick. And though I couldn't implement Nick's or Wally's moves in my actual games, I showed them off when coach Ed Megna wasn't looking at our 3-on-3 games.

Attached to each graduating Lawrenceville senior was a yearbook quote that was supposed to sum up that student. Here is the one given to Robert Peter (Bob) Ryan:

"What do you mean, study. The Colonials played last night."

G-d, I loved that league.

—Bob Ryan

PREFACE

This book had its inception in the early 1960s in Scranton, Pennsylvania, when our dads first took us to the Scranton Catholic Youth Center (CYC) to watch the Scranton Miners of the Eastern Professional Basketball League play. The Miners had Bill Spivey, Richie Gaines, Allie Seiden, and Tommy Hemans in their lineup, and unless you're a serious basketball junkie, 60 or older, and from either New York City, New Jersey, Philadelphia, or Kentucky, you probably never heard of those guys.

We don't recall the details of our respective first games (though one of us still has a program and scorecard from that game), but we do know that from the first game we were hooked on the Eastern League. We were hooked on the atmosphere in the smoky CYC, the raucous fans, the big, powerful men banging for rebound position underneath, the clever little guards deftly handling the ball and bravely driving inside into the stack of giants. We were hooked on the sweet *swish* of the ball falling through the net, the roar of the crowd, the taunts at the hapless referees who never seemed to do anything to please the home crowd. And we were hooked on the skill, toughness, and occasional antics of the men who were some of the best basketball players in the world, but whom few fans outside of the Eastern League had ever heard about.

For the next 10 years we spent winter weekend nights either watching them at the CYC, usually with one or both of our dads, or listening religiously to Miners' games on the radio (with "the Voice of the Miners," Ron Allen). Indeed, on at least one occasion the Miners and our religious obligations clashed. Jay clearly remembers when his parents made the mistake of scheduling his older brother Bruce's 1964 Bar Mitzvah party on the same night as a Scranton Miners home game against the Camden Bullets. Even worse, the game at the CYC was only a tempting one-block walk from the party venue. Solomonically, however, Jay's parents avoided a potential boycott by the guest of honor and agreed to let both sons, and their friends at the party, listen to the game on a pocket transistor radio.

We followed the Miners on the air to exotic places like Salesianum High School in Wilmington, Delaware, and rooted for them maniacally at the CYC against fierce rivals like the Camden Bullets with the incomparable Hal "King" Lear, the Sunbury Mercuries and the magical Julius McCoy, and the hated archrival Wilkes-Barre Barons with Levern Tart, Larry Jones, and Big Bob Keller (you probably never heard of those guys, either).

We knew the Miners' roster, the other teams' rosters, and the college histories of most of the players. We didn't care that it was the minor leagues. The proximity of the court to the bleacher-style seats at the CYC made the players more real and accessible to us than any NBA stars. They were pros performing so close that we could see the sweat pouring down their faces, the intensity in their eyes, their muscles gleaming. We got to watch them for maybe a buck or two a game, and they were ours.

The Eastern League—shorthand for the Eastern Professional Basketball League (EPBL) from 1946 to 1970, and then the Eastern Basketball Association (EBA) until it morphed into the Continental Basketball Association (CBA) in 1978—is a vanishing footnote in basketball history. Recent film histories of basketball have barely noticed it. The ESPN documentary *Black Magic*, about the history of African Americans in basketball, gives it a brief mention, while the 10-part ESPN documentary *Basketball: A Love Story* doesn't mention it at all.

The league hasn't fared much better in the basketball literature. Author Terry Pluto in his book about the American Basketball Association (ABA) titled *Loose Balls*[1] identifies the Eastern League as one source for players when the ABA formed in 1966, but doesn't fully capture just how many good players the ABA took from the league. Mark Johnson, whose father Andy played in the Eastern League after stints with the Harlem Globetrotters and in the NBA, devotes a chapter describing his dad's Eastern League experiences in his book *Basketball Slave*.[2] Prof. Ron Thomas includes a chapter on three great Eastern Leaguers who never got a chance to play in the NBA in his book on African American basketball pioneers, *They Cleared the Lane*.[3] And a 1971 *Sports Illustrated* article on the league titled "Toughing It Out around the Purgatory League," in listing several players who graduated from the Eastern League to the NBA or ABA, said, "The rosters tend to be, uh, flexible, the pay scale microscopic and the arenas prehistoric, but the players show lots of desire in the Eastern Basketball Association. Maybe because it's so nice to get out."[4]

As to fictional references, former Eastern League player and CBA coach Charley Rosen drew a comical and sometimes bawdy caricature of minor-league basketball in his book *Have Jump Shot Will Travel*,[5] based on his experiences in the league. Describing the players in the fictitious league portrayed in his book, Rosen said they were "to professional basketball as the Brooklyn Home for the Aged is to a hospital. All of them are incurably lame, some have diseased jump shots, some need hand transplants, and those in the wards are over the hill and halfway into the next valley."[6]

Perhaps the most affectionate tribute to the league came in a February 2001 *New York Times* article titled "The League of Dreamers Is No More," in which the writer, Harvey Araton, said: "A pugnacious basketball league that persevered in the manner of a large gypsy family for 55 years appears to have expired, leaving its scattered roster with only vivid memories and the satisfaction of having played for love of the game."[7]

Fifty-plus years ago, however, we and our boyhood friends could not have known the Eastern League's fate. Even if we had, we wouldn't have cared. Growing up in Scranton in the 1960s, with only eight or nine NBA teams and no cable TV, these athletes were larger than life to us then and remain so now. Kids in the big cites could worship Wilt, Russ, Oscar, West, and Havlicek. But in Scranton we adored the hunched-over, bespectacled persistence of Jim Boeheim (who perpetually had to push his glasses back up on his nose with one hand as he dribbled with the other), the deep set shot of three-point shooting specialist Bucky Bolyard (who amazingly had only one eye!), the magnificent athleticism of Willie Murrell (a 6'6" rebounding and scoring machine), and the instant offense of the prosaically named Swish McKinney. They were the players we'd emulate during our pickup games in the alley behind Wheeler Avenue or on the playground at Audubon Elementary School, pros one step away from the big time.

So when, after years of reminiscing about the Eastern League and frequently saying, "We should write a book," we actually decided to do just that. We entered the project thinking we were going to write a sentimental, sometimes comical, and mostly lighthearted book about the fun old days of minor-league basketball, filled with anecdotes about colorful characters who had a brief fling of low-level fame.

We were partly right, but mostly wrong.

Because as soon as we started interviewing former ballplayers and officials from the Eastern League and began to see the league through their eyes, we realized that the story of the Eastern League is much deeper, personal, nuanced, and socially significant. It's about serious basketball players competing in a tough, highly skilled, and physical league. It's about gym rats and playground ballers who would go anywhere, drive on snowy back roads through the night, and give up their weekends to get a good run against the best competition they could find, even in the most out-of-the-way places. It's about some of the best basketball players in the world and the limited opportunities they had to play at the highest level because of the relatively few spots available in what was still an emerging professional sport in the 1950s and '60s.

"I want people to know the Eastern Pro League . . . a lot of these guys belonged in the NBA,"[8] said Howie Landa, a former Eastern League player and coach, echoing the words of many other former Eastern Leaguers. (Sadly, Landa died in early 2020 and did not have an opportunity to read this book, to which he was an important contributor.)

The story of the Eastern League is also about great players whose opportunities to achieve their sport's highest level were restricted because of the ugly overtones of racism. It's about backward beliefs and unwritten quotas that relegated extraordinary players to careers in the shadows of professional sports rather than in the spotlights of Boston, New York, and LA. It's about talented young men who never had a chance to prove themselves at many of the top college basketball programs in the country, not because they didn't have the skill but because they were black.

The story of the Eastern League is about change. It's about small, largely white mining and factory towns in transition, adapting at first to a few black players on their teams, then learning to root for them, appreciate them, emulate them, and eventually take them in as their own. It's about the evolution of basketball, how the game was played in the Eastern League then and how it influenced the way the NBA game is played now. It's about subtle changes in attitude that have resulted in more open doors and opportunities.

The story of the Eastern League is about family men, successful professionals, coaches, teachers, businessmen, and the choices they made. It's about elite athletes who sometimes opted to begin their off-court careers rather than risk the uncertainties of careers in professional sports, but still wanted to keep playing at the next most competitive level they could find. It's about memories, roads taken, and glory days left behind.

Mostly, the story of the Eastern League is about men who adapted to their times and circumstances, most of whom have gone on to succeed in life with few, if any, regrets. Now, in their 70s, 80s, and 90s they have a story to tell, a story that might otherwise be lost. Our book gives these former players something they never thought they'd get—a chance finally to tell their story.

"I can't tell you how many times I've had other people associated with the league say . . . I need to write a book," said Rich Cornwall, a former Syracuse teammate of Boeheim's who played for nine years in the Eastern League. "I'm glad someone's finally doing it instead of talking about it."[9]

"I owe a lot to the Eastern League and to people like you that were in Scranton, and that remember that as vividly as I do," said longtime NBA referee Joe Crawford, a Philadelphia native who began his professional officiating career in the Eastern League. "I must think of the Eastern League . . . I probably think of it every day. . . . I'm so happy that you're doing the book because the league deserves it."[10]

The more we talked with former Eastern Leaguers, the more we realized that what we originally thought would be our story about our memories of the league was inevitably their story. And with that came the growing—and somewhat daunting—sense that they were entrusting us to tell it. We began to wonder whether in this, our first effort at writing a large-scale book, we would be up to the task.

It didn't help when Boeheim, as he described the "great players" and overall quality of the league, said, "It's hard to capture in a book just how good the league was and how good the players were."[11]

Nor did it help when Cornwall, asking how long it would take to write and publish the book said: "Listen, dude, we're not young anymore. . . . We want this done . . . while we're still above ground."

In the liturgy for the Jewish High Holy Day services is a traditional prayer called Hin'ni (pronounced "hin eh nee" and translated as "here I stand"), in which the congregation's prayer and song leader, called the cantor, beseeches the Lord to help him or her conduct the service properly and inspire the congregation, and that the Lord be moved by the congregation's prayers.

"Here I stand," the cantor implores, "even though I am unfit and unworthy for the task."

As we begin to tell the story of the men who played in the Eastern League, we feel very much like cantors. We hope, as Boeheim said, that we can describe just how good the Eastern League was and how talented were the players who competed in it. We hope we can describe the blue-collar cities and the fans and the atmosphere in the tiny arenas, the love and adoration the townspeople displayed for the players who gave their cities something to cheer about, even as the familiar industries and way of life around them were declining. We hope we can honor the perseverance of these elite athletes who learned to navigate the doors that were closed to them and nevertheless make successful lives for themselves and their families.

We also hope we can convey the sheer loss of talent, opportunity, and productivity that our country suffered because of outmoded racial attitudes. We hope we can explain how the Eastern League, in its way, contributed to change: change in the way the game of basketball was played, change in the skills required to play at the highest levels, and change in the attitudes of at least some of the people in the small towns around the league.

Mostly, we hope we can tell their stories. We hope you will understand what a tragedy it was that Bill Spivey never had a chance to become the greatest big man of his generation. We hope you can appreciate just how tough guys like Richie Gaines and Roman Turmon were, and the courage it took for defenders to stand in their way as they barreled down the lane. We hope you'll smile at the scrappiness and brilliance of Allie Seiden, the ultimate gym rat; respect the toughness and purposefulness of Carl Green; and admire the elegance of slender Tommy Hemans, whose scoring, rebounding, and grace elevated the game on weekends and the lives of children throughout the New York City schools during the week.

We hope you'll feel the thrill of seeing playground legends like Stacey Arceneaux, Herman "Helicopter" Knowings, and Joe Hammond in the flesh in a high school gym somewhere on a snowy night in Pennsylvania. We hope you'll appreciate the friendships of Howie Landa and John Chaney, Seiden and Green, and Stan Pawlak and John Postley, guys from different cultures and backgrounds, who played and traveled the back roads of the Eastern League together and bonded over their mutual respect for each other and the way they played the game. We hope you'll imagine the scoring brilliance of Julius McCoy, King Lear, Wally Choice, and Swish . . . and wish that somewhere you could find video of them in action and see just how sublime they really were.

So Hin'ni, here we stand, working together for the first time since we edited our eighth-grade class yearbook (precociously called *Those Were the Days* . . . yeah, right), about to tell the stories of the basketball players we watched, admired, and emulated as boys, but whom we didn't really get to know until we all were aging men and asked them to share their stories with us. May we be worthy of the task with which they have entrusted us, and may we bring to life their memories and our memories of the Eastern League.

ACKNOWLEDGMENTS

First and most important, we want to thank the former Eastern Leaguers who agreed to share their stories with us. Speaking with athletes and officials whom we idolized as children has been a special thrill. Learning about them as people and hearing their stories of their careers, the league, and what they did with their lives after basketball made this a much richer, more personal story. We are so grateful for their cooperation, assistance, candor, and enthusiastic support. In alphabetical order, they are: Walker Banks, Dick Bavetta, Waite Bellamy, George Blaney, Jim Boeheim, Hubie Brown, George Bruns, John Chaney, Rich Cornwall, Joe Crawford, Charlie Criss, Jim Drucker, Carl Green, Tom Hemans, Bobby Hunter, Harvey Kasoff, Steve Kauffman, Joe Lalli, Howie Landa, Maurice McHartley, Swish McKinney, Arthur Pachter, Stan Pawlak, Charley Rosen, Ray Scott, Willie Somerset, Tony Upson, Whitey Von Nieda, Bob Weiss.

A special thanks, too, to Art Pachter, the former owner of the Scranton Miners and Apollos, for not only sharing his inexhaustible collection of stories, but also his collection of photos that he had taken over the years. We recognize that Art's photos have given our photo spread in the center of this book a decided tilt toward Scranton, but his was the most substantial set of original photos that we could find using the various research tools available to us. And, having grown up in Scranton, we confess that the pictures of players we worshipped as kids had a special appeal to us. We are also obliged to disclose that Jay Rosenstein's father, Paul L. Rosenstein, was a longtime employee of Art Pachter's auto supply company in Scranton, and that when Jay and his brother Bruce were in high school they worked as statisticians at Scranton home games.

We were fortunate to find former fans from other Eastern League cities who remembered the league as fondly as we did. We've long admired Bob Ryan of the *Boston Globe* for his writing and his work as a television commentator. But who knew he had a similar childhood as ours and lived for Saturday and Sunday nights in Trenton the same way we did in Scranton? We are honored that he agreed to write the foreword for this book. Steve Kelley of the *Seattle Times* offered memories from his childhood as the son of one of the Wilmington Blue Bombers' owners. Imagine having Swish McKinney at your high school games yelling at you to shoot and spending a weekend in New York City with Art Heyman!

We talked to Hazleton fans turned sportswriters Ron Marchetti and Rev. Connell McHugh, who shared memories of their beloved Hawks, especially during the early years. Eddie White III, Brian Maloney, and Tim Maloney entertained us with stories of their respective grandfathers, who promoted pro basketball in northeastern Pennsylvania, magnified the Wilkes-Barre/Scranton rivalry, and were the kind of larger-than-life, small-town characters who built the Eastern League. Atty. Marvin Salenger and Felicita Pitt offered reflections on their friend and colleague Stacey Arceneaux.

We have talked or emailed with wives and family members of several former Eastern Leaguers. Mark Johnson's biography of his dad, *Basketball Slave: The Andy Johnson Harlem Globetrotter/NBA Story*, has been an especially valuable resource on the history of African Americans in professional basketball. Lee Pachter has welcomed us into her home and added her perspective to many of Arthur's stories. Their partnership is a thing of beauty. Their children, Judy and Jeffrey, have also lent support. Other family members who have provided assistance are Todd Bellamy, Troy Bellamy, Jonah Bronstein, Judith Green, Jill Greenspan, Robyn Landa, Pearl McKinney, Cleveland W. McKinney, Tony Upson Jr., and Arlene Von Nieda. Their interest in and support of this project are greatly appreciated.

We relied heavily on several sources for much of the historical, chronological, and statistical information in this book, starting with the Association for Professional Basketball Research website (APBR.org). Robert Bradley, the godfather of basketball research and founder and president emeritus of APBR, has been gracious with his time and expertise and reviewed a portion of the book. Chuck Miller, minor-league basketball historian and expert, shared notes and manuscripts from his unpublished "CBA Overall Guide," which has been a go-to reference. The NASL Jerseys website (nasljerseys.com) compiled by Dave Morrison and its listings of virtually every Eastern League player and team roster have helped us track player and team movements. Together, these sources—along with the *Eastern Basketball Association 1977–78 Official Guide*—have added a more granular level of detail than we could have achieved on our own.

We have also drawn on the ProBasketballEncyclopedia.com website, which is based on the work of basketball researcher Bill Himmelman, the blackfives. org website maintained by the Black Fives Foundation, and the peachbasket- society.blogspot.com website prepared by the Peach Basket Society. All three sites helped us gather biographical information on early Eastern Leaguers and on the history of African American players in professional basketball.

Throughout the process of writing this book, many members of the Eastern Basketball League (EBA/EBL) 1946–78 Facebook group, starting with the group's administrators, Jason Sereyka and Ed Kobak, provided valuable as- sistance. Jason and Ed have done a great service in creating and maintaining this page, which has some 1,000 members. Jason put us in touch with several former players and generously dug into his vast private collection to find photos and programs and allowed us to use them in this book. Other group members also provided assistance, including Jean-Pierre Caravan, whose background as a former employee of the Allentown Jets helped flesh out our knowledge of one of the league's premier franchises; Frank Thierer, another Allentown fan with an encyclopedic memory of the Jets and the Eastern League; Bill Mitchell and John Dimond, who provided photos from their personal collections; Jed Weis- berger, Arthur Quint, and Bruce Levy, childhood friends from Scranton, who have offered valuable suggestions; Matt Engel, who reminded us of the fervent Scranton/Wilkes-Barre rivalry; and Richard "Finner" Kane, Jim Marquette, Jim Nole, George Pawlush, and others whose recollections enhanced our memories and our manuscript.

It's good to have friends in the news media and sports information business. Buffalo newspaper and television sportswriter Jerry Sullivan reviewed a portion of the book and helped us get files from Rochester's short-lived Eastern League franchise. Bonnie Berko of ESPN, Jesse Dougherty of the *Washington Post*, Andy Fasnacht of *Lancaster Online*, and Bill O'Boyle of the *Times Leader* in Wilkes-Barre, Pennsylvania, provided contact numbers. Writer and former *Des Moines Register* columnist Chuck Offenburger shared stories of Stacey Arce- neaux and John Crawford. Mark Stewart of JockBio.com allowed us to use ma- terial from his site. Larry Dougherty of the Temple University Athletics Depart- ment, Pete Moore and Kelly Taylor at Syracuse University, and Nick O'Hayre of the Denver Nuggets helped us arrange interviews. And Borys Krawczeniuk, Pat McKenna, Marty Myers, and the venerable Guy Valvano of our hometown *Scranton Times-Tribune* offered information and assistance.

Other Scranton friends who helped us were Billy Timlin, who provided numerous contacts; Brian Clark and Margi Maloney Clark, who arranged an interview with her brother Brian; and Ken Meyer, Stanley Waleski, Joe Dente, Andy Brown, Jack Walsh, Tom McHugh, and Joe Agostinelli, who expressed enthusiasm for this project and offered suggestions.

Cindy Inkrote of the Northumberland County Historical Society provided photos, and an article she wrote a number of years ago helped re-create the atmosphere in the tiny Sunbury High School gymnasium. Former Harrisburg-area coach Jeff Thompson also offered information that helped enrich the story. Friend Steve Ross provided some valuable research assistance, as did Elisa Richardson of Newspapers.com.

Literary agent Jane Putch of Eyebait Management gave us confidence that our story was compelling and valuable advice on how to pitch it. Fellow Rowman & Littlefield authors Bijan Bayne and Douglas Stark offered encouragement and insight. Rabbi Adam Raskin helped with a Hebrew translation for the preface.

A special thanks to Rowman & Littlefield acquisitions editor Christen Karniski, who believed in our story and has helped us tell it better, and her assistant, Erinn Slanina, who has tirelessly helped us through all the details of bringing a book from manuscript to print.

Finally, our wives, Joan Sobel and Shelly Rosenstein. We could not begin to thank them enough for their support, encouragement, and all the many things they did while allowing us the time to work on this project. Joan pitched in as an IT guy, researcher, editor, and administrative assistant, and Shelly put her editor skills to use on reviews of draft text. We could not have done this without them. Daughters Marissa and Izzy Sobel and sons Greg and Michael Rosenstein also provided continuous support and encouragement and many good suggestions.

We also can't forget our moms, Gertrude Sobel and Harriet Rosenstein, for always having hot chocolate and a warm hug ready when we returned after frigid rides home. But we especially want to thank our dads, Isaac "Jack" Sobel and Paul Rosenstein, for bringing us (and Jay's older brother Bruce, who also provided encouragement for this book) to Eastern League games in Scranton and Wilkes-Barre starting in the early 1960s, when we were kids. If not for our fathers sparking our love of basketball, the Eastern League, and its players, this book would not have been written.

If we have failed to mention anyone who assisted us in this project, please know the omission is inadvertent and we are truly grateful for your help. And if, despite all the support from so many good people, there are any errors, omissions, or oversights in this book, they are ours alone.

Big Bill Spivey of the Scranton Miners goes for rebound over Harrisburg Patriot Stan Pawlak. Looking on from the second row at the far right are young coauthor Jay Rosenstein with his dad, Paul. *Source:* Arthur Pachter

1

WELCOME TO THE EASTERN LEAGUE

A Brief History and the Influences That Shaped It

Before Lebron, before Michael, and right around the time of Wilt, some of the best basketball players in the world traversed the treacherous mountain roads of Pennsylvania on winter weekend nights to play in high school gyms in gritty, blue-collar towns for $50 to $100 a game. Then, they'd drive home to New York, Philadelphia, and wherever else to get back by Monday morning— and their day jobs. Many of these players would be stars and first-round draft picks in today's 30-team NBA—but you probably never heard of them.

Welcome to the Eastern League.

The Eastern Professional Basketball League (EPBL) was born in 1946 amid a postwar boom of professional basketball leagues trying to capitalize on the popularity of big-time college basketball and suddenly plentiful entertainment dollars. Entrepreneurial businessmen and sports promoters "saw that after the war guys were coming back and they wanted to do something and they wanted to go out,"[1] said Scranton businessman Brian Maloney, explaining why his entrepreneurial grandfather, Joseph "Speed" Maloney, bought the Scranton Miners franchise in the American Basketball League (ABL) in the late 1940s, which eventually joined the Eastern League. "And these guys figured we could make a couple bucks."

In early 1946 two nationwide professional basketball leagues—the ABL and the National Basketball League (NBL)—already existed, and regional professional and local semipro leagues were popping up around the country. It was in that gold-rush kind of climate that the Eastern League was formed on April 23, 1946, six weeks before the Basketball Association of America (BAA) was launched in big cities around the country to compete with the ABL and NBL. (In 1949 the BAA would merge with the NBL to form the NBA.)

The Eastern League's organizers included Eddie White of Wilkes-Barre, Pennsylvania, and Robert Jamelli of Hazleton, Pennsylvania. Newspaper reports at the time indicated they had left the Penn State semipro league to form a more professionally run organization and avoid problems like frequent fights, hometown referees, and teams paying college athletes to play under assumed names (to protect the players' collegiate eligibility). Hazleton newspaperman William D. Morgan was elected as the league's first president.

The league's founders committed "to high standards, both in play and in conduct of business, and pledged to work at all times for the betterment of sports,"[2] according to an article in Morgan's newspaper, the *Plain Speaker*. They said the new league would discard the "rough and tumble" style of play that characterized professional basketball at that time and emphasize offense, citing "the success of college basketball at Madison Square Garden and other big arenas . . . as an indication that fans want to see basketball, not a 'modified form of indoor football.'"

White may well have had other reasons for founding the league. His grandson, Eddie White III, recalled: "There was a rumor that my grandfather wanted the Barons to get into the NBA [at that time the BAA]. The NBA was forming and starting, and Red Auerbach [then coach of the Washington Capitols in the BAA] was pissed off at the Barons and my grandfather . . . so he kind of blackballed him."[3]

"So," White continued, "that's why Harry Rudolph [another Wilkes-Barre area resident who became the Eastern League's head of referees and second president] and my grandfather said, 'Well screw it, we'll start our own league.' And they started the Eastern League. . . . I can remember as a little kid my grandfather would not root for the Boston Celtics because he was mad at Red Auerbach, because he said Red Auerbach was the reason Wilkes-Barre could not get in the NBA."

Teams from six cities tipped off in that initial 1946/47 season, including five from eastern Pennsylvania—Wilkes-Barre, Reading, Lancaster, Hazleton, and Allentown. (Scranton was awarded a franchise, but it was rescinded when the Scranton ownership group could not meet the league's 1,500-seat arena requirement.) The sixth franchise, Binghamton, New York, folded after seven games and moved to Pottsville, Pennsylvania. Basketball was popular in eastern Pennsylvania because "it was centrally located within an hour-and-a-half, two-hour drive from New York City," said Maloney. "At that time the [basketball] mecca was [New York City]. Nationwide, that was basketball."

In its early years, the Eastern Pro League, as it was often called, suffered growing pains. Teams changed hands and moved to different towns, sometimes several times in the same season. In 1948/49 the Reading Keys relocated to Allentown (which had lost its original team), played six games there, then moved back to Reading.

Eddie White's Wilkes-Barre Barons won the league championship in that initial 1946/47 season, defeating the Lancaster Red Roses in the three-game finals. Both teams bolted the league after the season to move up to the ABL. The Barons would become the ABL's dominant team, winning championships in three of the next five seasons (their streak interrupted for two seasons by their archrival and nemesis the Scranton Miners). Times being what they were, both Lancaster and Wilkes-Barre would eventually rejoin the Eastern League—Lancaster in 1948 after one season away, Wilkes-Barre in 1954 when the ABL folded.

At first, the Eastern League consisted mostly of local players from various colleges around Pennsylvania, as well as veterans of other professional and local semipro leagues. Players switched teams, switched leagues, and in some cases played on teams in different leagues at the same time. Writer and basketball historian Chuck Miller found evidence that the league suspended players for "double-dipping"[4]—playing for two teams in two different leagues during the same season—which was possible because the Eastern League played on weekends and other pro leagues had weeknight games. Some guys even tried to hide what they were doing by playing under assumed names. In 1951/52, the Eastern League and the ABL reached agreement to stop poaching each other's players.

In 1949, the BAA/NBL merger into the NBA reduced the number of professional teams and jobs available and brought more good players to the Eastern League, especially from the Philadelphia area. Sunbury Mercuries player-coach Stan Novak, a University of Pennsylvania alum and Philly area high school coach, brought several Philadelphia college stars with him to Sunbury (literally—they all drove to the games together), including Jack McCloskey (Penn) and Jack Ramsay (St. Joseph's), and made the Mercs one of the top teams from 1950 to 1954. McCloskey and Ramsay, of course, would go on to successful NBA coaching careers, and McCloskey was the general manager and architect of the championship Detroit Pistons' teams of 1989 and 1990.

During these early years Eastern League teams played exhibition games against ABL and NBA teams. They lost more often than not but usually stayed competitive. Eastern League teams also played exhibitions against independent barnstorming teams like the Harlem Globetrotters and the all-female All-American Redheads and All-American Cover Girls. The York Victory A.C. team played several exhibition games against the Masked Marvels, a team whose players wore masks and hoods. The Marvels were actually members of the Villanova University basketball team in disguise to protect their amateur status for college eligibility, including Paul Arizin, a future NBA star who would finish his career in the Eastern League.

Four significant events happened in the league during the 1954/55 season. First, Morgan, the league's president, resigned and was replaced by Harry Rudolph. Rudolph had sometimes officiated games with his son Mendy, who would go on to become a Hall of Fame NBA ref.

Second, the Wilkes-Barre Barons and Eddie White rejoined the league following the demise of the ABL and won their second championship. They would eventually win eight titles, tying them for most in league history and becoming one of the league's premier franchises.

Third, the Scranton Miners joined the league, replacing a Carbondale, Pennsylvania, franchise that folded three games into the season. (The previous iteration of the Miners owned by Maloney had withdrawn from the ABL in 1953, after turning down a chance to join the NBA.) The Miners, too, would become one of the Eastern League's flagship franchises. Their rivalry games with the Barons would become fierce and exuberant, filling both Scranton's CYC and Wilkes-Barre's massive Kingston Armory.

Last and most importantly, the league got an infusion of top-tier talent when several of the best former college players in the nation joined the Eastern League after they were implicated in gambling scandals and banned from the NBA. The league at first tried to block "the fixers," as they were often called, but eventually allowed them in.

The fixers presented a double-edged sword for the league. They tarnished the EPBL's image in the NBA's eyes. Eastern League officials had coveted a formal minor-league arrangement with the NBA, in which NBA teams would provide financial support for Eastern League teams to develop players for parent NBA teams and get players from the NBA in return. However any such plans were put on hold—along temporarily with Eastern League vs. NBA exhibition games—when the Eastern League welcomed the players the NBA had shunned.

On the other hand, the fixers gave the league credibility, if not in the eyes of NBA owners, in the eyes of serious basketball players who wanted to play against elite competition but couldn't land one of the very few jobs available at that time in the NBA—especially African American players.

Professional basketball had essentially been a segregated sport for its first several decades. Though a few black players had played in the NBL and ABL, the only professional options for most black players were barnstorming teams like the Globetrotters and the Harlem Rens. The NBA signed its first three black players in 1950, but the doors opened slowly. In 1955 and '56, the NBA's eight teams had a total of only nine black players.[5]

The Eastern League, however, had black players from the start. Three African Americans played for the Hazleton Mountaineers in the 1946/47 inaugural season, and in 1955/56, nine years before the NBA, Hazleton featured the first all-black starting lineup in organized professional basketball. African American players like Hal "King" Lear (Temple), Wally Choice (Indiana), Julius McCoy (Michigan State), Dick Gaines (Seton Hall), and Tom Hemans (Niagara) thrived by the late 1950s and are among the league's top all-time players. Many former players and observers said the NBA had an unwritten "quota system"[6] of no more than two or three black players per team, thus denying at least some potential NBA stars from getting a fair chance to play beyond the Eastern League.

By the late 1950s and early '60s, the league featured a wide-open, high-scoring style—enhanced with the adoption of the 24-second clock in 1955/56—and a tough, competitive reputation. With the ABL gone, the Eastern League—with the possible exception of the Amateur Athletic Union (AAU) leagues in the Midwest and West—was the next best alternative to the NBA (and the oldest league in the country thanks to its six-week head start on the BAA in 1946). Top-tier basketball players were drawn to the league either by choice, by necessity, or by word of mouth.

While the frequent movement of teams from town to town might suggest lack of fan support, the league was embraced by sports fans in many of the communities in which it played. Most of the residents of the league's small towns would never see an NBA or major college game in person, and televised sports was in its infancy. Local fans loved seeing former college and pro stars—many of whom they had read about in the papers—playing in person and representing their towns, and gave most teams a decided home court advantage.

For black players, however, the adulation only went so far. Though cheered and admired by home fans on the court, they sometimes faced off-the-court obstacles. Waite Bellamy, who later became one of the league's all-time top scorers with the Wilmington Blue Bombers, recalled coming to Scranton in 1963 and being turned away from an apartment rental when the landlord said, "We don't rent to coloreds."[7] Some black players who decided to live in the small, mostly white towns in which they played faced difficulty getting anything but menial jobs, even though they had college degrees.

The league survived a brief incursion in 1961 when Harlem Globetrotters owner Abe Saperstein formed a new American Basketball League (ABL). The ABL poached several top Eastern League stars. It folded, however, in 1962, and the players who had left returned, though not necessarily to their former teams.

The Eastern League did, however, retain one legacy of the ABL—the three-point shot. In 1964/65 the league owners adopted a 25-foot, three-point line. In its early years, three-pointers were a rare event, taken only by a handful of long-range shooting specialists like George Lehmann, who played for Sunbury, Allentown, and Trenton and would go on to a career as an outside shooter in the NBA and ABA.

Though the quality of play and players had improved substantially since the Eastern League's early years, the league still retained much of its seat-of-the-pants, ragtag style.

"Do you remember Sam Stith, Tom's brother?"[8] asked George Blaney, former college coach and NBA player who played five seasons in the Eastern League. "Tom played in the NBA for a long time, but Sam was a 6'2", 6'3" guard, was a very, very good player, was out of St. Bonaventure and was a good player in the league for a number of years. He played for Allentown one night and was traded to Camden after the game, so I played with him one night and played against him the next night. I'm pretty sure this is the G-d's honest truth, but the trade was for two basketballs, and I'm not sure if both of them were new, either."

Another unusual transaction involved the move of the NBA's Chicago Zephyrs to Baltimore in 1963. According to Harvey Kasoff, a co-owner and official of the Eastern League's Baltimore Bullets when the team folded after winning the league championship in 1961, the Zephyrs management "wanted to use the name Bullets, and our group had a patent on it. In other words, we owned the name Bullets. So they said, 'What do you want for the name?' So [the former Bullets president] says, 'Six season tickets, center court . . . and you can have the name Bullets.' And that's how they became the Baltimore Bullets [today's Washington Wizards] in the NBA."[9]

In 1962 the league got another boost when Arizin—a legitimate superstar who in 1996 was named one of the top 50 players in NBA history—decided to retire from the NBA and finish his career with the Camden Bullets rather than move to San Francisco with his Philadelphia Warriors and jeopardize his off-court career with IBM. Arizin played three seasons in the league, won an MVP Award, and led Camden to a league title.

By the early 1960s, Allentown's Jets had emerged as one of the league's perennial powerhouses and core franchises. The Jets won their first league title in 1961/62 behind Roman "Big Doc" Turmon's 32.5 points per game and repeated as champs the following year. They would win four more titles in the next nine years on their way to a total of eight, tying them with Wilkes-Barre for most in league history.

One reason for the Jets' success was an arrangement they had with the New York Knicks. Although the NBA and Eastern League still had not agreed on a league-wide working arrangement, the Jets had developed connections with the Knicks' management and became a proving ground for young players whom the Knicks wanted to develop before bringing to the NBA. The Jets weren't alone in getting former top college players on their rosters, as at least five former no. 1 NBA draft picks played in the Eastern League in the late '50s and '60s.

In 1965/66, the league expanded to 10 teams and two divisions and stretched as far away as New Haven, Connecticut. The following season it added teams in Hartford, Connecticut, and Asbury Park, New Jersey, and for the first time more Eastern League teams were located outside of Pennsylvania than in it. The Eastern League was solidly established as the second-best league around, just a step below the NBA.

Then it began to go downhill.

It started in 1967 with the formation of the American Basketball Association (ABA) as a direct competitor to the NBA. Looking for talent to fill its rosters, the ABA raided the Eastern League. Most of the Eastern League's top players—including Walt Simon, Levern Tart, Larry Jones, Hank Whitney, Willie Somerset, and Willie Murrell—left for higher salaries and the chance to play in a higher-profile, national league.

While the loss of talent didn't kill the league outright, it weakened it. Though many good players remained in the Eastern League, and some of the players who left eventually came back, the league had lost some of its prestige.

Its star power diminished even more as the NBA expanded. By 1970/71 the NBA was up to 17 teams while the ABA had 11, creating many more jobs for pro basketball players. By this time, too, racial quotas had ended, hastened by the ABA. Moreover, some players were going overseas to find work in emerging foreign leagues.

As the Eastern League's talent level declined, so did attendance. The small Rust Belt communities were suffering from the 1970s recession. Fans could stay at home almost every night of the week and watch NBA or ABA games on cable television. The small-town fans did not identify with the Eastern League clubs and players the way they had in the league's earlier days.

The league rebranded itself as the Eastern Basketball Association (EBA) in 1970, and Bill Montzman, Allentown's general manager, replaced the aging Harry Rudolph as president. League officials still coveted a formal working agreement with either the NBA or ABA or both, but settled for informal arrangements between individual clubs similar to the one that the Jets had with the Knicks.

In 1971/72 the league had shrunk to six teams, and in 1974/75 to four—Scranton, Allentown, Hazleton, and Cherry Hill, New Jersey (which had replaced Camden). *Sports Illustrated* said of a game that drew only 931 paying customers to Rockne Hall in Allentown, "The place bristled with indifference."[10] Player salaries—which had enjoyed a rise in the '60s, were back down to $50 a game, reflecting both the decline in talent and in paying customers.

In 1975, the league hired a 26-year-old Philadelphia tax lawyer, Steve Kauffman, as commissioner. Kauffman connected with the league through Stan Novak, who was still an Eastern League coach and part owner. Kauffman had contacted Novak hoping for an entry-level job and ended up becoming commissioner.

Two years later Kauffman was approached by a group of investors from Anchorage, Alaska, who wanted a franchise in the Eastern League. Kaufmann pitched the idea to the league's owners. Not all were eager to expand that far away, but ultimately the league let Anchorage in.

The expansion drew some attention to the Eastern League, and the new team was very popular in pro sports–starved Alaska. But the cost of travel was prohibitive to small-market teams, and old-line franchises like Scranton left the league.

The 1977/78 campaign ended with 10 teams in six states and the District of Columbia. Only three of those teams were from Pennsylvania. One of them, the Wilkes-Barre Barons, won the league championship by beating another, the Lancaster Red Roses, in the finals—just as in the old Eastern Pro League's opening 1946/47 season.

The following season the league, now under the direction of new commissioner Jim Drucker, changed its name to the Continental Basketball Association (CBA) to reflect its presence on both coasts. It continued until 2009, and would eventually get that long-elusive player development agreement with the NBA.

But the old, small-town Pennsylvania-based Eastern League that an ambitious group of post–World War II sports promoters had launched in Hazleton in 1946—the league that had at first provided recreation and entertainment for servicemen home from war, then a landing spot for some of the nation's brightest stars who got caught up in the sport's darkest gambling scandal, and ultimately for elite-level players unable to make the NBA because of numbers and race—that league was gone.

2

STARS OF THE EARLY YEARS (1946–1953)

It's 1946. The United States, riding the afterglow of victory in World War II, is feeling good. Young men have returned home from war. The economy is booming. People have some money in their pockets and are eager for entertainment. Young athletes whose lives, education, and athletic careers were interrupted by war want to get out of their military uniforms and back into their playing uniforms.

"We were all home from the war and everybody was hungry for sports," recalled Earl "Chick" Craig, in a 2001 interview with the *New York Times*.[1] Craig was a navy veteran who, before the service, had played basketball at collegiate powerhouse Long Island University (LIU) in Brooklyn.

The Eastern Professional Basketball League formed hoping to capitalize on this sports-hungry climate and the success of college basketball. The *Hazleton Plain Speaker*—whose Bill Morgan was the new league's president—announced that "Teams in New Eastern League Boast Many College Stars,"[2] and highlighted team rosters filled mostly with players from Pennsylvania schools. Many of the players were military veterans who had played on service teams during or after the war. Many were local boys, too, signed to play for teams in or near their hometowns. Some had experience in the professional and semipro leagues already operating in Pennsylvania, including the American Basketball League (ABL), the Penn State Professional League, and the Tri-County League. Indeed, so basketball-loving was eastern Pennsylvania at that time that some small towns like Hazleton and Wilkes-Barre would actually have two professional basketball teams—one in the Eastern League and one in the Penn State League.

In many ways, then, Stanley Lee "Whitey" Von Nieda was the typical early Eastern Leaguer. Von Nieda was from Ephrata, a small town near Lancaster. He played basketball at Penn State for two years before joining the army reserve and getting called up during the war.

"I had an incredible background in basketball in the service," Von Nieda said, as a paratrooper and playing with the Fort Benning, Georgia, paratroopers' basketball team.[3] In 1943/44 Von Nieda led the country, both college and service teams, in scoring. While in Berlin as part of the occupational forces, he played in a clinic conducted by several well-known college basketball coaches, including "the Baron," Adolph Rupp of the University of Kentucky.

"I participated in the clinic pretty well," Von Nieda remembered, "and Rupp said, 'You got to come to Kentucky.' I said I played at Penn State. He said, 'I don't care, I want you at Kentucky,'" and offered Von Nieda a scholarship.

But Von Nieda was determined to go back to Penn State. He got home in December 1945, and played in the Penn State League for Pittston, a small mining town between Scranton and Wilkes-Barre. He used an assumed name to protect his collegiate eligibility so he could finish his career at State College. A quick, 6'1" guard and deadly shooter, Von Nieda became one of the league's top scorers.

The Penn State League was a rough-and-tumble place, exactly the kind of hardscrabble semipro circuit from which the newly forming Eastern League hoped to distance itself. It wasn't just the players who were tough. The fans could be pretty rough, too.

"They nailed Art Hillhouse in the men's room," Von Nieda remembered.

Hillhouse was the 6'7" center for Pittston. He had played at LIU and eventually would play for the Philadelphia Warriors in the Basketball Association of America (BAA), before it became the NBA. But on this particular day he was playing for Pittston in a ramshackle, all-wooden gym in nearby Wilkes-Barre, and he took a pregame bathroom break. Big mistake.

"He went there," Von Nieda recalled, "and the Wilkes-Barre fans nailed [the door shut] in the men's room. And some of the Pittston fans went down to get tire irons to get him out of there, pry it open. . . . He didn't get out until about halfway through the fourth quarter. . . . So they took it seriously up there."

When Pittston's season ended, Von Nieda started working out at Penn State to get ready for the upcoming college season. But again someone came along tempting him to change his plans, this time Rothermel "Roxy" Wise, who had just bought into the fledgling Eastern League as owner of the Lancaster Red Roses.

"So Roxy Wise . . . called me and wanted me to play for them," Von Nieda said. "And I said, 'No, I have eligibility left with Penn State.' I fully planned on going back there to finish. . . . And he thought I was holding out for more money, I think. But I said, 'No, I just want to finish my collegiate career first.' And he kept upping the price a little bit. And so finally . . . he was up to $150 a game, which was a lot of money back then. Two games a week, and he promised there'd be an extra game a month, that he'd get an exhibition game or something like that. . . . So I wound up playing with Lancaster in the Eastern League that year."

Von Nieda, who already had established a reputation as a scorer, led the league that inaugural season with an average of 22.7 points per game—including a then-record 46 points in one game—much to the delight of Lancaster fans who loved rooting for the hometown kid.

"That's what I was to Lancaster. . . . I was a local boy, so I brought out a lot of support fanwise from the area. I think they were looking for all that kind of stuff," said Von Nieda.

Von Nieda's success also apparently caused at least some opposing coaches to employ innovative tactics to hold down his scoring. None more than Eddie White, one of the league's cofounders and a longtime owner and coach of the Wilkes-Barre Barons who won the championship in the EPBL's first year and then jumped to the ABL.

"He was into it," Von Nieda said of White. "He liked to win."

One of Von Nieda's signature scoring moves was a running hook shot.

"I was pretty accurate with it," he said. But when the Red Roses came to play Wilkes-Barre at the Kingston Armory, "unbeknownst to me, or anybody else, [White] would tilt the backboard just a little bit" to reduce Von Nieda's scoring ability.

Von Nieda found this out when, after the Eastern League season ended, White asked Whitey to join the Barons for a series of exhibition games against teams from the National Basketball League (NBL), which later would become part of the NBA. Von Nieda told White about his difficulty scoring in Wilkes-Barre, and White laughingly admitted why.

Von Nieda planned again to return to Penn State. But again, his basketball talent would get in the way. His performance in those exhibition games caught the eye of Leo Ferris, owner of the NBL's Tri-Cities Blackhawks (the predecessor to today's Atlanta Hawks). Ferris invited Von Nieda to his hotel room in Wilkes-Barre after one of those games and put down a wad of cash to induce the Ephrata boy to join the Blackhawks.

"Ferris, he gave me a bonus, a $2,000 bonus, up in Wilkes-Barre," Von Nieda recalled. "And I had to get a bus back to the school at Penn State for classes the next day. And so he said, 'Look, this is yours if you'll sign.' And there was $2,000 in cash. Well I never saw that kind of money at all. And so he said, 'I'll be right back,' and he left the room. And I'm sitting there by myself and I'm looking at my watch, and I got to make the bus. And I'm thinking the whole time if I left and left the money there, he could say I took it. And so I thought the best thing to do was, well, I'll take the money along and send it back to him. But I went back to the fraternity house, and we threw a party, and I didn't have enough money to send it all back then."

And that's how Von Nieda wound up getting into the NBL, and eventually the NBA, when the NBL and BAA merged in 1949. After two years with Tri-City and one with Baltimore, Von Nieda returned to Lancaster as player-coach for three seasons and was seventh in the league in scoring in 1950/51. As to college, he finally did finish his classes at Penn State but didn't do the student teaching needed to complete his degree.

Finishing second behind Von Nieda in scoring that first season was Bill Zubic of the Reading Keys. By the time the Eastern League began in 1946, Zubic was already a well-traveled veteran in Pennsylvania basketball circles. The *Hazleton Plain Speaker* referred to him as a "well-known star"[4] of the state's pro leagues, and indeed he was. Since graduating from high school in Philly in 1937, he had played in the ABL, Tri-County, and Penn State Leagues, with a break for military service during the war.

The 6'5" Zubic would be among the Eastern League's top scorers for the next four seasons, finishing first in both 1948/49 and 1949/50 and averaging over 22 PPG (points per game) for Lancaster. He was named four times to the all-league team and in 1950 won the first-ever Tommy Bell Memorial Trophy, given to the Eastern League's most valuable player. (Bell was a star Eastern Leaguer who died in 1949 at age 27. His last team, the Pottsville Packers, arranged a benefit game against top players from the league's other teams to raise money for Bell's widow, which became the forerunner of the league's annual All-Star Game.)

"I played with and against him many, many times," Von Nieda said of Zubic, "and he was a good ballplayer."

Casimir "Cas" Ostrowski of the Wilkes-Barre Barons was the EPBL's third leading scorer in the opening season, averaging 15.9 points per game. A native of the town of Wyoming, near Wilkes-Barre, he attended the University of Scranton for two years and then joined the navy in World War II. When the war ended, he returned home to play with Wilkes-Barre in the Penn State League in

1945/46 and then led the Barons to the championship in the Eastern League's opening 1946/47 season.

When the Barons moved to the ABL the following season, Ostrowski became one of that league's top stars. In 1951/52, Ostrowski returned to the Eastern League with the Pottsville Packers and was an all-league selection.

"He was a pretty smooth ballplayer," Von Nieda remembered. "He'd move around well so I could make a pass to him for an assist a lot of times. He could shoot the ball. He was no shrinking violet when it came to that."

Ostrowski had plenty of help from the Chanecka brothers, Bill and Steve, in taking the Barons to the 1946/47 championship. The Chaneckas were a bit unusual for the Eastern League in that they weren't native Pennsylvanians. They came from Binghamton, New York, about 75 miles north of Wilkes-Barre, just across the state line. Bill, the younger and taller at 6'4", entered the navy during the war, playing for a navy team based in Iowa. Like Ostrowski, he played briefly for Wilkes-Barre in the Penn State League after the war and then joined the Barons for that initial Eastern League season. He finished seventh in scoring to complement Ostrowski and paired with brother Steve to form a formidable backcourt.

Van Nieda had great respect for Bill Chanecka, saying that of the half dozen or so early Eastern Leaguers who he thought were good enough to play in the NBA, Chanecka was the only one who would have made it for sure.

Indeed, when the Barons jumped to the ABL starting with the 1947/48 season, Chanecka would become one of that league's top players, once scoring a league-record 58 points in a game, and was the ABL's MVP in 1949. In 1951 he returned to the Eastern League with Pottsville and played the next seven seasons for Williamsport, leading them to two league championships and being selected to three all-league teams.

The Harrisburg Senators joined the Eastern League in its second season and with them came Joe Cackovic, who would become the league's top scorer. "Cacky" was from the Steelton area outside of Harrisburg, the son of a Bethlehem Steel worker. He presumably joined the Eastern League right out of high school, since no record can be found of either college, pro, or military playing experience. He would be among the league's scoring leaders for the next four seasons and was a three-time all-league pick.

"Joe Cacky, he was all right," said Von Nieda. "He played for me at Lancaster when I came back. He was a good ballplayer. . . . And he wasn't with too many good players when he played at Harrisburg, and so consequently he didn't do as well as he could have or should have."

Good players weren't all the Senators lacked. They didn't have a true basketball arena in Harrisburg either, and had to split their games between the exotically named Madrid Palestra and the Zembo Mosque, two buildings that were large enough to hold a court and bleachers.

After the BAA and NBL merged in 1949 to form the NBA, the NBA began consolidating franchises. By 1953/54, it had reduced the number of teams from 17 to eight. The following year, the struggling ABL folded. Thus, the number of jobs available on major-league basketball rosters shrunk dramatically, and more good players from top college programs—especially from the Philadelphia and New York areas—looked for work in the Eastern League.

Stan Novak was one of the first to open the Philadelphia pipeline. Novak was a star for the University of Pennsylvania basketball team but left in 1944 to become a naval officer. He returned to Penn after his service to graduate and finish his playing career and then coached the Penn freshman team while getting his master's degree in education.

In 1949, while teaching and coaching at Springfield High School in suburban Philadelphia, Novak took a weekend job as player-coach of the Sunbury Mercuries. Novak's connections in the Philadelphia-area basketball community brought some of the league's best-known early stars to Sunbury. First it was former St. Joseph's player Paul Senesky and Temple alum Jerry Rullo, who in 1950/51 led the Mercs to their first and only Eastern League championship. Senesky was the league's top scorer that year with 21.5 PPG, while Rullo was eighth with 14.0. The league selected Rullo, a 5'10" playmaking guard, as its MVP.

The following season Novak brought fellow Penn alum Jack "the Giant Killer" McCloskey and St. Joe's grad Jack Ramsay to Sunbury, and for the next several years they would team with Rullo (in between his occasional trips to the NBA) to continue to make Sunbury one of the league's top teams.

McCloskey had played football at the University of Pittsburgh before leaving school to serve as a lieutenant in the Marines. After the war, McCloskey went to Penn where he played three varsity sports. A native of Mahanoy City in the northeastern Pennsylvania coal country, he began his Eastern League career with nearby Pottsville in 1948/49. In 1952/53 with the Mercs, McCloskey led the league in scoring with a 22.7 average and the following year finished third at 17.4. He was named the Eastern League's MVP after both seasons, the first and only player to do that for the next 20 years. He was picked to five all-league teams.

"He was a rugged kind of individual,"[5] remembered Rev. Connell McHugh, a Hazleton priest who grew up in Hazleton as a die-hard fan of the hometown Hawks and in recent years has written articles on the Eastern League for a Hazleton publication.

Ramsay, too, had his college education interrupted by World War II, serving in the navy before returning to St. Joe's. He began his Eastern League career in Harrisburg, teaming with Cackovic in 1949/50 to take the Senators to the championship finals, and the following season was named to the all-league team. Joining Sunbury in 1951/52, Ramsay paired with McCloskey to give the Mercuries a potent one-two scoring combination—"a pair of Jacks," as they were sometimes called—and was a four-time all-league selection.

"They were both very smart players," said Von Nieda.

McCloskey, Ramsay, Rullo, and Novak formed a tight group. They drove to games together and socialized off-court.

"Novak was the best man at Jack Ramsay's wedding,"[6] remembered Arthur Pachter, longtime owner of the Scranton teams in the Eastern League, for whom Novak would later coach. "They were all one big crew."

"They . . . were like thick and thin,"[7] remembered John Chaney, longtime Temple University coach and another Philly area player who would also play for Sunbury under Novak. "They were all responsible for building that league up."

In 1996, in commemoration of the 50th anniversary of the Eastern League's founding, the Continental Basketball Association (CBA) selected two all-time teams: One from the 1946–1978 era of the EPBL and EBA that is known as the Eastern League, and one for the CBA era. McCloskey and Bill Chanecka were named to the all-time Eastern League team, and Novak was picked as coach. Receiving honorable mention were Cackovic, Ramsay, Rullo, and Zubic.

And what of Chick Craig, the navy vet hungry for sports? He would be on the Allentown Jets' roster for that opening season in 1946/47 and enjoyed a nine-year career as a player, mostly with the Wilkes-Barre Barons. Like Novak, Craig would go on to a long, successful coaching career in the Eastern League and received honorable mention on the all-time team as coach.

The league's early stars represent a quaint and innocent era in professional basketball—a time of optimistic small-town promoters with big ideas, guys coming home from war eager to play sports, basketball-hungry fans rooting for their hometown boys, and a few big-city stars. The next era of Eastern League stars represents another side of sports, however, a darker side that would cast a cloud over a talented but tainted group of players and, with them, the league.

3

THE FIXERS . . . AND ONE FRUSTRATED SUPERSTAR

The New York college basketball scene was on a high after the City College of New York (CCNY) team won both the 1950 National Invitation Tournament (NIT) and the NCAA championship in games played at Madison Square Garden. Ed Warner, Floyd Layne, and Ed Roman were the heart of the 1949/50 CCNY team, under the legendary head coach Nat Holman, that won both championships in the same year—the first and only team ever to do that (because now the NIT serves as a consolation tournament for teams not selected for the NCAA tournament).

Meanwhile, over in Brooklyn, Long Island University (LIU), a perennial national power coached by the renowned Clair Bee, was having great success in the early '50s thanks to phenom scorer Sherman White, generally considered the best player in college basketball.

But in January 1951, Manhattan College officials notified New York City police that two former players had approached a current player—Junius Kellogg—to offer a $1,000 bribe for shaving points in a scheduled game against DePaul. Manhattan was a 10-point favorite, and the former players wanted Kellogg to ensure that the Jaspers won by a smaller margin. Detectives instructed Kellogg to go along with the scheme and equipped him with a wiretap to help seal the case. After the game, they arrested the two former players, who, under questioning, revealed connections that led police to gamblers bankrolling the operation, and from there, to players on other city teams who were taking bribes.

A month later, on February 18, 1951, which also was a month before the NCAA tournament, the college basketball world was shaken even more. This time New York City district attorney Frank Hogan and police arrested several current players from the beloved CCNY squad, including All-American forward Warner and star center Roman, as the team arrived by train at Penn Station at 2:00 a.m., after a game against Temple University in Philadelphia.

Two days after the CCNY arrests, Hogan apprehended Sherman White and other LIU players. This was one day after the *Sporting News* named White, who was averaging 27.7 points per game, the College Basketball Player of the Year. At the time of his arrest, White needed just 77 more points to set an all-time scoring record in college basketball. After suspensions were handed out, however, that would never happen.

In the coming months, more college players were charged with fixing games, including three who played at the University of Kentucky (UK) under coach Adolph Rupp. The most notable were Ralph Beard, a three-time first team All-American guard in 1947–1949 and an NBA All-Star with the Indianapolis Olympians by 1951, and Alex Groza, a three-time All-American center at UK and NBA Rookie of the Year with Indianapolis in 1951.

While gambling on college basketball games was common in those years, especially in the New York area, the illegal fixing of games by players was devastating to the sport. Fans were appalled by the number and quality of the teams involved, the arrests and downfall of so many great players, the media hype, and the dark, mysterious world of gambling and organized crime, including a relatively new way of paying players to engage in "point shaving." That meant corrupted players on a team that, for example, was favored to win by seven points (the "point spread") could play to win, but they would need to keep their team's margin of victory below seven points. By doing so—by not "covering" the point spread—the gamblers could profit big-time by betting on the opponent to keep it close and lose by less than the point spread.

For these young men in college, many of whom were poor or naive, it was much easier to say yes to a gambler offering a bribe when they weren't being asked to help their team get beaten.

LIU's White, who many basketball experts still consider one of the best college players in New York basketball history, led detectives to $5,500 in an envelope hidden behind a dresser drawer at the Brooklyn YMCA where he was living. According to basketball chronicler and former Eastern League center Charley Rosen in his book *Scandals of '51: How the Gamblers Almost Killed College Basketball,*[1] Judge Saul Streit called White a hardened criminal and made racial slurs before sentencing him to 12 months in the tough Rikers Island jail in New York City. White was released after about nine months. He also denied having any kind of prior record, and he and others for years would question whether racism played a role in his severe punishment.

Of the City College players, Warner got hit the hardest. Warner escorted police to $3,050 in cash, hidden in a shoe box in the basement of his aunt's house. He was the only CCNY player to be sent behind bars, six months at Rikers Island. Starting guard Al Roth, another CCNY fixer sentenced to six months in jail, handed over $5,060 from a safe deposit box, but the judge later agreed he could join the army instead. And Roman, whose attorney brought $3,000 to the authorities, and Layne, who took detectives to $3,000 buried in a flowerpot in his mother's bedroom, were among those who received suspended sentences.

But there was more punishment: all 32 players sentenced in the scandals were banned by the NBA. And no player was hurt more than Sherman White, who in 1951 was expected to be the New York Knicks' first-round "territorial" draft pick (a way for NBA teams to select popular players from colleges in their area), earn big bucks, and put championship banners at Madison Square Garden. But that hope would be crushed. Instead, White was barred from the NBA, and the Knicks lost in the 1952 and 1953 NBA Finals to the Minneapolis Lakers.

Similar gambling-related incidents led to NBA prohibitions of other college superstars around that time.

Jack Molinas, a colorful Columbia grad who could almost score at will, was drafted by the NBA's Fort Wayne Pistons in 1953. He did so well so soon that he was named as a rookie to the Western Division All-Star team in January of 1954. But before that contest could be played, Molinas was barred from the NBA for gambling on games. NBA commissioner Maurice Podoloff said Molinas bet on 10 Pistons games—all picking his team to win, not to lose—and that his winnings totaled $400. Molinas's defense was that bets he placed on the Pistons to win "were incentives to make me play better,"[2] reported Charley Rosen in his book *The Wizard of Odds: How Jack Molinas Almost Destroyed the Game of Basketball*, about Molinas's life on and off the court.

While Podoloff agreed that Molinas never intentionally lost any games, he refused to allow him back in the league. "The suspension is tantamount to life expulsion regardless of whether a crime has been committed,"[3] Rosen quoted Podoloff as saying. "The relevant point is that betting by a player is a violation of his contract, and that's why Jack Molinas was suspended."

And Bill Spivey, a seven-foot center at Kentucky from 1949 to 1951 who most basketball observers at the time thought was destined for future stardom as the next dominant big man in basketball, also was blocked from the NBA. An All-American and the leading player on UK's 1951 NCAA championship team, Spivey was accused by former teammates Walter Hirsch and Jim Line of joining them in taking bribes for point shaving. Spivey was never charged with point fixing, and in a perjury trial in New York in January of 1953 a hung jury favored Spivey by a vote of 9–3.

Even though Spivey was not found guilty of any wrongdoing and he passed two lie detector tests, in April of 1953 the NBA board of governors voted to ban from the league anyone implicated in the point-shaving scandal, including Spivey. He would never have the opportunity to become the NBA's best center after George Mikan and before "Wilt the Stilt" Chamberlain.

The NBA's loss soon became the Eastern League's gain. After the EPBL initially rejected "the fixers," the policy changed, most likely to improve attendance by bringing in more NBA-quality players. Hirsch, who played on three NCAA championship teams for the UK Wildcats, was the first of the scandal-tainted players to be accepted by the Eastern League, starting in the 1952/53 season with the Harrisburg Capitols.

Others soon found a home in the Eastern League, including three of the best former college basketball players in the country—White, Molinas, and Spivey. CCNY's Roman, Layne, Warner, and Roth also entered the Eastern League. In the words of Charley Rosen, the Eastern League "finally hit the jackpot"[4] when it began to admit the banned players.

While many Eastern League fans initially jeered at the fixers, they eventually became popular because of their talent.

"People kind of booed at first . . . but then there was a great enthusiasm for them," recalled Rev. Connell A. McHugh, who started attending Hazleton Hawks games in the early 1950s when he was eight years old and in recent years has written profile pieces on Eastern League players for a local magazine. "They [the fans] really enjoyed the basketball. It became very popular here. The players were very well liked—the quality of the basketball. They played hard."

It would be hard to overstate how much talent the banned players added to the league. Yes, they tarnished the Eastern League's image in the eyes of NBA owners and prevented the Eastern League from getting a minor-league-type arrangement with the NBA, whose owners did not want to be associated with the fixers in any way. But those players also elevated the competition, gave the league credibility in the basketball-playing community, and attracted more top players—especially African Americans—who wanted to go up against elite competition but couldn't find jobs in the NBA.

As John Chaney, longtime Temple University basketball coach and an Eastern League star from 1956 to 1962, put it: "Sherman White was the future of the Knicks. That man was something else . . . Floyd Layne—all these guys are All-Americans. Ed Warner. They were All-Americans, man!"

"I was always taken, always to this day, with the talent level of the Eastern Basketball League," said Ray Scott, an Eastern Leaguer in the late 1950s before an 11-year playing career in the NBA and ABA and three-plus years as coach of the Detroit Pistons. "But I was also taken with the sociological impact because you took the 'bad guys' from basketball and legitimized them. And no one in America was doing that. They were persona non grata."[5]

Scott added: "It was interesting to me as a kid, as a 20-year-old . . . to begin playing against Bill Spivey, who was an All-American at Kentucky. Ralph Beard. I mean All-Americans; I mean legendary All-Americans that were forced to play in the league because of the gambling . . . People forget that Sherman White was one of the greatest All-Americans of all time, to this day. And so you had Sherman White, you had the kids from NYU, Ed Warner and Ed Roman, and just incredible players. But those guys wound up in the Eastern League. So that was the first group. This was the group there was no future for them at all in the NBA."

In addition, these players established a conduit between the Eastern League and New York City's deep pool of talent. Star city players like Tom Hemans (Niagara), Stacey Arceneaux and John Crawford (Iowa State), Allie Seiden (St. John's), and Chet Forte (Columbia, who would later go on to fame as a sports television executive) joined the league. They and the fixers brought the kind of fast-paced, high-scoring, offense-minded game that the league and its fans craved.

White, Spivey, and Molinas had the longest and most productive Eastern League careers of the players implicated in the scandal. They offer perhaps the three most compelling stories.

Sherman White joined the Eastern League in the 1953/54 season with the Hazleton Hawks, averaged 29.1 points, and was named to the all-league first team. In 1954/55, he led the league in scoring with 27.2 points per game for Hazleton.

White eventually played in the Eastern League for 10 years (seven with Hazleton, two with Baltimore, and his final one in Wilkes-Barre in 1962/63), and he consistently averaged near 30 points a game.

Rosen, the author who played briefly in the Eastern League for Scranton and Camden in 1962, left no doubt about how good White was on the court. "Sherman White was amazing!" Rosen said. "He was the best basketball player in the country. He was the Dr. J, the Michael Jordan before either of those guys. He was amazing."[6]

"How do you compare somebody to Sherman White?" said Ray Scott. "Man, Sherman White was the best player, at one time the best player in America."

"He was way ahead of his time,"[7] Lou Carnesecca, the Hall of Fame coach for St. John's and the New York Nets, said when White died in 2011. "He was the first guy his size to play facing the basket. He was truly a great player and one of the best players of his time."

Jack Molinas entered the Eastern League in the 1954/55 season, signing with the Williamsport Billies and reportedly being the highest paid player in the league at around $150 a game. In his opening appearance, the 6'6" Molinas scored 34 points in a win over Hazleton. By the end of the regular season, Williamsport was in first place (but was upset in the first round of the playoffs) and Molinas finished second behind White in scoring, with an average of 22.8.

The next season, 1955/56, Williamsport again won the regular season and again lost in the playoffs, but this time Molinas took the scoring title with a 27.4 average, just ahead of White with 26.1, and he was named the league's Most Valuable Player.

"Flat out, Jack Molinas was one of the greatest players to ever play the game of basketball,"[8] said Hubie Brown, a former Eastern Leaguer and a longtime NBA coach and TV analyst, in *The Wizard of Odds*.

"Jack Molinas had as much skill as any basketball player I've ever seen," recalled Reverend McHugh. "He could play all five positions and play them well. . . . Had a one-hand push shot from three-point range today, and he had a deep corner hook shot which would be a three-pointer—a 25-foot hook shot! You wouldn't believe it unless you've seen it," McHugh said. "Jack Molinas was the smoothest player that there was. I've never seen anybody better than that."

The 1960/61 season was a busy one for Molinas as he was named player-coach for the Hazleton Hawks. Although he averaged 30 points a game, the team finished in last place. Molinas remained in the Eastern League for one more season, playing seven games with the Wilkes-Barre Barons and averaging 17.7 points.

Bill Spivey spent the early 1950s "barnstorming" in various exhibition games, opposing the Harlem Globetrotters and dabbling in the American Basketball League. He joined the Eastern League starting in the 1957/58 season and proved he was a superstar. The highlight of that first season for Spivey was scoring 62 points to lead his Wilkes-Barre Barons to victory over the Easton Madisons in the league championship game. The Barons repeated as Eastern League champions in 1958/59, and Spivey was the top scorer at 35.9 points per game and was voted the league's MVP. He then went to the Baltimore Bullets in the 1959/60 season and again led the league in scoring, this time with 36.3 points per game, but the team lost to Easton in the title series.

In early 1960, in hopes of ending the NBA's ban on Spivey and matching him with star guard Oscar Robertson, the Cincinnati Royals signed Spivey, age 31, to a contract. But after pressure from the league office, still citing concerns over Spivey's possible involvement in the point-shaving scandal at Kentucky, Cincinnati withdrew their offer. Spivey, in turn, sued the NBA, Podoloff, and the Royals for $820,000 in damages. He reluctantly settled out of court for $10,000.

While Spivey would never have the opportunity to play in an NBA game, he did once match up against Wilt Chamberlain in an exhibition contest played in Milford, Connecticut, in July of 1960. "It turned out to be more than an exhibition,"[9] Spivey told the *Louisville Courier-Journal*. "Wilt and I went at it. He wasn't playing around and neither was I." By game's end, Chamberlain scored 31 points and had 27 rebounds versus Spivey's 30 and 23.

Statistically it was an even game, which for Spivey meant that he could still hold his own against a spry 23-year-old, 7'2" dynamo who would become one of the all-time greatest centers. "[Chamberlain] was in good shape, having played regularly all season with the Philadelphia Warriors," Spivey added. "I had played just two games a week without working out, just grabbing planes for weekend games in the Eastern League."

The next season, 1960/61, Baltimore beat Allentown in the league finals. That gave a Spivey-led team the Eastern League championship in three out of four years. Spivey also led the Bullets with 28.3 points per game.

In 1961 Spivey jumped to Abe Saperstein's short-lived reincarnation of the American Basketball League and was a top scorer on teams based in Los Angeles and Hawaii. Then the ABL folded halfway through the 1962/63 season, and Arthur Pachter, the longtime owner of the Scranton Miners, immediately tracked Spivey down in California and convinced him to return to the Eastern League, this time with Scranton, where he played for five years.

That first season, Spivey played in only 13 games but averaged 24.8 points and 11.3 rebounds. His best year in Scranton was 1964/65, when as a 35-year-old he averaged 27 points and 13 rebounds and led the team to within one game of a championship (they lost to the Allentown Jets).

"In my estimation, the best player that I ever had was Spivey in his prime, when he first came here. He still had it," said Pachter.

In 1967/68, "Big Bill" finished his 10-year Eastern League career on the team where he started, the Wilkes-Barre Barons, averaging an uncharacteristic 10.4 points and 9.7 rebounds.

"Bill Spivey was probably one of the best post men of all time. Of all time," said Ray Scott, who as a young Allentown Jet battled against Spivey in the Eastern League for three years.

"He was really good, I'll tell you," said Jim Boeheim, who vividly remembers the one year he joined Spivey on the Miners. "I played with him in '66, he was probably about 38 or 40. He never worked out, he could barely . . . get up and down the court, but he could really play. When he got there, he was really good. He would have been a really, really good NBA player. . . . He was seven feet, he could handle it, he could pass the ball, he could shoot it from the foul line area, he had a nice hook shot. He really knew how to play."

But the frustrated superstar would never forget what he had been denied by the NBA. "I owe an awful lot to the Eastern League,"[10] Spivey said in an interview in the *New York Times* after he announced his retirement from professional basketball in 1968. "And especially to Harry Rudolph [Eastern League president]. He evaluated all the findings and allowed me to play when everyone else wouldn't."

4

BLACKBALLED

Race, the NBA, and
the Rise of the Eastern League

L ike much of life in the United States in the first half of the 20th century, professional basketball was segregated. As author Mark Johnson described in
his book *Basketball Slave*,[1] the early days of pro basketball during the first three
decades of the 1900s were characterized mostly by independent barnstorming teams rather than by organized leagues. These independent teams played
against each other, against local amateur teams, and all other comers—but the
teams were either all black or all white, not integrated.

The first two major professional basketball leagues were the American
Basketball League (ABL), which began in 1925, and the National Basketball
League (NBL), which started in 1937. They, too, were all white. But even as
these leagues were getting established, segregated independent teams continued to compete and remained popular—in many cases more popular than their
counterparts in the NBL and ABL. The most accomplished of the all-black
independent teams of that era were the New York Renaissance Big Five, who
were also known as the New York Rens and the Harlem Rens, and the Harlem
Globetrotters, who were a serious basketball team long before they became
known for their showmanship.

In 1939, the *Chicago Herald American* newspaper sponsored the first World
Professional Basketball Tournament in Chicago to determine the "world champion" from among the top professional leagues and independent teams in the
country, including all-black teams. The Rens won that first world championship tournament in 1939, beating the NBL's Oshkosh All-Stars, 34–25. The
Globetrotters won the championship the following year, and in 1943 another
all-black independent team, the Washington Bears, composed mostly of players
from the Rens, also won.

The first of the major professional leagues to integrate was the NBL—sort of. In 1942, with many basketball players off to World War II, the Toledo and Chicago franchises signed a number of African American players to fill out their rosters, including several members of the Globetrotters. Bill Jones of Toledo is generally considered the first African American to play on an integrated team. Four more black players joined the NBL in 1946, including William "Pop" Gates, the star of those world champion Rens and Bears teams.

The NBL tried another form of integration in the 1948/49 season, inviting the Rens to replace the financially troubled Detroit Vagabond Kings, who had folded early in the season. The Rens accepted the offer, moved the franchise to Ohio, and became the Dayton Rens. They finished out the season in the NBL as the first all-black team in organized professional basketball, with Gates as player-coach. But hampered by inheriting Detroit's 2–17 record, the Rens finished last in what would be the NBL's final season.

It's easy to understand why, in a fight for survival in its last years, the NBL would bring black players—and even an all-black team—to the league. The Rens and Globetrotters were the most popular—and arguably the best—teams in professional basketball. They drew large crowds wherever they played and offered a faster-paced, more exciting brand of basketball than the white professional leagues. The NBL was losing its competition with the Basketball Association of America (BAA). Indeed, four of its most popular teams, including the Minneapolis Lakers with George Mikan, had bolted for the BAA. The NBL was eager—desperate even—to attract fans.

The ABL also took its first baby steps toward integration in 1948. John "Boy Wonder" Isaacs, a star of those world champion Rens and Bears squads, played part of the 1948/49 season with Brooklyn in the ABL. Then, after the NBL's Dayton Rens experiment ended in 1949, Gates joined the ABL's Scranton Miners, as did former Ren and Washington Bear William "Dolly" King and several other African American players. They came to Scranton through their connections with the team's coach, legendary Yeshiva University basketball coach Bernard "Red" Sarachek. Brian Maloney, whose grandfather and father owned the Miners, said the African American players were initially not well received in Scranton.

"It wasn't that easy at first, my grandfather said, to have that many blacks. Sarachek . . . didn't care what color you were," Maloney said. "If you could do it, you're playing. . . . I know my grandfather got some heat from people for bringing in [black players]. . . . That was talked about, and it was talked about in the fashion that you're keeping a white boy from getting a [job]." However, Maloney said, the fans quickly came around, especially "once they started putting the ball in the hoop, if they were winning."

Win they did. The Miners would win the ABL title in 1949/50 and 1950/51.

"They were that good that they should have been [in the NBA]," said Maloney of the integrated Miners. "There was no question. And my father and grandfather said it." He and his brother Tim said that NBA owners had offered the Maloneys a chance to operate a franchise in Baltimore with their team. "And my father had said years later . . . that was one of his regrets. He said, 'I should have taken the professional team there [to Baltimore]. These guys would have beaten everybody,'" Brian Maloney said.

Despite the success of African American players and teams, however, the BAA did not integrate, not even after the Globetrotters defeated the NBL champion Minneapolis Lakers, 61–59, in a 1948 exhibition contest and split a two-game series with the Lakers the following year, after the Lakers had moved to the BAA.

Finally, in 1950—the year after the BAA and NBL merged to form the NBA—the NBA broke its color barrier and brought three black players into the league at the start of the season—Chuck Cooper (Boston Celtics), Nat "Sweetwater" Clifton (New York Knicks), and Earl Lloyd (Washington Capitols). A fourth, Hank DeZonie (Tri-Cities Blackhawks), joined the league after the season had started.

Integration would come slowly to the NBA during the 1950s and early 1960s, however. According to figures compiled by Johnson in *Basketball Slave*, the NBA would not have more than nine black players in any one season until 1956/57, when it had 14 among its eight teams.[2]

The Eastern League, meanwhile, had three black players, all on the same team, in its first season, 1946/47. Clayton, Isaacs, and William "Rookie" Brown—all veterans of the black barnstorming teams—played for the Hazleton Mountaineers that season. Clayton and Brown would remain in the league in 1947/48, with Brown averaging 11.3 points per game and being selected second team all-league. Also in 1947/48, former Globetrotter and Ren Frank Washington played for the Philadelphia Lumberjacks during their one season in the Eastern League.

It does not appear that any more African Americans played in the Eastern League until 1953, when players implicated in the point-shaving scandal, including Sherman White, Ed Warner, and Bob McDonald, joined the league, along with former Philadelphia high school player Bob Gainey. Floyd Layne would join the Eastern League the following year, and with that the doors appeared to open for black players much more quickly in the EPBL than in the NBA. During the 1955/56 season, the Hazleton Hawks became the first integrated professional basketball league team with an all-black starting lineup: White, Layne, Tom Hemans, Jesse Arnelle, and Fletcher Johnson. The NBA would not have an all-black starting lineup for another nine years—the 1964 Celtics—and after that, not until the 1971 Milwaukee Bucks.

Moreover, by 1960, when the NBA was about 20 percent black, the Eastern League was mixed and perhaps even predominantly black. As reported in *They Cleared the Lane: The NBA's Black Pioneers*, by Ron Thomas, one of the part owners of the Allentown Jets, John Kimock, estimated that the league was about 70 percent black in the early 1960s.[3]

Why the disparity in African American players between the NBA and the Eastern League from the late 1940s through the early '60s?

Part of it, as Johnson and Thomas explained in their respective books, was the relationship between NBA owners and Abe Saperstein, owner of the Globetrotters and a former part owner of the NBA's Philadelphia Warriors who remained close to the Warriors' influential owner, Eddie Gottlieb. Essentially, the understanding between Saperstein and the NBA was that Saperstein would have "first dibs" on talented black basketball players for the Globetrotters. Even after the NBA integrated, Saperstein continued to keep black players under contract, and if an NBA team wanted one of those players, it would have to pay Saperstein.

Gottlieb and other NBA owners were willing to placate Saperstein in those early years because they needed him and the Globetrotters to succeed. By this time, the Globetrotters were considered the best basketball team in the world (as their 1948/49 games with the Lakers demonstrated), renowned for their skill and their showmanship. As former NBA coach and television commentator Hubie Brown, himself an Eastern League player in the 1950s, said of the Globetrotters: "They were the premier players of the time. . . . Every guy on that team could have played in the [NBA]. People forget that. People forget how good those guys were."[4]

The Globetrotters drew hundreds of thousands of fans worldwide. NBA teams, meanwhile, were struggling. To help attendance, NBA owners made a deal with Saperstein whereby the Globetrotters would play exhibition games in doubleheaders with NBA games. During the early years of the NBA, the Globetrotter games were the main attraction, with the NBA game getting second billing. These doubleheaders filled arenas and helped the fledgling NBA survive financially.

Former players and other observers offer several reasons for the slow pace of integration in the NBA, most of which have to do in some way with race.

One was the owners' belief that white fans—who comprised the large majority of NBA fans at that time—would not come to watch a team with multiple black players. In a conversation that Thomas described in his book, one NBA team owner explained to an African American player in the early 1960s that until there were more black fans in the stands, NBA teams would be predominantly white.[5]

But perhaps at least some NBA owners misjudged their fans' willingness to watch teams with black players. By most accounts Eastern League fans supported their teams during the league's heydays, even with rosters that were mixed or predominantly black. Longtime Hazleton fan Ron Marchetti recalled that "it was no big deal"[6] at the time when the Mountaineers started five African Americans in 1955/56. Moreover, several years later when six of the nine players on the 1962/63 Eastern League champion Allentown Jets were black, the Jets were one of the biggest draws in the league, regularly filling Rockne Hall.

Then there were various versions of the explanation that the "style of play" of black players did not fit with the NBA game. The theory was that black players, most of whom at that time came from small, historically black colleges and universities, favored a more individual, creative, and showy style of play and did not play the kind of structured, team-oriented game that players from major college programs did. Also, since most NBA coaches at the time came from major college basketball programs, they were used to that structured style of play and wanted players who could play it. As *Boston Globe* sportswriter and ESPN basketball analyst Bob Ryan observed: "The coaches were predominantly ex-players who had known only one way how to play."[7]

But just because coaches were used to running offenses that involved intricate passing, cutting, and screening doesn't mean that players who favored that style were better than players who could create their own shots and play above the rim.

"No question about the [black] players being able to innovate and create for themselves," said John Chaney. "We had great players like Wally Choice. . . . Oh man, he was a great player! All of these players were great in their own right. . . . They should have been [in the NBA]. It's a darn shame."

Moreover, the argument that black players didn't fit the NBA's style also reflects a kind of stereotyping. The terms "undisciplined" and "playground ball" were often used, terms that were fraught with negative, racial connotations.

"There were people that had a wrong impression of the way black players played,"[8] recalled Stan Pawlak, a white player who broke into the Eastern League in 1965 and enjoyed a 12-year career. "I'm brought up in the city of Camden [New Jersey]—Camden High. And even I as a young kid always thought, well, we're the smart players, they're the athletic players. I learned quickly that that was bullshit. . . . I mean that was such a, again, something that was so ridiculous it's not funny. Maybe people had the idea that they didn't work as hard or something. But that's all stereotypes that exist to this day. . . . It's just not the truth."

In addition, the NBA during those early days did not have the kind of sophisticated scouting system that it has now, through which scouts could find talented black players at even obscure schools. Scouts had to rely on the advice of players and coaches they knew, who came from the same major colleges they went to.

Also, major college basketball programs were generally not recruiting black players during the 1950s and '60s. The small, historically black colleges and universities, mostly in the South, were the only schools available to most black players, and neither scouts nor white NBA players knew much about them.

"I was the most valuable [high school] player in the city [Philadelphia] . . . and I went to a black school in the South [Bethune-Cookman]," recalled John Chaney, Hall of Fame former basketball coach at Temple University and a star Eastern League player in the 1950s. "I was not even recruited for one of the schools in the city, for the white schools. Temple had one black player, LaSalle had one or two black players. . . . So there was just limited access, no visibility, which I think was the biggest cause."

Said Waite Bellamy, a Florida A&M grad who was drafted and cut in preseason by the St. Louis Hawks in 1963: "A lot of small, black college players were in [the Eastern League] because [NBA teams] didn't give us so much of a choice, or much of a look anyway." Bellamy became one of the Eastern League's top scorers with Wilmington in the late '60s and early '70s.

Thus, as Johnson wrote, "in the 1950s and '60s, the NBA was letting black players in—in Noah-like fashion, two by two."[9] As many former Eastern League players and observers put it, the NBA had an unwritten but implicit quota on the number of black players per team of no more than two players, which gradually increased over time.

"When I got out of Niagara in 1956, it was widely known and practiced that NBA teams limited the number of black players on each NBA team,"[10] said Tom Hemans, one of the members of that all-black starting five in Hazleton and a 15-year Eastern League veteran. "Without question race was the major factor that kept talented black basketball players out of the NBA."

"Each team was trying to limit the number of black players they had on the team," recalled Bellamy, "even to the detriment of having some white players on the team that were not as good."

"They already knew who was going to play and who wasn't going to play,"[11] recalled Cleveland "Swish" McKinney of the St. Louis Hawks' camp during the preseason of 1964. "You could come on a team, and you look around [at the number of black players], 'Aww, jeez, am I going to make this here?'"

"Quotas existed," said Ryan. "Nobody can deny it."

Thomas explained it this way in *They Cleared the Lane*:

> The feeling was that the magic number varied from owner to owner, from franchise to franchise. From 1950 to 1955 only two teams—the 1952–53 Baltimore Bullets and 1954–55 Syracuse Nationals—had more than one black player on their rosters, and both of those topped out at two. The 1955–56 season saw a small step up to three on [the] Knicks . . . and on the roster of the Rochester Royals. . . . The next season Rochester became the first team to have four blacks at one time.[12]

George Blaney agreed: "I would say, definitely, there was a quota in the NBA at about that time. . . . It went from each team had one, and each team had an unwritten rule they wouldn't start black players. And then they started, it got to be, you could have four black players on the team. And then finally Red Auerbach started the five black players at Boston and that kind of broke the cycle."

The owners' concerns about how fans would react to African American players not only influenced how many black players were chosen to play in the NBA, but also how they were expected to play when they got there.

Earl Lloyd, who became the first African American to play in an NBA game during the 1950 season, recalled in his autobiography *Moonfixer: The Basketball Journey of Earl Lloyd*, that "nobody said it, but it was whispered how most of the black guys who made it early in the NBA were big, physical guys who weren't expected to be cerebral. They let white guys run the team on the floor, and they sent the black guys under the hoop to do the heavy labor, which fit the pattern in this country for a long, long time."[13]

John Chaney recalled that when the New York Knicks signed their first African American player, "Sweetwater Clifton, he was no more than someone they threw the ball in and cut off of him and he had to give it back."

Wrote Mark Johnson of his father Andy's role with the NBA Warriors: "Like most of the blacks who entered the NBA in the early years, Dad was given a role that he was expected to play. . . . He was supposed to pass the ball, get the rebound, and not let his teammates or himself get beat up. But Dad was not to be a star. He was required to water down his abilities and not play *his* game."[14]

"Andy was somebody that could shoot the ball, but he wasn't allowed to shoot in the NBA," confirmed his longtime friend Chaney.

"Rim runners," Chaney called players like Lloyd, Clifton, and Johnson. "They run from one rim to the other rim and the coach never has to worry about writing up any plays for them because the play never went through them at all." But, as Chaney observed, "they were players that did things that made you win."

That could explain why, during the 1950s and early 1960s, a nucleus of black players with prolific scoring ability entered the Eastern League. The top four scorers in Eastern League history, and eight of the top 10, are African American players who entered the league between 1954 and 1963.

Three players whose names almost always come up when discussing Eastern Leaguers who should have had NBA careers, but didn't, are Hal "King" Lear, Wally Choice, and Dick Gaines. Thomas devoted a chapter to them in his book about black NBA pioneers.[15] All were collegiate stars and all, unlike most black players of that era, played at major college programs: Lear at Temple, where he played in the 1956 Final Four and set a then record by scoring 48 points in a third-place game (which are no longer played); Gaines at Seton Hall, where he played in the NIT championship game twice and graduated as Seton Hall's fifth leading career scorer; and Choice at Indiana University, where he became the first African American captain of the Hoosiers' basketball team.

But all three had strikes against them—in addition to race—at least in the thinking of the times. All three were scorers and didn't fit what NBA teams wanted from black players. Lear was a shooter and, at six feet tall, considered a bit undersized to play shooting guard. Gaines was a burly, physical 6'3", 230-pounder whose game was driving inside and posting up. Neither was the kind of "feeder" who would dish the ball to other scorers. Choice was a 6'4" 'tweener who could score inside and outside with an assortment of shots, but he wasn't the classic forward.

All three played in NBA training camps, but only Lear made it onto a regular season roster. He was drafted in the first round by the Philadelphia Warriors in 1956 and made the team out of training camp, but played in only three games before being cut. The Warriors had only one other black player on the roster at the time, Jackie Moore.

"Lear was one of the greatest shooters in college basketball," said Chaney. "He was one of the great players. . . . I would have to say that people like that [were] kept from reaching their level that they should have been."

Gaines was drafted by Syracuse, which already had a talented backcourt as well as two other black players on the roster. He was cut before the season started, was told that he was going to get picked up by the Knicks, but it never happened.

Choice was drafted by the St. Louis Hawks, but instead went into the service and played on an AAU team. He had a tryout with the Knicks when he got out in 1958 but got cut. The Knicks had two other black players on their roster at the time.

"I don't know why Wally didn't go [into the NBA], because he could play," recalled Howie Landa, a player and coach in the Eastern League in the 1950s and '60s. "The black kids had a tough time. . . . There was a limit in the NBA at that time on the black players."

As Ray Scott, a former Eastern Leaguer, NBA All-Star, and NBA head coach, said about Lear, Gaines, and Choice, "you don't have to be incredibly brilliant to figure out what was going on."

Lear, Gaines, and Choice all went on to excel in the Eastern League and, for much of their careers, played together for the Easton-Phillipsburg Madisons. Lear scored 50 or more points in a game 10 times—the all-time Eastern League record—and was the 1957 MVP and fourth all-time leading scorer. Gaines was the league's Rookie of the Year in 1958 and its seventh all-time scorer. Choice averaged 41.3 points per game in 1961/62, the best ever in Eastern League history, scored 69 points in one game, a record that held until 1976, and was the 10th all-time scorer.

The list of players—mostly black, but many good white players, too—who former Eastern Leaguers say could or should have played in the NBA is long and inherently subjective. But most observers would include the league's top three all-time leading scorers on that list: Julius McCoy, Stacey Arceneaux, and Tommy Hemans, who was also the league's top all-time rebounder. Chaney, too, is often mentioned as a player who should have been in the NBA.

"John Chaney was a great player in the Eastern League," said Ryan. "There wasn't any question that John Chaney, as he was then, today is comparable in this league [to] a 10-year NBA player. . . . He was pretty damn good."

Many black former Eastern League players from the late '50s and early '60s who are mentioned as NBA-caliber talents had one thing in common—star quality. They were dynamic individual players who stood out—and that was the problem.

"Too outstanding was not going to work,"[16] said former Globetrotter Bobby Hunter, who was released from the New York Knicks' training camp in 1965 and briefly played for Wilmington in the Eastern League. "So if you were more balanced . . . you would be picked on a team. Point in example: Cleo Hill. There's no way in hell that he doesn't make an NBA team. Race and the team's attitude—no sale."

Cleo Hill was a multitalented 6'1" guard from tiny Winston-Salem State University in North Carolina. He could run the floor, score from outside and inside, leap, rebound, and block shots—and he did it all with flair. As Thomas wrote, "of the many black players who should have been but weren't in the NBA, Cleo Hill is spoken of in almost Jordan-esque terms."[17]

"He was like . . . [Russell] Westbrook," said Waite Bellamy. "He was so quick up and down the floor."

"He was murder," said author and former Eastern Leaguer Charley Rosen. "The guy was a great player!"

The St. Louis Hawks drafted Hill eighth in the first round of the 1961 NBA draft and brought him to training camp. What happened from there has been the subject of various articles and a segment in the ESPN documentary *Black Magic* about African Americans and basketball.

Hill dazzled in training camp with his multiple talents, including his outside shot, which the Hawks sorely needed. "I got [newspaper clippings about Hill] in one of the scrapbooks that I got somewhere," said Chaney. "He was devastating! He was killing them scoring, you know what I mean. . . . Cleo was something else, man."

Unfortunately for Hill, he joined a veteran team anchored by its "Big Three" star frontcourt players, Bob Pettit, Cliff Hagan, and Clyde Lovellette. Hill averaged in double figures during preseason and, after an inconsistent start to the season, began scoring in double figures again as well as displaying his passing and rebounding skills.

But, as various versions of the story go, the team's veterans became unhappy because Hill's speediness downcourt and scoring ability cut into their scoring opportunities, and because of the attention Hill was getting for his exciting style of play. Moreover, Hawks coach Paul Seymour supported Hill and directed his veterans to get the ball to him or else get benched. The veterans reportedly complained to Hawks owner Ben Kerner, who sided with them and told Seymour to cut Hill's playing time. Seymour refused and, 14 games into the season, Kerner fired Seymour.

"Paul told me he was forced to cut him or get fired, and he got fired," recalled Syracuse University coach Jim Boeheim, who played for Seymour for one season in Scranton.

Hill, after averaging almost 11 points per game under Seymour, finished the season as a part-time player under new coach Fuzzy Levane, who had been coaching in the Eastern League. He averaged 5.5 PPG, his confidence shot. The following year the Hawks cut Hill in training camp and he ended up playing five seasons in the Eastern League with Trenton, Bridgeport, New Haven, and Scranton. He would never play in the NBA again.

As Thomas described in his book,[18] Kerner, members of the Big Three, Levane, and others close to the Hawks offered various reasons for what happened to Hill: The Hawks needed a point guard, and ballhandling and passing weren't Hill's strengths. Hill wasn't a great defensive player. The veteran players didn't like the attention that a rookie was getting, or what they perceived as his lack of deference to the veteran stars. Added Hunter: "It didn't help him blocking one of Bob Pettit's layup attempts" in preseason camp.

Moreover, points were especially important to the veterans, whose salaries—relatively modest by today's standards—were linked to how much they scored. If they followed Seymour's orders and allowed Hill to score, that would have cost them points and, ultimately, money. So, most observers said, the Big Three froze Hill out, not passing him the ball. Over the years Hill would say this was the main factor in the conflict, telling Thomas: "When people say it was black and white, that wasn't it. It was the points."[19] But St. Louis's history with African American players should also be noted. While the NBA took its first black players in 1950, St. Louis did not have one until 1958: Sihugo Green, who finished his professional career in the Eastern League after an eight-year NBA career. In 1956, the Hawks drafted Julius McCoy (Michigan State), Wally Choice (Indiana), Willie Naulls (UCLA), and—wait for it—Bill Russell (University of San Francisco). They didn't keep any of them, trading Russell to the Celtics (for Hagan and center Ed Macauley) and Naulls to the Knicks (for guard Slater Martin).

"We were getting [newspaper clippings] where Julius would be scoring, you know, 17, 20 points a game in the [Hawks' training camp] or whatever," recalled Chaney. "But try to remember, St. Louis was one of the last teams that came along in terms of being integrated. There was no place to stay, life was hard, and they were really racist in the St. Louis area. And that was one of the reasons why he didn't make it."

In 1959, the Hawks drafted Tom Hemans and traded him to Cincinnati (which Hemans refused to join when they would not honor St. Louis's promise of a "no-cut" contract). Two years later when Hill joined the Hawks, three other African American players were on the roster—Green, Lennie Wilkens, and Fred LaCour—but Green was traded to Chicago, Wilkens was in the army most of that season, and LaCour left the team. The following season, with Wilkens back, the Hawks did keep six black players—a high for an NBA team at the time. But for the next couple of seasons at least, they also continued to cut talented black players who would go on to star in the Eastern League—Bellamy in 1963, and McKinney and Maurice McHartley in 1964.

To African American players of that era, the Cleo Hill story is a cautionary tale, a reminder of what could happen at that time to a black athlete who dared to shine.

"Cleo Hill really was a star," said Ray Scott, who like Hill was a first-round draft pick and broke into the NBA the same season. "And so Cleo, wrong time, wrong place, because in his time that he was in St. Louis, St. Louis was a bastion of segregation. . . . No one saw marketing Cleo Hill as a star in St. Louis. It just didn't fly."

Though Hill would play for five years in the Eastern League after a brief stop in the short-lived American Basketball League (ABL), he was not the same player. He scored 23.1 PPG for New Haven in 1966/67 but averaged in the low teens for his other four seasons, playing on three different teams.

"He was still a good player [in the Eastern League] but he was not the same," remembered Bellamy. "Mentally, you lose your confidence. And what happened, it was just a shame. He was still a good player because I played against him. But he was not the same."

Said McHartley: "Sadly enough—because I played against Cleo in college, too—he was never the same guy after that. I mean, I couldn't believe it."[20]

The NBA's rejection of talented black players was the Eastern League's gain. As Hemans said, it "created a pool of highly talented black players, many of whom had 'starred' at various highly ranked colleges. Consequently, Eastern League teams recruited those black players, many of whom were more talented than many white players on NBA teams. . . . But in fairness, there were also some better white players in the Eastern League as well. . . . When given an equal opportunity to play basketball, black players featured prominently in the Eastern League; as they do now in the NBA."

Said Scott: "I was also with Tommy Hemans and Stacey Arceneaux, and you know, these, these great players, but that were just—I don't know—systemically they couldn't play in the [NBA] or what have you . . . [but] we got that overflow from the NBA to the Eastern Basketball League. So you had really good guys, guys that had played in the NBA."

And in contrast to the NBA, race generally did not seem to be a significant factor in determining who made it into the Eastern League, at least not by the 1960s. Kimock, one of the Allentown owners, told Thomas: "There was no discrimination as far as [Eastern League] club owners were concerned. . . . Everybody wanted to win a championship. I think if you went with a solid white team, it would have finished last."[21]

"Art Pachter wanted the best ballplayers on the floor at any time, and he had great coaches that wanted the best ballplayers," said Willie Somerset of Scranton's team owner. "The management was 100 percent. That wasn't Art's bag at all. He wanted the best team, and the best team filled up the coliseums and the arenas."[22]

Said Pachter: "There were loads of black players, as well as loads of white players. . . . I remember the first game that we had starting all five black guys. Tommy Hemans was my coach; it was one of those times when we had a player-coach . . . and he started five black guys. That was what he wanted to do."

"In the Eastern League, I don't ever remember anybody having any thoughts about race in the Eastern League, to be honest with you," said Blaney. "You know, black players started, black players played hard, but I can't remember any quotas or anything."

This isn't to say the league was entirely color blind in assembling its teams.

"We had many, many good white players," Bellamy said. "Many excellent white players. We did have the same kind of situation, though. We always wanted to keep a few white players on each team whether they sat on the bench or what. . . . You tried not to have an all-black team."

And by all accounts, race was not an issue between black players and white players. Players carpooled together and bonded over their competitiveness and respect for each other's games.

"When we came together, we would play hard and we wanted to win and there was good crowds and we had a good time," Somerset recalled. "We didn't think about discrimination or who was on the ball club or who was not. We were just concerned about winning."

"When you're playing basketball like that, you and your teammates don't have any kind of negative relationship—white players, black players, none of that stuff," said Bellamy. "We understood that—all the black players understood the dynamics of having to have a couple of white players on the team, which was accepted. And we had no racial incidents that I could remember on the court, on the team, or anything like that."

Said Joe Lalli, a popular Scranton-area athlete who played two seasons for his hometown team: "Black players, white fans in the Eastern League. From the perspective of a white boy from Dunmore, PA, I knew nothing except to show up and play a game of basketball with black players while being cheered on by fans, whether white, black, tan, or whatever color they might be."[23]

"I roomed with Chaney. Chaney and I were very close," recalled Landa, who like Chaney was from Philadelphia and had grown up in similar basketball circles in the early 1950s. "Chaney played at Ben Franklin High and I played at Central. But we were very close, and we drove together and everything."

Looking back, some black players from that time view their experience in the Eastern League as a coming-of-age, learning from older black basketball pioneers how to deal with the disadvantages they experienced and to succeed in spite of them. In an interview with Zack Burgess on the website JockBio

.com, Sonny Hill, a former Eastern Leaguer and highly respected Philadelphia sportscaster and youth basketball organizer, recalled his first year with the newly formed Allentown Jets in 1958:

> I was the only black player on the Jets for the first part of the season. Soon, my good friend Ray Scott dropped out of [the University of] Portland, and I told the coach I had a guy that was 6-foot-9 who could play. So then it became the two of us. Jim Tucker was also on the Jets. He and Earl Lloyd were the first two African-Americans to play on an NBA champion, with the Syracuse Nationals in 1955. Tucker mentored us. He took us under his wing as young guys. We were just coming out of our teenage years.[24]

Scott also remembered Tucker: "He was an All-American at Duquesne. And Jim Tucker was a professional, I mean he was a well-educated, erudite, handsome man, well dressed, and you saw him as a 20-year-old and you said: 'That's the kind of guy I want to be like. I want to have that class. I want to have dignity.'" Scott also observed and learned from men like Carl Green, Charlie Hoxie, and Roman "Big Doc" Turmon, former Globetrotters who were playing in the Eastern League and had traveled the world.

"The way they handled things always interested me," Scott said.

Remarkably, most of the African American former Eastern Leaguers interviewed did not express bitterness at the obstacles they faced in getting to the highest levels of basketball. Perhaps that's because so many African Americans of that time, especially those who had come from the segregated South, had already lowered their expectations.

"We were pretty happy with what we were doing competing against the other segregated schools," said Bellamy. "At that time we just wanted equality. We were not thinking about integration."

Said McHartley: "I had opportunities to play against some great players [in the Eastern League], and actually that made us all better and not even thinking about it as 'this ain't the NBA.' But it was, so to speak. Had we been in a position, or had the [NBA] been more open to more players, there was a whole lot of guys that would have made it. I mean a lot of guys that would have made it. But, you know, there wasn't enough room so you had to go where you had to go, fit in where you had to fit in."

"There was a much better quality [of player] in the NBA," acknowledged Somerset, who played briefly for the NBA Baltimore Bullets in 1965 before entering the Eastern League, "but then it was true, there were some ballplayers that deserved to be in the NBA. But at that time it just wasn't here. It wasn't the right timing at that time."

By the mid-1960s, the NBA was integrated. That's not to say teams were no longer race conscious in building their rosters, but most observers said quotas for black players had ended. Fans in NBA arenas had become accustomed to watching and rooting for black players. Teams seeing the success of the Celtics sought to compete. They needed players who could counter the Celtics' fast break and play above the rim with Russell.

"Absolutely," said Charley Rosen. "Red Auerbach broke the quotas."

In 1967, when the American Basketball Association emerged and needed good players to fill their rosters, they looked for the best ballplayers they could find—including some 30 Eastern Leaguers, most of them black. Such players were perfectly suited for the ABA's up-tempo, entertaining style, and had played with a three-point line in the Eastern League since 1964.

Looking back, Scott said, "The whole world has changed. That whole basketball world has changed. . . . Because when I say it changed, it changed sociologically. You know, it was unthinkable that on a team of 10 players, that eight of them would be African Americans."

Said Chaney:

There wasn't access and opportunity. At that time most of the players came from big colleges, and a lot of our black kids were not in big colleges at that time. So access, opportunity were not there. . . .

There were so many great players that certainly were capable of playing in the NBA, that you often think of what . . . kind of people working in the NBA at that time would allow this talent to go astray like that, or to find themselves not recruiting them? I thought there were great players that should have been in the NBA, but they neglected to recruit them.

Racist views held this country in a position where it couldn't move. This country could have moved a lot faster. . . . The world, a lot faster if it was able to get rid of these issues. . . . There was so much talent that was lost because of these social issues that tend to get in the way of people being successful. It's a shame. It's a shame.

5

THE GLORY YEARS (1954–1967)

The Second-Best League Around

The NBA's ban on Sherman White, Jack Molinas, Bill Spivey, and other players tainted by the college point-shaving scandal brought one group of highly talented basketball players to the Eastern League. The NBA's racial quotas brought another. Two other factors helped to fill the Eastern League with exceptional talent and lift the EPBL of the mid-1950s through mid-1960s to just a notch below the NBA.

First, the number of jobs available for top-tier professional basketball players had shrunk. The NBA had dropped from 17 teams in 1949 (when the BAA and NBL merged) to eight teams in 1955/56, as a number of franchises had folded. It would only have nine teams in 1961/62 and 10 in 1966/67. Moreover, the ABL disbanded in 1954, and Abe Saperstein's attempt to start a new ABL in 1961 lasted only one full season, leaving the NBA alone as the only full-time professional league.

Roster sizes were also much smaller than today's 15-man squad. According to statistics compiled by basketball historian Robert Bradley, NBA teams carried 10 players from 1947 to 1960, then increased their roster size to 11.[1] As a result, a lot of very good basketball players were competing for somewhere between 80 and 99 NBA jobs.

This numbers game created a gold mine of talent for the Eastern League.

"All EBL teams were competitive," said Tom Hemans, a longtime Eastern Leaguer in the late 1950s and early '60s. "In my first year in the EBL, the NBA only had eight or nine teams. . . . This . . . produced a highly skilled talent pool [outside of the NBA] from which EBL teams could select players. And this was an annual occurrence! So how many players could be added to EBL's already stacked rosters?"

"While the Eastern League can be talked about as what the G League is today," said George Blaney, a former college coach and NBA player who played five seasons in the Eastern League, "I think it was more like an NBA league because most of those players would be in the NBA today if it were the way it is. You had Hal 'King' Lear and Bobby McNeill and Paul Arizin and Stacey Arceneaux and Wally Choice and Alan Seiden. . . . You just go on and on with the names of the players and the types of players who played in the league."

"You can imagine what the [NBA] would be like today if they cut it down to nine teams and only carried like 10–11 players," said Bob Weiss, a longtime NBA player and coach who played for Wilmington in the 1960s. "It would be all all-stars. . . . There was no ABA, there was no Europe. I mean, [the Eastern League] was it."[2]

"Where else could they go?" said Arthur Pachter, longtime owner of the Scranton Miners and Apollos. "The quality was here."

Second, and perhaps difficult for modern-day fans to believe, playing NBA basketball was not especially lucrative in those days. Most NBA players had to work off-season jobs to support themselves financially, and they had to plan for income after their basketball careers ended. For fringe NBA players, it made financial sense to take a full-time job, get a head start on their postplaying careers, and earn extra money playing weekends in the Eastern League—especially if they had a family—rather than risk the uncertain job security of playing in the NBA.

"Those guys were only making . . . [no more than] $10,000 a year," said Temple coach and former Eastern Leaguer John Chaney of NBA player salaries in the mid-1950s. "Those guys had to get another job. You couldn't live off the money you were making in the NBA at that time. No way. No way they could do it. . . . They had to get extra jobs and work."

Hemans, who was a teacher in the New York City public schools during his Eastern League playing days, said "my combined [Eastern League and teaching] income was more than the NBA contract I signed with the St. Louis Hawks. This fact also impacted upon my decision to play in the Eastern League and at the same time work towards a professional career." When the Hawks traded him to the Cincinnati Royals after training camp in 1959 and the Royals would not honor the "no-cut" contract he signed with the Hawks (after initially saying they would), he declined to sign with Cincinnati.

"I felt deceived and I refused to pursue the matter any further with them," said Hemans. "I was also [at the time] moving upwards professionally in New

York City; and between my Eastern League salary and my employment with the city, I was making much more money than the NBA contract I signed with St. Louis. I also thoroughly liked being able to enjoy life at home with my family and friends, working on my career and playing professional basketball in the Eastern League. . . . I played in the EBL and never looked back."

Hal "King" Lear provided a similar rationale to author Ron Thomas for not pursuing an offer from the New York Knicks the year after he was cut by Philadelphia. As quoted in Thomas's book *They Cleared the Lane*, Lear said: "They said, 'This is the NBA.' I said, 'Nonetheless, if I'm going to put myself out, I want a two-year contract at X amount of money. If you can't do that, then sayonara.'"[3]

At the time, Thomas wrote, Lear was a management trainee for the city of Philadelphia, earning $3,000. Plus, he was earning money on weekends playing in the Eastern League, and more playing for a barnstorming team in Philly. "I made $10,000 playing basketball and another $3,000 at the job when others were making $3,000 for playing [NBA] basketball," Lear said. "I wasn't going to give up $13,000 for $3,000."[4]

Stacey Arceneaux, the Eastern League's second all-time leading scorer, played seven games with the Hawks in 1962. But he "quickly learned that he'll make more money playing in the Eastern League and getting a job than he would playing professional basketball in those days,"[5] said Marvin Salenger, an attorney for whom Arceneaux worked as a negotiator for many years after a long career as an insurance claims adjuster.

Syracuse University basketball coach Jim Boeheim also decided to pursue his nonplaying career rather than an opportunity to play in the NBA. Boeheim started playing for Scranton during the 1966/67 season under former NBA coach Paul Seymour. When the 1967/68 season began and Seymour became head coach of the NBA's Detroit Pistons, he offered Boeheim a roster spot. Boeheim looked at Detroit's roster and saw guards Dave Bing, Jimmie Walker, and Tom Van Arsdale.

"I knew I'd be the fourth guard," said Boeheim. "I was getting into coaching and starting to like coaching. I knew I could hang on in the NBA, but I wasn't going to play. I'd already made up my mind to be a coach. . . . I was working and I was coaching. I just didn't think I could go and so I stayed in the Eastern League. I played four more years . . . it was a great experience."

"He played like he coaches," said Joe Lalli. "He was understated."

In 1969, Boeheim was hired by Syracuse as a graduate assistant coach, and for the last three of his six years in the league (all with Scranton), he split his time between playing for the Miners and coaching at SU. He became head coach of

Syracuse in 1976, won an NCAA championship in 2003, was inducted into the Naismith Memorial Basketball Hall of Fame in 2005—and he's still coaching the Orange.

Former Eastern League and NBA referee Dick Bavetta recalled:

> There were a lot of people—players, of course, some referees—that didn't want the rigors of being in the ABA or being in the NBA, either as a referee or as a player, and traveling, being away from their family. So, legitimately, sometimes you'd run into someone and say, "Gee, how come you didn't play in the NBA?" And [they'd say], "Well, I wanted to be with my family," and then you walk away and you roll your eyes. But the true story is that what he's saying is true. . . .There were a lot of players and a lot of coaches, a lot of people who didn't want that lifestyle. And it's not because the talent level wasn't there.[6]

The most prominent example of a player deciding to leave the NBA and play part-time in the Eastern League for financial and non-basketball career reasons was Paul Arizin.

Arizin was NBA royalty. A Villanova grad, he played with the Philadelphia Warriors from 1950 to 1962. He averaged 21.9 PPG during the 1961/62 season, was the NBA's third all-time leading scorer with 16,266 points, the first NBA player to average 20 or more PPG in nine straight seasons, and a perennial all-star.

But at the end of that 1961/62 season, the Warriors moved to San Francisco, and Arizin, at the age of 34, decided to stay home in Philadelphia and retire from the NBA so he could take a job for IBM and play weekends for the Camden Bullets in the Eastern League. He played for three seasons in Camden, averaging over 20 PPG, being named MVP in 1963, and leading the Bullets to the league title in 1964.

With so many talented players finding their way to the Eastern League for so many different reasons, basketball fans in these small towns had a remarkable privilege. They got to watch a tough, competitive, serious league with some of the best players in the country—in the world, really—up close in mostly intimate gyms for a few bucks a ticket.

"The league was loaded," said Boeheim. "It's hard to capture in a book just how good the league was and how good the players were."

Boeheim was correct, of course. It is tough to capture in a book just how good the Eastern League was, especially from 1954, when the players implicated in the point-shaving scandals first joined the league, to the formation of the ABA in 1967. But here's how some former players, officials, and fans described those glory years.

"It was one incredible, incredible league," said Ray Scott, who played for three seasons for the Allentown Jets after he dropped out of the University of Portland and, under NBA rules in effect at that time, could not be drafted until his class graduated. "We were committed to play against seasoned basketball players and guys that had professional experience and guys that were All-Americans."

Said Chaney: "There were so many great, great players who could perhaps fill the NBA with great players today. . . . It's unimaginable that many of them would be playing [in a minor league today]. . . . Sherman White . . . [Dick] Gaines and Wally Choice, all them guys from New York."

"Guys from all over college basketball," said Howie Landa, Chaney's backcourt partner and traveling companion for the Sunbury Mercuries in the mid-1950s. "There was some great players there."

"My first year with the Hazleton Hawks," said Hemans in his written responses to interview questions, "we had a team of outstanding players led by the 'great Sherman White.' The level of competition. Every player was very talented. . . . No question this was professional basketball competition at its best! . . . The overall level of competition was equal to the NBA teams and players. There were many Eastern League players who were either equally talented or more talented than many NBA players. This was a fact known by the NBA, its players and those with knowledge of the game."

He added: "A major difference between the two leagues at that time was that the NBA teams had more talented [centers,] bigger and taller men than those on the average Eastern League team, except, for example, when Bill Spivey played for the Wilkes-Barre Barons and later the Scranton Miners. The roster of players on those particular teams could compete with the roster of players on any NBA team. The same for the Allentown Jets. Or even the Hazleton Hawks with the great Sherman White with whom I had the great pleasure to play."

"The top 20 players [in the Eastern League] were all NBA-type players," Boeheim said. "There just wasn't quite enough room in the NBA. I think there were 10 [NBA] teams then. . . . So it was a great league. Competition was terrific. Every team had good players. . . . There were just a lot of good players in the Eastern League. A lot."

Weiss, a Penn State grad who was cut from the Philadelphia 76ers camp in 1965, recalled: "One of the Kaufman brothers [Wilmington Blue Bombers' owners] called me and said . . . 'We'd like you to come play for us, we think you could help us.' And I kind of think to myself, 'Think I could help you? I'm an NBA player,' not realizing how tough the Eastern League was."

But Weiss had to fight for playing time when he first joined the Blue Bombers, with Freddie Crawford (who played several years in the NBA), Waite Bellamy, and Maurice McHartley all in the backcourt.

This isn't to say that the Eastern League was just as good as the NBA during this mid-1950s to mid-1960s era or that every Eastern Leaguer belonged in the NBA. But the top layer—and maybe the top two layers—of Eastern League players certainly had NBA talent at that time, especially when you compare the size of the NBA then to today.

"If you think of 80 [NBA players then] . . . versus 450 guys today, a lot of those guys [in the Eastern League] would have played in the NBA [today]," said Hubie Brown, whose professional career started with Rochester in the Eastern League in the 1950s. Brown went a step further in discussing this point with author Charley Rosen, saying, "Many of the guys in the Eastern League would be NBA All-Stars if they played today."[7]

"I know some ballplayers that should have been in the NBA but were playing in the Eastern League," said Willie Somerset, who played briefly for the NBA's Baltimore Bullets in 1965 before joining Johnstown of the Eastern League, "and they just didn't fit the roster of a certain ballclub, or the coach's technique, or the coach, or they just weren't ready at that time."

"The sheer numbers obviously speak for themselves," said sportswriter Bob Ryan. "So whether it was—maybe luck of the draw what team you tried out for, what the coach liked, and it's probably always defense, too. That's always been a thing that separates guys, the ability to and willingness to play defense."

Perhaps the best assessment of the relevant talent levels of the NBA and Eastern League came from Arizin, who once told Allentown fan Frank Thierer, "The 80 best players in the country played in the NBA, and after that you had the Eastern League."[8]

One major difference between Eastern League teams and those in the NBA was practice. In the Eastern League, basically, there wasn't any. Eastern Leaguers were weekend players. They played on Saturday and Sunday nights and then went back to their full-time jobs. Some teams might try to have a practice on Friday nights for players who could make it, and some guys who lived and worked in the towns they played in would get together on other nights. But otherwise, they hit the floor without a lot of structure.

"The basketball was pretty much pickup because you never had any practices," said Weiss. "You played two games on a weekend and you'd never get to practice. We did have like a little bitty training camp the next year, but it was very short and so it was just kind of a freelance, learn how to play basketball. But it was some very talented players."

Little practice time also meant not a lot of sophisticated offenses or defenses, just basic basketball that emphasized individual skills.

"The game itself . . . was more fundamental," said Hemans. "Quick passing, give and go, back door plays, pick and roll. In my opinion, in my time, those major differences provided for better and more exciting true basketball play and for a more intense and 'skill'-based game in terms of overall offense, defense and rebounding."

"It was great," said Rosen. "You know, nobody practiced. Just one-on-one, and run, isolation, and nobody played defense."

Seattle Times sportswriter Steve Kelley, whose father was one of the part owners of the Wilmington Blue Bombers, wrote, "The quality of basketball in the EBL . . . was remarkable. Every team played up-tempo. The league was a run-and-gun thrill ride."[9]

In many respects, the Eastern League was a winter version of the summer playground tournaments and leagues that thrived during this era, such as the Rucker League in New York City and the Baker League in Philadelphia. Many Eastern Leaguers competed along with NBA players and playground legends in those summer leagues, measuring themselves against some of the best players in the country, then bringing that style of play to Eastern League gyms in the winter.

"They had these tournaments all over the metropolitan area," said George Bruns, a former Eastern League player and coach who played for the New York Nets in 1972/73. "You'd show up with guys and you never knew who the heck was going to be on the team. Teams—they could show up with anybody. I played in a tournament [and] Jack Molinas was in it and Alan Seiden. They were kind of at the end. But you'd go to a tournament and they could show up with Wilt."[10]

"At some point you find yourself playing against everybody that you know that can play, or you find a way," McHartley said of his participation in summer leagues. "Because everywhere there were some great players, I wanted to go."

"I knew by what I did in the Baker League and stuff like that that I could play anywhere," said Stan Pawlak.

That wide-open, playground league style of ball was a hit with Eastern League fans.

"Nobody was bashful," recalled Hazleton, Pennsylvania, sports commentator Ron Marchetti, who grew up in the 1950s as a Hazleton Hawks fans. "Everybody shot. But even though they didn't practice I think they played well together."

Said Sonny Hill when interviewed for the website JockBio.com: "In the Eastern Basketball League, you could let your total game be played. Whereas if we went to the NBA, you would have been required to play within the parameters of a structure."[11]

In addition to the quality and style of the game, former Eastern Leaguers also recalled how tough it was.

Blaney, who played one season with the New York Knicks before coming to the Eastern League, said one reason for the league's physicality was "players frustrated [about] not being in the NBA, and along that same line, players wanting to get to the NBA. The competitive aspect of that was enormous. You were playing against another team that maybe had a guy who you were competing against to get to the Knicks or the 76ers or whatever team was looking for a player at the time. There were call-ups at that time, too. Guys went up and down from the league, so it was a very competitive league."

"I remember thinking that these guys really bang!" said Hemans. "Like in New York City's playgrounds!"

"In the league when I first started you didn't go inside," recalled Boeheim. "Tom Hoover and John Postley—there was a bunch of big guys, and they didn't want you coming in there. There was blood a lot of nights that first year. There was a lot of blood and a lot of fights. It was a tough league."

Referee Dick Bavetta said some former college players had a difficult time adjusting to the Eastern League's physicality. "It was a tougher brand of ball . . . than they were used to from the colleges. So they learned pretty quickly . . . that it was a tough league to play in."

Recalled Blaney:

> I think the first year I was at Trenton, I think we played something like 27 or 30 games, something like that over the course of the year, and I would venture to say that we had at least 20 fights in those 27 or 30 games. I mean, they were fights. They were not just grabbing and holding.
>
> I remember probably one of the first fights we had, and I think it was against Camden. Pickles Kennedy, from Temple, he was playing on Camden and a fight breaks out. Guys are up in the stands. People are coming out of the stands. Guys are jumping on tables. Tables are being overturned. The police are being called. Pickles grabs me and almost starts hugging me, and he said, "Move with me to the center court." I'm like ready to hit him and he's like just bucking me, being nice, and we get to the center court, the circle, and he said, "This is the safe place on the court." And he says, "I'm a lover, not a fighter." So he taught me how to avoid getting killed in a fight.

Carl Green, who played six years for the Globetrotters and nine in the Eastern League, remembered some run-ins with Bill Spivey and the talented—and tough—1959–1961 Baltimore Bullets. "Spivey . . . I had a headache for two weeks, man, he hit me with an elbow in my temple," said Green. "It took me two weeks to get rid of the headache." But Green said he got his revenge in the next game against Baltimore, scoring 38 points and holding Sherman White to 12. "This was physical, man."[12]

The Eastern League's style of play also produced some high-scoring games. Final scores in the 130s—and higher—were not unusual.

"One of the things I tell people . . . we scored in one game 175," McHartley recalled. "People say, 'Aw man, y'all had 175?' and I say, 'Yeah, we scored 175, and I still got the write-up to prove it.' And I think the night before we might have scored like 145. . . . So that was a league that I say wasn't a whole lot of defense played."

As entertaining as that style of play was for the fans, the players seemed to enjoy playing it just as much, if not more.

"We scored a lot of points back in those days," Pawlak said. "But it was tough basketball. I mean these guys were really good. I relished playing in the games, I really did! It was for me a terrific, fun time."

"I can't tell you how much I enjoyed playing in that league," said Boeheim. "It was just great basketball. I really liked it."

One feature that made the Eastern League just a little more fun for players and fans was the three-point play. After the ABL folded in 1962 (and Lear, Spivey, and other players who had bolted returned to the Eastern League), the Eastern League decided to reincarnate one of the ABL's innovations—the three-point shot. On June 1, 1964, Eastern League owners agreed to adopt the rule that all shots made from 25 feet or farther would count for three points.

During the first few seasons after the rule went into effect, three-pointers were rare. Only a handful were attempted during most games, and usually by one or two players on each team who were considered three-point specialists. That first season, Brendan McCann of Allentown led the league in three-pointers with 31 in 28 games. Two years later, George Lehmann of Trenton led the league with 60.

McCann and Lehmann were among the small group of three-point marksmen who would dot the league in the mid-'60s. Others included Blaney, York Larese, Gene Hudgins, Bobby McNeill, Jim McCoy (Julius McCoy's brother), and Bucky Bolyard (who had a glass eye, which led to occasional quips about his "great shooting eye").

"I used to bust [Blaney's] balls," said Ryan. "Three-on-0. First guy I ever saw come down on a fast break and shoot a three. Three-on-0. I may have been wrong. Maybe three-on-a-half. But I know damn well, I'd never seen it. It was a new phenomenon. Never saw anybody that didn't advance to the basket when that was the option. That was a new thing. And George was the one who did it."

Blaney, for his part, said Lehmann was the first guy he ever saw shoot a three on a 3-on-1 fast break. "I had never seen anyone else ever do that. I played in a game when he made 10 threes. That's back in the '60s. I mean, that's unbelievable."

Boeheim, too, would earn a reputation as a good three-point shooter. "Hey, man, oh you talk about a shooter, listen, we used to talk about him all the time," said Tony Upson. "Because he wore those little thick glasses, you know, and running around looking like somebody who shouldn't even be on a team—he'd be shooting you down, boy."[13]

In a 1971 *Sports Illustrated* article, former NBA player "Mike Riordan remember[ed] from his one year at Allentown coming downcourt on a three-on-one, and the lead guy pulls up for a 25-foot three-pointer. He misses, gets the rebound, dribbles behind the line for another shot. 'I couldn't figure out what he was doing till I remembered he was in a race for the scoring title,'"[14] Riordan reportedly said.

One measure of the Eastern League's talent during that golden era was the number of players who either worked their way up to or came down from the NBA and played in the Eastern League. While the league didn't have a formal minor-league arrangement with the NBA, teams in the big league were allowed to "farm out" one or two players to Eastern League clubs to get experience while preparing for a chance to play in the NBA. This created a pool of NBA-quality players shuttling to the EPBL and, sometimes, back again.

Several Eastern Leaguers who played in the NBA have already been mentioned, including Arizin, Scott, Andy Johnson, Weiss, Cleo Hill, Sihugo Green, Arceneaux, McCann, Blaney, McNeill, Larese, Freddie Crawford, Lehmann, Somerset, and Lear (albeit only in three NBA games).

Other Eastern Leaguers from that 1950–1960s era who also played in the NBA included Riordan, Bob Love, Paul Silas, Nate Bowman, Joe Strawder, Barney Cable, Art Spoelstra, Danny Finn, Zeke Sinicola, Joe Holup, Bob "Zeke" Zawoluk, Dick Ricketts, Jim Tucker, Larry Hennessey, Tom Stith, Al Butler, John Barnhill, Alex "Boo" Ellis, Walter Dukes, John Richter, Tom Hoover, Hubie White, Cal Ramsey, Art Heyman, Larry Jones, Sonny Dove, Jim Ware, Jim "Bad News" Barnes, Ben Warley, and Gene Conley (who was also a Major League Baseball pitcher). Established NBA stars K. C. Jones of the Boston Celtics and Larry Costello of the Philadelphia 76ers also made brief appearances in the Eastern League—Jones for eight games with Hartford in 1967 and Costello during the 1965/66 season with Wilkes-Barre before returning to the 76ers.

"You blended in the guys that were right on the edge of playing in the NBA," said Scott. "Really good guys, guys that had played in the NBA . . . That just made an incredible thing."

Some teams were especially loaded with NBA-level talent.

"I mean, think about it, on that Wilmington team Tom Hoover played in the NBA. Freddie Crawford played in the NBA. Bob Weiss played in the NBA. I played in the ABA. And that was just from that particular team," recalled McHartley of his 1965/66 and 1966/67 Blue Bombers, who won back-to-back league championships. They also had NBA veterans Cable and Ellis (1965/66).

"We were so good," recalled Bellamy. "Somebody was encouraging somebody in the ABA to just adopt our entire team. We would have been competitive. If somebody had that vision, to grab all of us and sign us, the basic core of the team, you know, and put us in the ABA, we would have been very competitive right away."

The Blue Bombers weren't the only team loaded with NBA-level talent. The Allentown Jets of that same mid-1960s era had Johnson, McCann, Stith, Larese, Lehmann, and future ABA stars Walt Simon and Hank Whitney. Arizin's teammates at Camden from 1962 to 1965 included Lear, McNeill, Hoover, Gaines, Dukes, Strawder, Blaney, and Ira Harge, who would become an established ABA big man. And the Easton-Phillipsburg Madisons of the late 1950s had Lear, Choice, and Gaines leading them to the 1959/60 league title.

Just to give an example of the NBA-level talent in the EPBL during this era, the league's top 10 scorers in 1960/61 were:

Hal Lear, Easton	39.7 PPG
Boo Ellis, W-B	37.9 PPG
Ray Scott, Allentown	33.4 PPG
Roman Turmon, Allentown	31.9 PPG
Jack Molinas, Hazleton	30.0 PPG
Dick Gaines, Easton	29.5 PPG
Bill Spivey, Baltimore	28.3 PPG
Wally Choice, Easton	27.4 PPG
Stacey Arceneaux, Scranton	27.2 PPG
Tom Hemans, Williamsport	26.0 PPG

With the exception of Spivey, who was banned from the NBA because of the point-shaving scandal, every one of those players had some NBA experience, at least in preseason.

The Eastern League also became a home for ex-Globetrotters, many of whom tired of the Trotters' grueling travel and performance schedule of upwards of 1,000 games per year. Johnson, Turmon, Chaney, Hudgins, Tom "Tarzan" Spencer, Carl Green, and Charlie Hoxie were all veteran Eastern Leaguers who had at least some experience with the Globetrotters, who at that time still attracted many of the best African American players.

Several high-round NBA draft picks from that era were either sent to the Eastern League or went there after getting cut from NBA teams. Bill Green, the no. 1 draft pick of the Celtics in 1963 and eighth overall, decided not to play in the NBA because of a fear of flying and spent eight years in the Eastern League.

"He was a terrific athlete," Boeheim said of Green, who was also drafted by the Dallas Cowboys and the Boston Red Sox.

John Richter, the Celtics' no. 1 pick in 1959 and sixth overall, played one season in Boston and then 10 in the Eastern League with the Sunbury Mercuries, becoming one of the league's top rebounders and formidable post players. Other NBA no. 1 picks from that era who played in the Eastern League were Cleo Hill, St. Louis Hawks, 1961; Sihugo Green, Rochester Royals, 1956 (drafted one ahead of Bill Russell); and Tom Hoover, Philadelphia 76ers, 1963.

"Due to the abundance of highly skilled players, if you made a team in the Eastern League you had to be exceptionally talented," said Hemans. "I personally witnessed outstanding 'college all-stars' who legitimately could not either make an Eastern League team or complete a season with an Eastern League team."

Perhaps Boeheim said it best when describing the league's talent.

"There were great players," he said in an interview on the Syracuse.com website. "Guys you never heard of because they didn't play in the NBA, but the NBA didn't have the room for all the quality players that you have today. So they played in the Eastern pro league. The talent was unbelievable."[15]

6

STARS OF THE GLORY
YEARS (1954–1967)

S o with all that talent, all those guys in the mid-1950s to mid-1960s who were close but not quite right for the NBA, or who were kept out, or who kept themselves out—who were the best?

In 1996, in commemoration of the 50th anniversary of the Eastern League's founding, the Continental Basketball Association (CBA) named two all-time teams: one from the Eastern Professional Basketball League/Eastern Basketball Association era from 1946 to 1978; the other from the CBA era. Players named to the EPBL/EBA-era team who starred during the 1954–1967 period were Hal Lear, Stacey Arceneaux, Tom Hemans, Julius McCoy, and Roman Turmon.[1] Other players from that era who received consideration were Paul Arizin, John Chaney, Wally Choice, Alex "Boo" Ellis, Dick Gaines, Art Heyman, Jim Huggard, Bob Keller, George Lehmann, Brendan McCann, and Bob McNeill.

What's immediately apparent from the list is that whoever selected those teams decided not to include players implicated in the 1950s college point-shaving scandal. In any discussion of star players from that era, Bill Spivey, Sherman White, and Jack Molinas are inevitably mentioned near the top. Spivey was the best center in the league for almost a decade. He's the sixth all-time leading scorer in Eastern League history, an MVP, led the league in scoring in back-to-back seasons from 1958 to 1960, and even in 1964/65 at age 35 averaged 28 PPG. White is the eighth all-time leading scorer and in 1954/55 led the league in scoring and was selected MVP, while Molinas is the 12th all-time scorer and was the league's top scorer and MVP in 1955/56. White was first team all-league for five seasons in a row, while Molinas made either first or second team all-league for seven straight seasons.

Spivey, White, and Molinas would no doubt have been NBA stars, and are considered among the best players of their generation. As described in chapter 3, they were dominant talents in the Eastern League, always at or near the league leaders in scoring and in other statistical categories, as well as in the estimation of their peers. Their talent and stature gave the Eastern League legitimacy and credibility in the professional basketball world. They belong in any discussion of the league's all-time best players.

Following are profiles of players who, with Spivey, White, and Molinas, are mentioned most often when discussing the Eastern League's top players from the time when the "fixers" joined the league to the formation of the American Basketball Association (ABA). The players are listed roughly in the order in which they joined the league.

HAL "KING" LEAR

"The best player in the league played for Easton—Hal Lear from Temple." That's what former Eastern League player and coach Howie Landa said. As described in chapter 4, Lear was one of the best players that the city of Philadelphia produced in the 1950s and finished his collegiate career at Temple earning some All-American honorable mention. Landa and others who saw him play believe that Lear deserved more than the scant three-game NBA career he had with the Philadelphia Warriors.

"I think Lear got screwed," said Landa, mincing no words. "He could really score. . . . They just felt that even though he was a scorer he couldn't play in the NBA."

Teaming with Wally Choice and Dick Gaines to form a high-scoring Big Three for the Easton-Phillipsburg Madisons, Lear was the Eastern League's preeminent scorer in the late 1950s at a time when the league had an abundance of scorers. He led the league in scoring during his rookie season, 1956/57, with a then-record average of 40.3 PPG and won the MVP (the league did not introduce a Rookie of the Year Award until the following season). He would finish third in 1957/58 (behind Larry Hennessey, with whom he competed for a spot on the Warriors, and Molinas); third in 1958/59 (behind Spivey and Tom Hemans); and second in 1959/60 (behind Spivey) before winning the scoring title again in 1960/61 with an average of 39.7.

Of the 40 times that an Eastern League player scored 50 or more points in a game, Lear had 10 of them. He finished his career as the fourth all-time leading scorer in league history. Not only could Lear light up the scoreboard, but he often ranked among the league's leaders in assists, too.

Easton-Phillipsburg—with a lineup that in addition to the Big Three also had Jay "Pappy" Norman, a former teammate of Lear's at Temple, and Charlie Ross, a hometown star from Easton High School and Lafayette College—would win a share of the regular season title in 1957/58 (when they, Wilkes-Barre, and Hazleton finished with identical 18–10 records) and the postseason championship in 1959/60.

"Easton was loaded," agreed Landa. "I mean the funny thing about it, I picked up Hal Lear when he came out of the bathroom, and Jay Norman would set a screen as he came onto the court, I swear to G-d, man!"

"That Easton team used to be a really big story," recalled Hubie Brown. "Easton used to score a ton of points."

John Chaney attributed Lear's scoring prowess in part to his quickness, especially his first step.

"You couldn't keep him" from driving to the basket, said Chaney of the slender Lear, who stood 6'0". "If he could see the basket he's going to score."

He could also score from outside, playing for most of his career before the league adopted the three-point shot in 1964. He was, though, the beneficiary of the three-point rule in the short-lived American Basketball League (ABL), where he starred during its slightly more than one season.

Lear's talent was so sublime as to seem almost effortless.

"Lear was unbelievable," recalled Hazleton fan and sports historian Ron Marchetti. "But [he] was the only player that never sweat. He'd be playing the whole game, no perspiration on him. I can't believe that. And he was a great shooter. . . . He controlled the outside."

"King Lear was the best!" said Stan Pawlak. "The most difficult guy to play against of anybody. . . . I remember the guys that I wasn't capable of dealing with. They left an indelible mark. And he was just a guy that had an off-speed way of handling the ball. . . . He was really difficult for me to handle."

WALLY CHOICE

If Lear was Mr. Outside for Easton-Phillipsburg, then Choice—an all-Big Ten player at Indiana University who also played for the Globetrotters—was Mr. Inside. In his four seasons at Easton with Lear and Gaines, Choice averaged 25 or more points per game each year, topping out at 27.9 PPG in the Madisons' championship 1959/60 season. He was first team all-league once during that time and second team twice.

But it was after Lear and Gaines left for the ABL in 1961/62 and the Madisons moved to Trenton that Choice became a scoring star. He averaged 41.3 points per game that season, the best ever in league history, and scored 69 points on March 4, 1962, against Sunbury, a record that held until 1976. He led the league in scoring the following season, too, averaging 34.1 PPG, the final year in which he played.

Boston Globe sportswriter and ESPN basketball commentator Bob Ryan was a teenager in Trenton and remembered attending the Colonials' first game and Choice's scoring line, including 20 free throws. "He was a classic '50s product," Ryan said. "Inside guy, 6'5", powerful, kind of an Elgin Baylor body, maybe even stronger, and his game was inside. Obviously, you make 20 free throws, you're getting fouled because you're not doing it from facing up the basket. And that was his game. And of course the world was different, and you could be a 6'5" power guy. And he was very good at what he did."

As Lear told author Ron Thomas in *They Cleared the Lane*: "Most players had one shot. . . . [Choice] could shoot jump shots, he could shoot hook shots, shot a one-hand set, and could drive to the basket."[2]

Landa said Choice was among the Eastern League players who he believed "belonged in the NBA. . . . I don't know why Wally didn't go because he could play . . . the guy could outright play."

Ryan, too, thought Choice had NBA ability but said: "I mean, look, they all had a reason why they weren't in the NBA. There weren't many jobs, we all know that, we all know the story. . . . So there's a lot of good basketball players out there that had . . . strengths and weaknesses, and whatever was the deal with Wally. . . . All I know is he was unstoppable, at least in my eyes."

Choice also developed a reputation as something of an on-court instigator.

"He'd kind of work up the crowd," recalled Hazleton sports aficionado Rev. Connell McHugh. "Like when he'd come to Hazleton, when the referees weren't looking it was almost like [pro wrestling]. He'd give somebody a push and all that. He deliberately worked people up and then once in a while, too, he'd cherry-pick and he'd go down there and wait. That used to aggravate the people—he'd deliberately work the fans. He was a good guy himself."

"He was murder, because they hated him," said Landa, adding that opposing players and even fans would sometimes try to invade the team's locker room after games, looking for Choice. "They would come in and want to fight him. Oh my G-d, but he was a great shooter and scorer . . . they were so jealous of him. He was something. He didn't take shit from nobody, I'm telling you."

JULIUS MCCOY

His contemporaries describe Julius McCoy with almost a sense of awe, and his ability to score inside despite his relative lack of size was such that even his true height gets lost amid the legends.

"I mean Julius McCoy. He scored any way. He was 6'4"—maybe—under-sized but he just scored inside against anybody," said Jim Boeheim.

"Julius, he's a 6'1" post guy who nobody could guard," recalled Pawlak. "So here's a guy averaging like how many zillions of points a game as a 6'1" post player. But then when you realize how good a player he was at Michigan State you realize how good this guy was. . . . Able to score inside on anybody. Nobody really stopped him."

"He was like maybe 6'4". Maybe. And a post player," said former Eastern Leaguer Richie Cornwall. "I remember my teammates prior to playing against him telling me that this guy Julius McCoy, he doesn't even look at the basket. He just turns and shoots and he consistently makes shots. And I'm saying like, 'Yeah, OK' or whatever. And . . . we played him and he played entirely with his back to the basket and it was uncanny how he would just turn and use the backboard to make shots. . . . He was a tremendous talent, he really was."

"My G-d," said Chaney simply. "Nobody stopped Julius."

For the record, McCoy was listed as 6'3". He came to the Eastern League in 1958 after an illustrious college career at Michigan State, where he earned All-America, first team all-Big Ten, and team MVP honors in 1956, finishing his career as the Spartans' all-time leading scorer at the time. He played six seasons with the Williamsport Billies (with a brief foray to the ABL in 1961), and then six seasons with the Sunbury Mercuries. By the time his Eastern League career ended, McCoy was (and still is) the league's all-time leading scorer with 7,754 points, a two-time league scoring champion, and the 1965/66 MVP when he led the league with 33.6 PPG.

In many ways, McCoy and his brother and teammate, Jim, epitomized the Eastern League. They were big-time players (Jim went to Marquette) perform-ing in the smallest of towns in tiny little gyms. They never won a championship in the Eastern League, but in a league where the home teams usually won, play-ing against them in Sunbury was a very tough out.

"Just small gym, small town," said Boeheim talking about Sunbury and the McCoys. "They each got 30 every night they played."

While Jim at 6'1" was an outside shooting guard, Julius was a post player. He could hit the medium-range jump shot, but he wasn't a shooter—he was a scorer. His bread and butter came on twisting, spinning moves to the basket, throwing left-handed shots up off the backboard at odd angles, which would usually go in. He could also shoot fouls, which he would draw by the bushel with his work around the hoop.

"He has more moves than a Chinese lantern on a windy day," was how former Scranton Miners' radio play-by-play announcer Ron Allen used to describe McCoy.[3]

What made McCoy's unusual arsenal work for him were his long arms, big hands, body control, and unexpected quickness. He had been a champion sprinter and a star running back in high school, and had actually been recruited by Michigan State and Penn State to play football before deciding to focus on basketball for the Spartans.

"He could always get that shot off," said Willie Somerset, who played briefly in the NBA before becoming an Eastern League and ABA star. "No one could block it. He was quick and nobody could block that shot."

"Man he would go to the hole," said McHartley. "He was real deceptive. . . . Real deceptive."

He was also very strong.

"He had great, great strength," Pawlak said. "Without question the strongest guy in the league. And he would be able to use his body to keep the big guys away from him. He used to have a little half-hook that he could make consistently. And he just would get that ball in the post. Didn't come out of there very much. . . . Once he was in there, he was going to score points. . . . He was a unique player."

"Julius McCoy was one of the highest-level basketball players I've seen," said Swish McKinney, who also became a prolific scorer in the league. "The other guys that I knew . . . it was easy to figure them out and know what they could do and what they could not do. . . . I studied a lot of players. I studied a lot of players. And Julius McCoy, he's probably the only one, only one" who McKinney said he could not figure out.

McCoy played in the St. Louis Hawks' camp in 1958 but didn't make it to the NBA. Some of his contemporaries say he was simply undersized.

"He really was very talented, [but] he was an in-betweener, like size-wise," said Cornwall. "He couldn't really be a guard and he couldn't really be a big person."

Others, however, like Somerset, who came from the same town in western Pennsylvania as the McCoys and was close friends, disagreed. "He did not get a fair, fair shot into the NBA," Somerset said. "[The Hawks] had at that time . . . some other good ballplayers, but he would have overshadowed all of them."

ROMAN "BIG DOC" TURMON

If Bill Spivey was the best pivot man in the league in the late '50s and early '60s, then Roman "Big Doc" Turmon was the baddest.

"Fearsome, 6'6", bull-in-the-china-shop kind of player as I recall," said Bob Ryan. "Scary. I don't know if he was a bad guy or not, but he was a scary guy."

"He was one tough guy under the boards," recalled Harvey Kasoff, part owner of the Eastern League's Baltimore Bullets. "He could play in the NBA."

Turmon's size and demeanor could be intimidating, and he used both to his advantage. He was a football and basketball player as well as a shot-putter at Clark College in Atlanta, and then played with the Harlem Globetrotters for five years. In 1959/60 he left the Globetrotters to join the New York Knicks and became one of the first of many players sent to Allentown through a personal connection between Knick scout and later coach Red Holzman and Allentown Jets' co-owner/general manager Frank Wagner.

Turmon made an immediate impact on the Eastern League, leading it in rebounding his first season as he would for the next four seasons. He finished second in scoring behind Wally Choice in both 1961/62 (32.5 PPG) and 1962/63 (32.7), leading the Jets to back-to-back league championships and being named MVP in 1962.

The Eastern League record book is dotted with great individual performances by Turmon, such as a March 1961 contest in which he scored 38 points and grabbed 37 rebounds as the Jets defeated Williamsport, 163–137. Earlier that season, he scored a then-league-record 68 points—and Hal Lear had 57 for Easton—in a 153–139 shootout win for the Jets.

In 1964, a pay dispute with Allentown's ownership ended Big Doc's playing career, even though he finished the 1963/64 season averaging almost 24 PPG. As Scranton owner Art Pachter explained, to keep Turmon from signing with another team, the league instituted a rule that if a player didn't sign his contract by the third game of the season, he would have to sit out the season. Effectively, that meant players either had to take the salary their teams offered them, or they would lose a season without playing or getting paid. That provision became known around the league as "the Roman Turmon rule."

Turmon sat out that 1964/65 season and never returned to pro basketball. In his five seasons with the Jets he was named first team all-league three times and second team once, and would amass 3,686 points, becoming the league's 23rd all-time scorer.

DICK GAINES

No player in the Eastern League was tougher than Dick Gaines, who was also called "Richie" or "Chink." At 6'3" and 230 pounds or more, Gaines was strong, physical, fierce, and fearsome.

"He was . . . like Charles Barkley," said author and former Eastern Leaguer Charley Rosen. "He was like a bowling ball when he drove. He was tough. From Seton Hall. Tough player." Recounting a story about Gaines in his autobiography *Crazy Basketball*, Rosen wrote: "Gaines is my teammate and I'm afraid to step on his shadow."[4]

A Scranton Miners' program from the 1963/64 season put it this way: "A rough, tough player who neither asks nor gives no quarter, Richie plays to win at all times."[5]

Gaines relied on strong drives to the basket for most of his points, but could also hit the long-range jumper.

"I was always going toward the basket,"[6] Gaines told Thomas in *They Cleared the Lane*. "I tried to get as close as I could and if that couldn't do it, I would pull up and shoot the jump shot. I used to love to get there with the big guys."

His hard-charging style was the perfect complement to Lear's outside scoring and Choice's inside play in Easton-Phillipsburg. He won the league's first Rookie of the Year Award after the 1957/58 season when he finished sixth in scoring with 24.3 PPG, and averaged 24.9 the following year and 28.3 in the Madisons' 1959/60 championship season. After a brief stint in the ABL, he returned to the Eastern League and had his best season in 1961/62, averaging 32.4 PPG with the Camden Bullets. He finished his 11-year career as the league's seventh all-time scorer with 5,474 points.

"Chink was a real good player," said Hubie Brown. "He scored a ton of points."

"He definitely should have been playing in the NBA," said Bobby Hunter of Gaines, who was drafted by the Syracuse Nationals (as described in chapter 4) but did not play in the NBA.

JOHN CHANEY

Contemporary basketball fans recall John Chaney as the fiery, Hall of Fame coach of Temple University, an elder statesman of Eastern and Philadelphia basketball. But before that, Chaney earned his reputation as an equally fiery, wiry, and slick 6'1" guard who played and coached in the Eastern League for 12 seasons, mostly in tiny Sunbury.

Sonny Hill, in an interview with the sports website JockBio.com, said: "I tell people all the time, he was a far better player than he was a coach! He was ahead of his time."[7]

Chaney was a double-figure scorer, topping out at 19.1 PPG in 1956/57, and was considered among the league's top playmakers. His game was about speed, deft ballhandling, relentless defensive pressure, and ball-hawking.

Known as "Chick," Chaney was admired as much for his tenacity as his talent. His backcourt running mate for the Mercuries and traveling companion from Philly, Howie Landa, said he sometimes had to keep the slender Chaney from getting into fights.

"He's a character and a half," said Landa. "Chaney was a good player. . . . He was so skinny at the time it's unbelievable."

STACEY ARCENEAUX

Unlike most of the other players named in this chapter, Stacey Arceneaux actually played in the NBA, for seven games with the St. Louis Hawks in 1962, totaling 50 points and 32 rebounds. That brief stint came about halfway through Arceneaux's 14-year career in the Eastern League, after he had already established himself as one of the league's most prolific scorers and won an MVP Award. Arceneaux quickly realized that he could make more money by staying with his off-court career as an insurance claims adjuster and playing pro basketball on weekends, so he returned to the Eastern League.

But there was no question about his talent.

Arceneaux was one of "the guys that were right on the edge of playing in the NBA," Ray Scott said.

Arceneaux was a New York City high school legend when he joined the Scranton Miners in 1956. How great a legend?

"I took a client of mine to Madison Square Garden to see a basketball game," said attorney Marvin Salenger, for whom Arceneaux worked for many years as a claims negotiator. "And sitting just by chance below me was . . . Stacey. The friend I had taken was a Taft [High School] graduate and without saying anything to me, he says 'Oh my G-d!' And he ran down the stairs and he says to Stacey, he says 'Stacey, I went to high school with you. You're the greatest player!' . . . It was like him seeing Babe Ruth. That's how famous Stacey was in all the boroughs."

In 1954, Iowa State University recruited Arceneaux and fellow New York City high school star John Crawford (who also would later become an Eastern Leaguer). But when Arceneaux got there, the school learned that he did not have enough credits to enroll. The coaches wanted Arceneaux to stay in Iowa to complete the required credits, but Arceneaux decided to return home to New York.

"From what I understood, he was one of the few black people at Iowa State, and he was really and truly uncomfortable," said Salenger.

Arceneaux was a 6'5" forward who could score inside and outside.

"Great shooter," recalled Reverend McHugh. "He had a terrific bank jump shot. I can remember one game for Hazleton here he had 58 points on 29 field goals. Banking them in. Unbelievable shooter."

"I got to watch Arceneaux a lot with the Camden Bullets, in Camden Convention Hall," said Pawlak, who grew up in Camden. "He was just a spectacular scorer. Just unbelievable scorer. Could score from anyplace. Big, tough guy."

Arceneaux would be in the league's top 10 scorers for eight straight years, topping out at 31.1 PPG in 1961/62 with Hazleton. He was also a top rebounder, often averaging among the league's leaders with double figures. In 1960 he won the MVP Award playing for Scranton, and he was named first team all-league four times and second team once. When his career ended in 1968, he was the league's all-time leading scorer with 7,735 points, but he was later surpassed by Julius McCoy.

TOM HEMANS

Hemans was one of those players who was so quietly, steadily efficient that he sometimes gets overlooked. But by the time his 14 years in the Eastern League—mostly with Hazleton, Williamsport, and Scranton—were over, he had amassed 7,641 points and was third all-time in scoring behind McCoy and Arceneaux. He was also first in career rebounds and led the league in rebounding four times.

"Tommy Hemans was outstanding," said Hubie Brown, who played at Niagara a couple of years behind Hemans. "Tommy Hemans should have been in the NBA. . . . He . . . had all kinds of great post-up moves, was terrific off the dribble, had a jumper, could block shots, run, outstanding athlete, great rebounder. He proved that with what he did in the Eastern League."

Brown said the slender, left-handed Hemans is "very bright. He had a very high basketball IQ . . . and was an outstanding student at school. Now there's a guy that should have been in the NBA."

Hemans "was very popular here," recalled Reverend McHugh of Hemans's time in Hazleton. His popularity continued in Scranton, and he was selected by Scranton fans as their "Most Popular Miner" two seasons in a row.

"A good left-handed jump shot, a good foul shooter, good all-around player and fast," said McHugh.

Hemans's trademark was a sweeping left-handed hook, but he did everything well. He got selected to either first or second team all-league teams seven times.

"His play at all times has been exceptional and many times sensational,"[8] said his bio in the 1963/64 Miners' program.

In 1967/68, the Miners appointed Hemans as their coach. "It was a natural," that season's program said. "Tommy exemplifies all the drive and spirit necessary in a professional basketball player."[9]

RAY SCOTT

Ray Scott (who, like Gaines, was sometimes called "Chink") is one of the Eastern League's great success stories. A Philadelphia native, he left the University of Portland in his sophomore year and, because of NBA rules in effect at the time, could not be drafted by the NBA until his college class graduated.

So Scott played in the Eastern League for three seasons with the Allentown Jets, until the Detroit Pistons selected him as the fourth player in the 1961 draft. He enjoyed a nine-year career starring with the Pistons and Baltimore Bullets in the NBA and two seasons with the Virginia Squires in the ABA. Later, Scott was the Pistons' head coach for three and a half seasons.

"Ray Scott was the high scorer of the team," said Hubie Brown, who played with Scott in Allentown. "He was so outstanding, because he could really score. He was a great outside shooter, good rebounder, good on the break, had a mid-range game, post-up game."

"He definitely was one of the best players that I ever played against," said Tommy Hemans. "Very strong, smooth, tough rebounder and an excellent ball handler and passer."

Brown said Scott "was the total package. He was an excellent teammate. Everyone got along with him. He was just biding his time at that time playing in the Eastern League."

During his time in Allentown, the 6'9" Scott led the Jets in scoring and teamed with Turmon to form a formidable frontcourt. In 1959/60 he was eighth in the league in scoring and third in rebounding and in assists, and in 1960/61 he was third in league scoring with 33.4 PPG and finished second to Turmon in rebounding.

PAUL ARIZIN

Arizin, a 6'5" forward, only played three seasons in the Eastern League, but his impact was so great that he has to be counted among the league's all-time best. Imagine if a perennial NBA all-star like Dirk Nowitzki or James Harden left the NBA in his prime to finish his career in a weekend league. That's essentially what Arizin did when, as described in chapter 5, he decided not to move with his Philadelphia Warriors to San Francisco in 1962 and instead stayed home in Philly working for IBM and playing basketball on weekends with the Camden Bullets (reportedly for over $300 a game, making him the league's top-paid player).

In Camden, Arizin combined with fellow Philadelphia area basketball greats including Lear, Norman, Bobby McNeill (a former Knick, Warrior, and Laker who played collegiately at St. Joseph's), Alonzo Lewis (LaSalle), Tom Hoover (Villanova), and Sonny Hill, as well as Dick Gaines (in 1962/63), to turn the Bullets into one of the league's top teams. They would either tie for or win the regular season title in each of his three seasons, and in 1963/64 won the post-season championship. Arizin won the MVP Award in 1963 and was first team all-league twice, second team once, and averaged 27.4, 25.8, and 23.5 PPG.

Author Charley Rosen played briefly on that Camden team, too, and recalled the first time he met the great Arizin at a practice session in a freezing gym. (A version of this story also appears in Rosen's book *Crazy Basketball*.)

> So we're practicing and he's not there. Suddenly the door opens and in he comes. And meanwhile we were getting a little warm. We took off our coats, we took off our gloves, we took off our hats. And we're running up and down in shorts and shirts. We're warm.
>
> He strips down to his shorts and his shirt and jumps on the court. And I happen to be guarding him. . . . And it's freezing and you could see your breath and everything. There's no way he had any feeling in his hands—in any part of his body—that's how cold it was. And he proceeds to hit about 10 jump shots in a row. It was one of the best exhibitions of shooting that I have ever seen.

ANDY JOHNSON

Andy Johnson was already an established professional player when he joined the Allentown Jets in 1962/63. He had played four seasons with the Harlem

Globetrotters starting in 1954/55 and four seasons in the NBA—three with the Philadelphia Warriors and one with the Chicago Packers.

But Johnson—who was still under contract to Abe Saperstein and the Globetrotters and had been "loaned" to the NBA—fell victim to a squabble between Saperstein and the NBA that kept other NBA teams from signing him. So he played for the Philadelphia Tapers in Saperstein's ABL in 1962 until they folded and then entered the Eastern League with the Allentown Jets, quickly becoming an all-around star.

"He scored, he assisted, and in addition to allowing others to stand out, he was able to shine as the team's captain,"[10] wrote his son, Mark, in *Basketball Slave*.

Johnson teamed with Turmon, scoring sensation Walt Simon, playmaker and long-range shooter Brendan McCann, and big men Tom Stith and Hank Whitney to make the Jets the league's dominant team for most of the 1960s. They won league championships in 1963, '65, and '68, and Johnson won the MVP Award in 1964, even though he was only the third leading scorer on the team averaging 20.7 PPG.

In a 1965 playoff game against the Camden Bullets, Johnson held his old Philadelphia friend and teammate Paul Arizin to only three field goals. Mark Johnson said one reporter called his father "the most complete player he had ever seen."[11]

WALT SIMON

A slender, 6'5" swingman from historically black Benedict College in South Carolina, Walt Simon joined the Allentown Jets in 1961 after getting drafted and waived by the New York Knicks. A natural scorer, Simon was a consistent 20-per-game man for the talent-laden Jets and led the league in scoring in 1964/65 with 29.3 PPG, topping Julius McCoy by one point and winning the league MVP Award. His highest average was 33.3 PPG in 1966/67, his last season before leaving for the ABA, and his 4,073 points put him 17th on the Eastern League all-time list.

Former Globetrotter and Eastern Leaguer Bobby Hunter was in the New Jersey Americans training camp with Simon in the ABA's first season. "He . . . controlled the . . . camp," Hunter recalled. "He was great coming off the bench and he played each of his positions very well. Then he'd rebound and played a pretty good defensive game." Simon starred for seven seasons in the ABA with the Americans, New York Nets, and Kentucky Colonels.

"Walt Simon could play," said Maurice McHartley, who competed against Simon in the ABA and Eastern League.

HANK WHITNEY

When Abe Saperstein's ABL went defunct during its second season in 1962/63, Hank Whitney was the prize pick in the dispersal draft that the Eastern League held to allocate former ABL players.

Art Pachter, owner of the Scranton Miners, recalled that league owners "decided that we'll pick names. . . . Certain names weren't in the list [because] . . . they were too expensive. . . . Hank Whitney, that was the first name everybody wanted. Allentown drew first. They got him."

A powerfully built, 6'7", 230-pound power forward/center, Whitney could run the floor, rebound, and score inside. He finished consistently among the league's top rebounders and had his top scoring season in 1966/67 with 28.4 PPG. Whitney played on two championship Jets squads and made all-league twice.

In 1967 he left the Jets and joined the New Jersey Americans of the new ABA, scoring 16.0 PPG and grabbing 12.9 rebounds. He would play three more seasons in the ABA before returning to the Eastern League in 1970 for a final three, and finished 22nd on the league's all-time scoring list.

BOB MCNEILL

If there's a prototype of the tough, crafty, Philadelphia point guard, it's Bobby McNeill. A product of St. Joseph's University where he was known as "an assist machine"[12] according to his bio on the St. Joe's Athletics website, he played three seasons in the NBA with the New York Knicks, Philadelphia Warriors, and Los Angeles Lakers, averaging five points and three assists per game.

In 1962, McNeill opted not to return to the Lakers and joined fellow Philadelphian and IBM employee Paul Arizin to play with the Camden Bullets.

"Remember, the NBA didn't have any money back in those days," said Pawlak, himself another great Philadelphia-area guard. "I mean, Bobby McNeill's another one who everybody said was an NBA player and he worked for IBM. . . . And he was as good as any guard I played against in that league."

McNeill and Arizin teamed to lead the Bullets to either first or tied for first in their three regular seasons together, and in 1963/64 Camden won the postseason championship. McNeill finished no lower than third in assists in each of his seven seasons in the league with Camden, Trenton, and Allentown (where he would win another league championship), and won the assist title twice with 6.7 per game in 1964/65 and 6.3 in 1966/67.

He could also score, both from outside (including three-pointers) and in gritty drives to the basket. McNeill finished 15th on the league's all-time scoring list with 4,449 points, topping out in 1965/66 averaging 27.5 PPG to finish second behind McCoy. His consistent excellence made him a six-time, first team all-league selection.

LEVERN "JELLY" TART

Levern Tart was on his way to becoming one of the best guards in the Eastern League when he left for the Oakland Oaks of the ABA in 1967.

A star at Bradley University, Tart was drafted by the Boston Celtics in 1964 and was the last player cut in training camp. He joined the Wilkes-Barre Barons and made an immediate impact, finishing fifth in the league in scoring at 23.9 PPG (right behind Rookie of the Year Swish McKinney). The following two seasons he averaged 23.6 and 29.2, and was named first team all-league both times.

Tart teamed with former Philadelphia 76er Larry Jones to give the Barons a potent backcourt. Jones was the better outside shooter, with Tart the fearless driver who relied on his strength and body control to make seemingly impossible finishes around the rim. At 6'3" and 195 pounds, he was like a slimmer but still solid facsimile of Richie Gaines.

"[Tart] just elbowed me one night," recalled Boeheim. "I think I woke up the next week. He was as physical as anybody I'd ever seen. . . . I didn't even know what day it was. He was a good player."

Tart was among the ABA's early stars. He was a two-time ABA All-Star and played for six teams in four years. He averaged 19.4 PPG and for a time held the ABA's single-game scoring record of 49 points until Jones broke it with 52.

"He could score, he was quick," said former Wilmington star Waite Bellamy, a fellow Floridian who recalled seeing Tart play in high school.

"Jelly and I ended up playing with the Nets in New York together for a while," recalled Bellamy's former backcourt mate McHartley. "And that was somebody else [who] never saw a shot they wouldn't take."

When his ABA days were over, Tart returned to the Eastern League for a season with Hazleton in 1973/74.

"I remember playing against Tart," said Pawlak. "He came with a great reputation, but you found out that these guys that came back were not as good as they were. They didn't kill the league when they came back."

WILLIE MURRELL

Murrell played only two full seasons in the league before leaving for the ABA and then returned for part of a season. But in his two full years in the league, he was such a dynamic force that it would be impossible not to include him here.

"He was a great athlete," said Scranton owner Pachter. "I mean, Murrell would get a rebound and he would be the first guy down on the other end and he'd score the basket. He was just . . . a phenomenal athlete."

"He rebounded. He could score. He was a really good player," said Boeheim, who as a rookie in 1966/67 played on the Miners with Murrell. "Willie was probably the toughest guy to guard in the league all around."

Murrell, a 6'6" forward, was a 1964 All-American at Kansas State. He led the Wildcats to the NCAA Final Four, where they were eliminated by UCLA despite Murrell's 29-point, 13-rebound effort. The St. Louis Hawks picked him fourth in the draft, but he didn't stick.

He burst upon the Eastern League in 1965/66, leading the league in rebounds with 18.8 per game and scoring 20.3 PPG, but lost the Rookie of the Year Award to Bob Love. The following season he was the league's dominant player with a 20–20 average—scoring 22.3 PPG and repeating as rebounding champ with 20.3. He led the Miners to the championship finals, where they lost to Wilmington in five games, and was the league's MVP.

"He was clearly the best player in the Eastern League" that year, recalled Boeheim. "Easily the best player . . . He was just a beast inside rebounding."

But the following season Murrell was gone to the ABA's Denver Rockets. He would play three seasons in the ABA with Denver, Miami, and Kentucky, averaging 13.1 PPG and 7.3 rebounds. "He played in the ABA, but he could have easily been in the NBA," said Willie Somerset of his former teammate.

In 1970/71 he returned to Scranton for part of the season, but he was not the same dynamic player.

7

TOUGH GUYS, CHARACTERS, AND URBAN LEGENDS

R ay Scott paused when asked to name some of the Eastern League's "char-acters": "You know, it's funny. When you say characters, it seems like that denotes a level of entertainment or showmanship. . . . These were hard-nosed guys who, when they drove up on Friday night, they came for business on the weekend. . . . They were serious basketball players."

Scott, a former Eastern Leaguer, NBA star, and head coach, is right. The Eastern League was loaded with serious basketball players, highly skilled ath-letes who took their craft seriously, played hard, and were among the very best in the world.

Nevertheless, some players developed reputations for qualities other than— or at least in addition to—their talent and became part of the Eastern League's folklore. Stories abound about the toughness of one player, or the temper of another, or some guy's unpredictable behavior, or zany sense of humor, or some other trait for which a particular player became noted—the kind of thing that when you mention their name, former players or fans will say, "Oh, did you hear about . . . ?"

So, with due respect for the talent and seriousness of the players named, this chapter shares some of the most irresistible stories that are still told about a few of the toughest, most amusing, and at times most colorful players to grace the courts of the Eastern League.

In a league distinguished by its toughness, no one was tougher than Dick Gaines. At a solid 6'3" and 230 pounds (at least), his game was all about intimi-dation and physicality.

"He scared people," said basketball writer Bob Ryan. "Extremely physical guard . . . Fullback body."

It wasn't just his size that was scary. He looked the part.

"Fu Manchu," recalled Ryan from his teenage years as a Trenton Colonials fan, referring to the mustache Gaines styled at times in his career. "He was a forerunner of the early Fu Manchus."

Further enhancing Gaines's reputation for toughness was his off-court occupation as head of the physical recreation program at Rahway Prison in New Jersey.

"Can you imagine, he work[ed] for a prison system," said Art Pachter, former owner of the Scranton Miners for whom Gaines played for two seasons. "He'd be perfect for . . . that."

"I remember one time I got into it with him," said John Chaney. "He was a tough, tough player. Got angry with me for scoring, and had the nerve to come up and grab me around the waist and pick me up and carry me to half-court."

Charley Rosen said that Gaines used to carry a gun in his gym bag, and recalled the following story from Rosen's brief playing days with the Camden Bullets (a version of which he also included in his autobiography, *Crazy Basketball*).

> George Blaney was on the Trenton Colonials, and I knew him when he was a rookie with the Knicks. . . . So we're playing there like back to back, Trenton and Camden. . . . So, George, who was a good shooter, was killing Gaines. Killing him. Driving on him, hitting shots. Killing him, killing him, killing him.
>
> After the game Blaney came over to me and said, "Charley . . . after the game Gaines came over . . . and he said, 'You do that to me again tomorrow night and I'll kill you.'" And George said, "Ha ha ha, he's only kidding right?" And I said, "No, he's not. He's armed." So I think George had like four or five points the next night. That was the EBL.

Blaney, a former head coach at Holy Cross, Seton Hall, and University of Connecticut who played five seasons in the Eastern League after a season with the New York Knicks, recalled a different run-in with Gaines:

> He was a monstrous competitor and a great, great player. So it was the first time I was playing against him, the first time I was ever seeing him. And on the first play down he throws an elbow at my head. So I came down the other end and threw an elbow at his head. And he said, "After the game! After the game!" I hit the parking lot quicker than anybody could ever see and was out of there! So that was another life lesson I learned. It was after the game you'd better get out of there.

Rosen shared another Eastern League adventure (also published in *Crazy Basketball*) involving Allentown's imposing center, Roman "Big Doc" Turmon. The setting is one of Rosen's first games in the league, and he's sent in as a sub:

So . . . I go into the game and Roman Turmon is the center. . . . And what is he, 6′8″ [actually 6′6″], 260, all muscle. So the first play of the game that I'm part of, he goes into the low post. I'm behind him. I can't see anything else, you know, he's so big. I was like 6′8″, 230 in those days. He gets the ball. He catches it with one hand, with his right hand. With his left hand he reaches behind him, grabs me by my arm, like under my armpit, lifts me up off the floor, throws me out of bounds. I don't remember if there were mats against the wall, I don't remember that. Throws me against the wall, I wind up on my ass. He wheels and dunks the ball. Basket's good, foul on me. . . .

Welcome to the Eastern League.

Gaines and Turmon were bona fide stars, top scorers, and among the very best players in the league. They used their reputations for toughness to try to intimidate other players. But even Gaines and Turmon knew better than to mess with some of the league's "enforcers," guys like Andy Johnson and Carl Green, who were talented players but also protected their teammates from opponents who tried to get rough.

"Andy Johnson played that role," said Chaney. "Every team had one. They were the guys that would keep the game clean because they were rough."

Carl Green concurred.

"He's strong as hell, man," Green said of Johnson, his former teammate on the Trotters. "[Gaines] was one of the toughest players in the league. But let me say this to you. Chink had guys scared and run over them and everything. But when it came to certain guys, Chink stopped. You take Andy. Or he had a lot of respect for Sherman [White]. And different guys."

Green said that Turmon, notwithstanding his reputation for toughness, deferred to Johnson when they were Allentown teammates. Turmon was the Jets' acknowledged leader "until Andy got there. When Andy got there, his whole attitude changed. Nobody fooled with Andy."

Green, himself, was another guy not to be messed with.

"I ain't bother nobody, but I ain't backing down for nobody," Green said.

"Carl was something special," said John Chaney, who played with and coached Green in Williamsport, uttering the one word that best characterized his former backcourt mate: "Tough."

One of the biggest enforcers in the league was Wilmington's 6′9″ Tom Hoover.

"On that team with Wilmington our protector was Tom Hoover," said Maurice McHartley. "Hoov didn't mind killing somebody, so to speak. The funny part about Tom, nicest guy I ever met off the basketball court. Off the basketball court. On the basketball court . . . he'd tell you in a minute, 'Man, send [the player you're guarding] down the middle.' Ok, Hoov, here he come."

Hoover was a Villanova grad who had a two-year stint with the New York Knicks in the NBA and two-plus years in the ABA in between terms in the Eastern League. Hoover's teammates enjoyed the protection he provided. Recalled Bob Weiss: "We had Tom Hoover . . . and I mean we had some melees. . . . He was our enforcer and really a great guy. You did not want him getting mad at you. He used to box, too. He was a boxer and a comedian, too. He did stand-up comedy and boxing. So if you didn't laugh at him, he'd beat the shit out of you."

Hoover was happy to set screens for his team's shooters, but they'd better make their shots.

Recalled Swish McKinney: "Tom would say, 'If you don't make these baskets, you won't be able to get out of here. All these shots I'm giving you, you put them in the basket.'"

Hoover's teammates may have thought of him as a nice guy off the court, but to opposing teams and their fans Hoover was "mean, rotten," said Pachter. "He was tough."

"Big" Bill Green, the top draft pick of the Celtics in 1963, never played in the NBA—but more on that later. A powerfully built, athletic 6'6" All-American center/forward from Colorado State who was also drafted by the Boston Red Sox and the Dallas Cowboys, Green developed a reputation as an intimidator during his eight seasons in the Eastern League, where he played mostly for Wilkes-Barre and Scranton.

"He would play in the post and I would go down there and steal the ball from him on occasion," recalled Joe Lalli, a 5'8" sparkplug who played two seasons with the Scranton Miners. "He once said to me, 'If you come down here again to steal the ball I will break your nose.' I never heeded his warning."

Even Green's teammates were leery of him.

"I was scared to death of him," said Stan Pawlak, who played with Green on the Barons for three seasons. "Every time I did throw it in to him . . . it would never leave. . . . He would maneuver in there with that big body, and he would somehow score. So if I didn't throw it into him, I knew I was going to hear about it. He made me nervous, he really did."

Pachter said he "traded [Green] for Dick Gaines—one bad guy for another. I was like Al Davis. I loved those guys."

Perhaps no Eastern League player looked more imposing than John "Dynamite" Postley. He was listed as 6'5" but seemed bigger, mostly because of his muscular, chiseled frame. And then there was the reputation—that he killed a man in prison—and the scar.

"I played against a guy named John Postley, who killed somebody," said Jim Boeheim. "He came out of prison and played in the league. He was big. They say—now this is hearsay but pretty strong—that Wilt was afraid of John Postley. John played in the summer league in Philly and they said Wilt did not mess with John Postley. He was a big, strong, tough guy. I drove in one time, made a shot, he looked at me, says, 'Rook, you'd better not come in here anymore,' and I never went in there again on John Postley."

Pawlak, Postley's former teammate on the Wilkes-Barre Barons, got to know Postley well:

> John, just by his presence, was intimidating. I mean if you didn't see this guy's body—he was built like an Adonis. . . . I had a lot of experience playing with him in the Philadelphia Baker League, so John and I were friendly. . . .
>
> There's so many legends about John but the one thing you didn't have to worry about was nobody would mess with him. . . . I've read stories where he's 6'9" and stuff like this. We do know he was in prison at one point.

And about the scar? Pawlak said, "John had a keloid scar on his back from one shoulder down to his waist. It was that long a scar. And the story went that somebody tried to cut him in prison and the dead man resulted in that guy who tried to cut him. That's how I heard the story. I wasn't there in the prison, so I can't tell you how much of it's true, but he did have the scar."

Pawlak recalled that players were not the only ones afraid of Postley: "I was married; my wife used to travel with me. And she would keep stats. At the end of each game he would always run to her to see how many rebounds [he had]. He didn't trust the stat guy, so my wife Julie would always give him like four or five more rebounds than he had, just not to make him angry. And then he would go back to the stat guy and say, 'This is right. You're wrong. Her stats are right.'"

So while Postley often ranked among the league's top rebounders, one might be advised to view his stat totals with some skepticism.

Ken Wilburn was an undersized but tough inside player, a wiry 6'6" forward from historically black Central State University in Wilberforce, Ohio. He was perennially one of the league's top rebounders and scorers during his career that began in 1966 with Trenton, included stops in the NBA and ABA in 1967–1969, and then lasted into the early years of the CBA, mostly with the Allentown Jets.

"Kenny was brutal," recalled former NBA and Eastern League referee Joe Crawford. "He would take people's heads off. No, I mean really take their heads off. He was as tough a guy as I have ever reffed, and I'm talking about the NBA. He was really tough."

Of course, no catalog of Eastern League tough guys is complete without mentioning John Brisker's brief interlude in the league.

Brisker was a notoriously contentious ABA and NBA player in the early 1970s who was often ejected for fighting. He was so volatile, he even fought with his teammates. Walker Banks, who played with Brisker for Pittsburgh in the ABA, recalled being sent down to the Eastern League after an altercation with Brisker.

"John was dirty to me," Banks said. "I mean he literally tried to hurt players. I blocked two of his shots, he came up behind me and slugged me in the head. I'm reaching up, got blood on the side of my face and in my hand."[1]

In February 1974, Seattle Supersonics coach Bill Russell sent Brisker to Cherry Hill for three games as a disciplinary measure. Brisker, whose contentiousness sometimes overshadowed his talent, scored 58 and 51 points in the only two full games he played.

"He was the best player I ever played against," said Pawlak. "He was stronger, he was faster. I don't think I've ever felt foolish playing basketball except for that day."

But it wasn't just Brisker's talent that impressed Pawlak. "I was afraid of him. . . . He was mean. . . . This is a guy that you don't want to mess around with. You just don't want to."

Long before Brisker's brief stay, the Eastern League had a number of players who developed reputations for their mercurial natures and on-court antics.

Old-timers were quick to mention Danny Finn. A 6'1″ guard who left St. John's University after a couple of seasons, Finn played three years in the old ABL with the Scranton Miners from 1950 to 1953, then parts of three seasons in the NBA with the Philadelphia Warriors before being released in 1954/55. He then spent the next seven seasons in the Eastern League, primarily with Wilkes-Barre and Hazleton.

"Danny Finn was a crazy guy," said John Chaney, who teamed with Finn in the Hazleton Hawks' backcourt in 1960/61 and 1961/62. "He would come down the court . . . and clown and shoot the ball backwards."

"He was a character," recalled Hazleton fan and sports chronicler Ron Marchetti. "Danny Finn was always in an argument. He always cried to the officials.

But he was a good player." Marchetti said he even remembered "Danny Finn sitting on the rim of the basket."

Many fans loved Finn's unpredictability and temperament, and in that gritty coal country, many found his frequent fights and various other antics entertaining.

"I remember Danny Finn got in a fight with George Feigenbaum," Marchetti said. "They went out the doors and out into Fifth Street in the snow and they're slugging it out . . . unbelievable. That was during a game. They went out there with their uniforms."

"I think that hurt Danny," said Chaney of Finn's behavior, which usually wore thin on coaches and teammates wherever he played. "He was just getting involved with so many dumb things on the court. He wasn't . . . as serious as all of us were."

Chaney never had to worry about not being considered serious or competitive. Indeed, he had a reputation for his combativeness, and together he and Finn must have been quite a duo to watch when they teamed with the Hawks.

"Chaney was nuts," said Harvey Kasoff. "I mean, he was a wild man. So was Danny Finn. . . . They were wild guys. They would dive for loose balls. They would incite the crowd. They were exciting."

Chaney's backcourt mate for the Mercs, Howie Landa, said Chaney would sometimes get so heated that "as he got older he wanted to bite everybody in the league." Chaney laughed when told that Landa said he threatened to bite opponents.

"I would attack you, there's no question about that," Chaney said, "because I had a lot of pride in making stops. Stopping you from penetrating. Always pride on playing the better players on the teams. And always got into a ruckus with them one way or the other, because they just didn't like the nagging."

Chaney said, "I had to do that because Howie was not the kind of defensive player that I was. He was just a great offensive demon. He was great."

The diminutive, 5′9″ Landa may not have had Chaney's defensive tenacity, but he could be feisty when necessary—like the night he took down Bill Spivey:

It was my sixth year in the league, and we were playing . . . at Wilkes-Barre. And Spivey turns around, gets a rebound, and then knocks one of the players on my team right in the jaw, knocked him right to the floor. . . .

So . . . I took off at half-court, because I was back on defense. And went in the air—went in the air!—and grabbed Spivey around the neck and knocked him down and went into a scissors right at his throat. And I swear . . . he was turning colors. And finally they got me off and he chased my ass around the court. I mean, it was unreal! But I'll remember for the rest of my life that I took down the seven-footer.

Landa said that even though he didn't score, the local paper gave him two points for the takedown.

Allie Seiden was another player that old-timers remembered as a mixed blessing, a tough New York City basketball playground and gym rat with all the talent in the world, but maddening to play and get along with.

"Alan Seiden," said Bob Ryan. "Something about him. People loved to hate him, as I recall."

Seiden was a New York City high school superstar—for many years the highest-scoring high school guard in city basketball history—who starred at St. John's University. He led the Redmen to the 1959 National Invitational Tournament (NIT) championship (when the NIT was as prestigious, if not more so, than the NCAA tournament), and was an All-American.

New York City sportswriters and brothers George and Peter Vecsey were longtime friends of Seiden and have written about his life and his career. Peter Vecsey recalled in a column in the *New York Post* how he first saw Seiden play in high school as a "5-foot-10 senior who never seemed to stop scoring or swaggering." But, he wrote, Seiden also "had a knack for making things worse."[2]

The St. Louis Hawks drafted Seiden in the second round of the 1959 draft. But stuck behind Hawks veterans Slater Martin and Jack McMahon and relegated to feeding Hawks stars Bob Pettit and Cliff Hagan when he did play, Seiden wanted more playing time and didn't have the patience to wait his turn. So he quit the Hawks.

The following season, Peter Vecsey wrote, "the consensus captain of the All-Time Basket Case Team"[3] was offered a tryout by the Detroit Pistons. But again, despite showing NBA-level offensive skills, too many experienced players were ahead of him and Seiden was the odd man out and the last one cut.

He got one more chance the next year when the Syracuse Nationals offered him a roster spot. But again, Seiden was his own worst enemy. He demanded a written guarantee. The Nationals looked elsewhere, and Seiden's NBA bridges were burned.

Perhaps hampering Seiden, too, was his close association to two players implicated in gambling scandals, Jack Molinas and Eddie Gard. George Vecsey, in a *New York Times* article titled "A Fallen Star of the City Game," wrote that "although Seiden did admit to being approached by gamblers once while at St. John's, he was never accused of anything illegal."[4]

So Seiden played in the Eastern League for six teams in nine years, both dazzling with his talent and infuriating with his temperament. His nickname, "Little Poison," described both his game and his personality. Simply put, he was annoying, argued with teammates who didn't pass him the ball, or otherwise caused trouble.

Landa recalled a game in which Seiden would bring the ball downcourt and "wave Wally Choice over, like, 'Get out of my way, I'm coming down the right side.' So at halftime I came down and Wally Choice had him up against the locker choking him. I said, 'Wally, it isn't worth it. It isn't worth it. Let him go! Let him go!' I kept Seiden from being killed."

Recalled Blaney:

Alan and Wally didn't get along at all. So, we're getting off a bus one time after a game up in Sunbury, I believe, and they had been arguing in the back of the bus about something. . . . Wally gets off first and Alan is coming down the steps, and Wally comes up to him, as he's up on the last step, and puts his hands right in his chest, in his coat, and lifts him off the step and points his other finger right in his face and says, "Don't you ever speak to me again." And he didn't. We played the rest of the season. They played fine together, but they never spoke again.

Still, Seiden had his supporters, none more loyal than Carl Green. "Al Seiden . . . he was like a helluva dude. . . . But a stand-up dude," said Green, who first saw Seiden play as fellow New York City high school stars and played with him on Williamsport, Scranton, and other Eastern League teams.

Green said many of Seiden's detractors were envious of his talent and skill. "They was jealous of him. They were jealous that this boy was smart at the game and could play the game. He could score. . . . So they was jealous of him."

Peter Vecsey described Green as Seiden's "Eastern League protector."[5] Green relished that role, even to the point of taking on some of the toughest guys in the league. He recalled a game against Easton: "They was beating [Seiden] up one night so bad, Wally Choice and Chink [Gaines] and them, man, and he went through and they hit him and he was bleeding from the mouth. So Wally Choice, I hit him. He said, 'Damn, man, Carl, stop,' and I said, 'Shit man, y'all beatin' my man up.'"

Another night, Green recalled, "Tom Hoover, I had to get him. He hit Al hard. I wasn't even in the game. So after the game, Hoover said, 'I'm riding back with you.' I said—me and Alan were in the car—I said, 'No, you ain't riding back with me. You fucked my man up.'"

Scranton owner Pachter recalled the night Seiden led a players' revolt. "We lost in Scranton very bad on a Saturday night, and I didn't think—the players didn't put out. I don't know what the deal was, but you could see they just did not put out."

Green, who was also on that team, said it had to do with coaching. Pachter had hired former Wilkes-Barre Barons owner and coach Eddie White, who was also one of the league's cofounders, to coach the Miners. But Green, Seiden, and other players were unhappy.

"We got Spivey, Tommy Hemans, John Crawford, Alan Seiden, myself, and a bunch of other guys on this team," said Green. "So here's a team, you're supposed to win. . . . All of us could play. . . . And everybody's arguing because Eddie White didn't know what he was doing."

Pachter got wind that the players were planning to boycott the following night's game, so "after the game I went into the dressing room and I fired five or six of them. One was Alan Seiden." Pachter did not know why the players were protesting, but of one thing he was certain: "Seiden was the whole instigator."

Art Heyman was another tempestuous New York City player. His one year in the Eastern League produced a disproportionate share of folklore.

No one questioned Heyman's talent. He was the consensus College Player of the Year at Duke in 1963 and was the first overall pick by the New York Knicks in the 1963 NBA draft. But his turbulent behavior and frequent fights soon outweighed his value as a ballplayer. After a bit more than two seasons in the NBA, Heyman was in the Eastern League in 1966/67. He led the league in scoring averaging 33.6 per game for the Hartford Capitols (with a brief stop-over in Wilmington), and his 39 points in the 1967 All-Star Game is the league record. The following season he was in the ABA, where he would play for five teams in three years.

"Art Heyman was crazy,"[6] Boeheim said in an interview on the Syracuse. com website. He recalled a game when Scranton was playing Heyman's Hartford Capitols. "He came down and warmed up with us. I said 'Art, what are you doing?' He said, 'I don't like those (bleeping) guys. They're assholes.' He was crazy."

Seattle sportswriter Steve Kelley got to know Heyman from a different perspective—as the son of one of the Wilmington team's owners.

"Heyman used to sit at the end of the bench and play solitaire," Kelley remembered in an email exchange.[7] "One night he came up to me at halftime and asked me to get him a hot dog. He was an all-American at Duke and is in the Duke Hall of Fame, but he was undersized and not particularly quick. He didn't like sitting on the bench.

"But he was always nice to me," Kelley continued. "The summer after the championship season he met me at Penn Station and took me to a Yankees' game. The year we won the championship Art Heyman gave me his trophy. I wish I had kept it."

When it comes to Eastern League characters, however, one name that inevitably comes up is George Lehmann.

"George Lehmann—the shooter," said Bob Ryan. "I heard all the George Lehmann stories when I got to know people like [George] Blaney later on. Yeah, George was a legend, absolutely."

Again, no question about Lehmann's ability.

"George Lehmann was one of the great shooters of all time," said Hubie Brown, one of basketball's top talent evaluators. "He was a great three-point shooter in the ABA. He was right up there with Louie Dampier, Freddie Lewis . . . he was that great of a shooter."

"He was an exceptional shooter," said former Eastern Leaguer and Globetrotter Bobby Hunter, who played with Lehmann in Philadelphia's summer Baker League and later conducted shooting clinics with him sponsored by a sneaker company. "He hit 78 jump shots in a row in the rain in a North Carolina fair. . . . We were having a jump shooting contest, and I hit 28 jump shots in a row, which I didn't believe. And he hit 78."

People talk about Lehmann much as they would a gunfighter: not only because of how well he shot, but also because of how cocky he was about his shooting and how quick a trigger he had—and not just as a shooter.

Said Howie Landa, who coached Lehmann in the Eastern League:

George Lehmann was unbelievable. He shot the hell out of the ball. . . . During the game he'd go on a fast break and pull up and shoot threes. . . and the guys would come to me and go, "Howie, this guy's nuts. I mean we're wide open. Can you tell him?" . . . So I eventually pulled him over and said . . . "I know you're the greatest shooter in this damn league. You don't have to prove it to me. But when they're wide open can you throw them the ball?" And he said, "Howie . . . my damn fucking three-pointer is better than their layups."

Maurice McHartley recalled competing with Lehmann in the St. Louis Hawks' training camp: "He came to camp in St. Louis while I was there. Me and George had history, too. . . . We had a couple of fights during the course of our time. Because George could play but—he was an exceptional shooter, he could really shoot the ball, but . . ."

Then there's the well-traveled story about Lehmann burning down a gym.

"What stories do you have on George Lehmann?" asked his former Trenton Colonial teammate Tony Upson. "Well here it is. Got cut from his high school team and he set the gym on fire, burned the gym up."

"Well, that's the rumor, that's part of the folklore, supposedly," said Ryan. "I've been told that . . . part of the story is that he burned down a gym. That's interesting on your resume."

Several other former players referred to the story about burning down the gym but asked that it not be attributed to them. "Don't mention my name, all right?" said one. "Because I live in a wooden house."

And Hunter said he had not heard the story. "[Lehmann] set fire to a lot of gyms," he quipped, "but I don't remember him doing it physically."

Various versions of the story have circulated over the years. Some said it happened in high school. Some said it happened at Wake Forest, which Lehmann attended before going to Campbell University in North Carolina.

"George Lehmann . . . You probably start with the story that he burned the school down, right?" said Stan Pawlak, a South Jersey resident like Lehmann who used to work out with him and their friend Gary Williams, former University of Maryland coach. "My version of it is different. My version of it is he snuck in the school, there were no lights, that he lit a newspaper to see where he was going, and when they caught him he dropped the paper that was on fire to run away."

Some Eastern Leaguers were legends even before they got to the league. Herman "Helicopter" Knowings was already a summer Rucker League legend in Harlem when he joined the Eastern League for two seasons from 1967 to 1969. A product of Benjamin Franklin High School in New York City who never went to college, Knowings stood around 6'5" (though he's been described as anywhere from 6'4" to 6'7"), had an ultralong wingspan, and he could jump. Boy, could he jump!

"Played against him many times," said Pawlak. "He could jump like crazy. He wasn't the greatest player in the world but he could jump."

"He could really get up," said former Eastern League and ABA player George Bruns. "He could block shots, really get up."

"He could jump out the gym,"[8] remembered Charlie Criss, who played five years in the Eastern League before enjoying an eight-year NBA career. "Oh yeah. He could take money off the top of the board. He could jump."

That "taking money off the top of the board" thing was part of Helicopter's legend. As the story goes, Knowings once picked a quarter off the top of a backboard to win a bet. Over the years the story was embellished to say he took the quarter and left change.

Tony Upson didn't buy into the legend, however. "I saw him play, and played against him, and that business of him going to the top of the backboard and getting a quarter off the backboard, I think that's a little, as they say, over the top. But a heck of a rebounder, you know. Powerful jumper, though."

Knowings was a great shot-blocker and—again, reputedly—once blocked three straight shots by NBA stars, including Willis Reed, in one sequence in a Rucker League game.

But it was his dunks that drew oohs and aahs and entertained fans. One of his creations was called the "double scoop with the cherry on top," in which he got airborne north of the key, made two complete revolutions in the air, and then stuffed the ball backward, that is, the cherry on top.

Of course, legends being legends and hard to confirm, some of the myths about Knowings have been attributed to another former great Eastern League leaper, Jackie Jackson.

"Speaking of dunking, hold the phones," said Bob Ryan. "Jackie Jackson. Oh my G-d! He's the legend of legends—to this day! Jackie Jackson was famous! He was the guy—6′5″—he was the guy they famously said could—I don't care who else tells you it was about, it was not, it was about Jackie Jackson—the guy who could take a quarter or dime or whatever off the backboard. It wasn't Herman 'Helicopter' Knowings, it was Jackie Jackson. I'll argue that one."

Jackson spent two seasons in the Eastern League and one in the old ABL before going on to a long career with the Globetrotters.

"Jackie Jackson would have won a whole lot of those dunk contests when they started," said McHartley. "I mean because his imagination about dunking was off the charts. I mean off the charts!"

Some basketball aficionados consider Joe "the Destroyer" Hammond the greatest streetball player of all time. Eastern League fans got to appreciate his talent for parts of three seasons from 1969 to 1973 with the Allentown Jets and Garden State Colonials.

"I'm sure there are stories about Joe Hammond," said Pawlak. "Joe Hammond is a legend. . . . Joe Hammond is a New York Rucker player who was known for his drug activity. But he could really play. Everybody said he was the best player in New York. And every once in a while he would play in the Eastern League, and he would come down and play and then you wouldn't see him anymore. Because he was making so much money in New York. He's a legend. He's a New York legend, like a big one."

"I know refereeing in the Rucker League over the years a legend in that league was a gentleman by the name of Joe Hammond," said Dick Bavetta. "He could show up at halftime of a game and score 34 points in the second half."

Hammond attended Taft High School in the Bronx, but he dropped out of school in the ninth grade. The Los Angeles Lakers picked him in the 1971 Early Entry draft, but he turned them down, and he also turned down a three-year ABA contract offer.

Bavetta recalled that Hammond "was offered to come to the Lakers, different teams to try out with a $10,000 guarantee or something. . . . That all became part of the folklore. He was offered positions, to come try out for teams, and he said, 'I make more than that with what I'm doing here on the street.' . . . Financially, it would have been a loss for him to play professional basketball, and I'm sure he's not the only one."

A 6'3" guard, Hammond "was burning up the EBA before he ran into trouble with the Allentown management,"[9] according to a 1971 *Sports Illustrated* magazine article. He would later run into trouble with gambling and drugs.

A few more Eastern Leaguers got known for some unique features of their lives or their games.

York Larese had what must be basketball's craziest style for shooting free throws. Nobody else came close to matching the way the 6'4" Larese took foul shots. Since his college days at the University of North Carolina, there was no such thing as ready, aim, fire off that foul shot. Instead, he was famous for accepting the ball from the ref and—without hesitation and almost without looking—launching it at the rim.

"I had a vivid memory of [Larese] because in the history of basketball I don't think there was ever anybody like it, ever, anywhere," said Bob Ryan. "Fastest free-throw shooter ever. He almost would yank the ball and throw the referee in with it. The quickest release ever shooting free throws I've ever seen."

Larese, who played one season in the NBA for the Chicago Packers and the Philadelphia Warriors (1961/62) before settling in for seven years in the Eastern League, reportedly was timed taking between 0.8 and 1.1 seconds to hoist each foul shot. His speedy grab-and-go earned him the nickname of "the Cobra." His unique delivery didn't damage his statistics. Larese made about 80 percent of his foul shots in college and in the pros. He was also one of the league's top three-point shooters—though he used a more conventional shooting style for that.

Nick Werkman, a former Seton Hall star who led the nation in collegiate scoring in 1963 and played four years in the league, also had an unusual shooting move.

"He would throw the ball off the backboard and run after it, and rebound it and then lay it in," said George Blaney. "So if you were guarding him and you kind of stopped him, he would just throw the ball off the backboard and run after it and dunk it or lay it in. In the Eastern League he did it from half-court one night. He threw the ball at the backboard, he caught it and laid it in."

Wilmington's high-scoring guard Maurice McHartley always played with a toothpick in the corner of his mouth. "It was a bad habit I picked up," said

McHartley, who would play four years in the ABA. "It was one of those little flat toothpicks; it wasn't the round kind."

He said he never had any injuries involving the toothpick.

Walter Dukes was an established NBA player by the time he got to the Eastern League in 1963. He had played eight years in the NBA following an All-American career at Seton Hall and three years with the Globetrotters. A seven-footer, Dukes could run the floor and was considered one of the first of the "athletic" centers, set a single-season NCAA rebounding record in 1952/53, and led Seton Hall to the NIT championship. In the NBA he averaged 10.4 PPG in his career, consistently grabbed double figures in rebounds, and was twice selected as an NBA All-Star.

At age 33, when he joined the Camden Bullets, he was still considered a tough opponent—but not just because of his basketball ability.

According to Art Pachter, Bill Spivey told him, "The player I hated playing against the most in my entire career was this guy from Seton Hall—Walter Dukes."

"Why?" Pachter asked.

"Because he always had such bad odor, you couldn't guard him. You had to stay three feet away from him."

"You're kidding me! That stinky?" said Pachter. "No way!"

"Yes!" replied Spivey. "He was that bad."

Charley Rosen confirmed Dukes's notorious body odor.

"The thing about Walter Dukes, he had this body odor that would freak people out. Guys didn't want to guard him. They didn't want to touch him. Wilt Chamberlain had the same thing. But Walter was famous for his body odor."

Finally, there were the comical moments that characterized the small-town, minor-league atmosphere of the Eastern League.

"You ever hear the Wilmington Blue Bombers-George Sutor story?" asked Pawlak.

George Sutor was a guy that played at LaSalle, who at one point tried out for the [Philadelphia] Eagles, but was a 6'8" big guy who played center for the Wilmington Blue Bombers. They have a halftime show of a weightlifter, and this weightlifter—muscle-bound, Arnold Schwarzenegger type—he's got mats out there with all these weights. . . .

And people are clapping and he's lifting this stuff over his head. Well the halftime ended and George comes out . . . and the guy's heaviest weight is still left out there on a mat, it hadn't been moved yet. And [Sutor] looks at it, and he lifts it over his head with one hand, after this guy had been struggling and groaning. And he puts it down and the weightlifter's embarrassed. And I think the story went on that the weightlifter challenged him, and of course I wasn't there for the challenge.

Stories and personalities like the ones described in this chapter made the Eastern League fun, relatable, intimate. It created a bond between players and fans that has grown over the years. The folklore made the Eastern League folksy. The people made it memorable. As Ray Scott put it when discussing some of these stories:

"You see, that's the lore. . . . And so there were so many life lessons. That's why I guess when you were talking about the characters, there were the characters, of course. But there were so many people with character."

8

LIFE IN THE
EASTERN LEAGUE

Jim Boeheim remembered the drives back to Syracuse on snowy Sunday nights.

"It was unbelievable," said the Syracuse University basketball coach of his trips between Syracuse and Scranton on Interstate 81. "I remember many nights going up the road five and 10 miles an hour, tops. Tops! . . . More than a couple nights I had to open the car door just so that I could see that I was on the road. And I was going like five miles an hour. It took me four to five hours to get back from Scranton several nights. It's a two-hour drive. It's a tough road. [Interstate] 81's a tough road in the wintertime. Awful road! I saw 30, 40 cars off the road many nights. I made it through. I made it through somehow."

If there was one thing practically every Eastern Leaguer had to get used to, it was long-distance driving on weekends at all hours of the day or night, with or without teammates, with or without treacherous snow, and with or without expenses being paid for gas or lodging. Just some of the risks they took off the court to compete at the highest level they could.

"Guys were coming from all over the place," noted former Eastern League center Walker Banks. "So guys would be late. They'd have accidents and everything else trying to make it to the games."

Scranton team owner Art Pachter recalled that carpooling was the best way for players to get from place to place and save gas money. "The Philadelphia players . . . would meet at the end of the turnpike [at the] George Washington motel right in Plymouth Meeting, meet there, park their car there, four or five guys, one car. . . . The New York guys used to meet [in] downtown New York.

So most of them came together. . . . And it was nothing for somebody from my team to be coming in the car with somebody from the other team."

According to author and former Eastern Leaguer Charley Rosen, often when night games ended and carpools formed again, "somebody would be picked after the game, driving back after a game . . . [who] had to stay awake to talk to the driver. You'd have to have one guy sitting in front who would stay awake and bullshit with the driver so he wouldn't fall asleep. That was a big requirement in order to get a lift."

Joe Lalli, who played two years in the Eastern League for his hometown Scranton Miners while working in Washington, DC, was fortunate enough to live to tell his stories of driving alone late at night without a designated talker to keep him awake.

"I almost killed myself twice . . . falling asleep," he said. "I mean, you play the ball game. The game, let's say, started at seven or eight, and you're out of there at eleven or eleven thirty and I have a four-and-a-half-hour drive back to Washington because I'm going to teach the next day."

Driving and not flying wasn't a problem for Bill Green, the top draft pick of the Celtics in 1963, who never played in the NBA because of a sudden fear of flying. Green, a 6'6" forward out of Colorado State, was used to airplane travel until a couple of horrifying flights in his senior year. During the preseason, Green got encouragement from the Celtics and professional help, but he still wouldn't step foot on a plane, not even for the NBA.

As he told *Sports Illustrated* in 1986, "The fear just built to the point where I couldn't take it anymore. I made up my mind: I wouldn't do it."[1] A year later Green joined the Eastern League, where he drove from his New York home to games on weekends for eight seasons, mostly playing with Wilkes-Barre and Scranton and developing a reputation as an intimidator.

Players and coaches also occasionally found themselves in the awkward position of giving rides to refs. Dick Bavetta remembered driving from Brooklyn with fellow referee Ray Lara for a game in Hartford when a tire went flat not far from Bloomfield High School, the home court of the Hartford Capitols. As Bavetta and Lara prepared to hitchhike to the game, Hartford coach Pete Monska drove by with his wife, family, and All-Star guard George Bruns. Monska stopped the car, stuffed the two refs in the backseat, and drove the few miles to Bloomfield High.

"As the visiting players were emptying the bus, we were getting out of the car," Bavetta said. "The visiting team stopped in their tracks in amazement as we were thanking and hugging Pete, Mary, two daughters, and George Bruns for the ride to the gym."

Eastern Leaguers during the 1973/74 season also clearly remembered going to great lengths to keep gas in their car during the so-called Arab oil embargo that occurred after countries, in retaliation for United States support for the Israeli military during the ongoing Arab-Israeli war, imposed a ban on sales of oil to the U.S.

Walker Banks recalled that when he and former Drake University star Al Williams were driving together during the oil embargo as teammates on the Hamilton (New Jersey) Pat Pavers, "You couldn't get gas after a certain time or . . . if you had half a tank or more they wouldn't give you any gas. Well he and I would spend all night on occasion in the car parked at a gas station, parked along the turnpike somewhere . . . in line with other cars until the gas station's open. I actually have pictures of that—a picture of us pumping gas in a basketball suit."

Referee Joey Crawford said he would "jump off the turnpike, get a dollar or two dollars or whatever it was" and then hope to find more gas down the road. And Charlie Criss, then playing for the Hartford Capitols, recalled getting help "to siphon gas out of somebody else's tank to put in my car so I could get back home."

Driving distances were the downfall for the Rochester (New York) Colonels, who joined the Eastern League for the 1958/59 season but dropped out after losing their first eight games. The car and travel expenses from players' homes to Rochester and to and from away games (the shortest was 200 miles from Rochester to Scranton, the longest 400 miles to Baltimore), the wear and tear on their cars and bodies, the terrible snow and low fan turnout at home games all quickly added up to be too much for the organization.

Hubie Brown, who played guard at Niagara University and landed a spot on the Rochester team, said, "We had mostly guys that played up in colleges up in western New York. But unfortunately, they didn't anticipate how difficult it was to commute first to Rochester, and then get from Rochester to Pennsylvania to play these teams. And then get back again after Sunday's games, you know, without trying to get killed with all the snow. I thought it was too bad because they had a pretty good team."

John Chaney recalled, "My G-d, we would travel and then pull into the snow, risking our lives pulling into Hazleton where the mountains were, with me and Howie Landa."

Charlie Criss had his own snow survival story. "We had an accident one time, slid off the road down an embankment because of the snow and ice on our way back home and hit a tree. No, nobody got hurt. . . . If it wasn't for the snowbanks, it would have been worse than what it was."

Banks had this memorable scare: "I went over a cliff one night coming back from Wilkes-Barre . . . to Harrisburg. . . . I hit a solid sheet of ice and went over, and the thing that saved me from really getting injured, it was a lot of snow on the ground, which slowed the car down. . . . I had to duck down in the car because I didn't know what was going to happen. And so when I finally raised my head up a little bit I was trying to look and see if I saw any angels or whatever—I was hoping it was angels."

He added, "I was able to get a tow truck. Had to pay the guy $100 to bring me back to Harrisburg. So there goes my one game."

In fact, money was tight for most Eastern Leaguers, and that meant many of them needed the additional income from playing in the league to supplement their wages from other jobs. The pay for Eastern League players—depending on the era—typically started around $35 per game. The top players could make $150 or more—if they got paid at all, which, for some teams, was not always certain. And if players were lucky, ownership might occasionally kick in a little extra cash to help pay for gas or for an overnight stay at a motel, especially when weather conditions were treacherous.

Also uncertain was how long a player could count on a steady salary in the Eastern League given that hardly anyone received no-cut contracts. As Hubie Brown recalled, "They paid you in cash right after the game. You got so much if you started, so much if you're a reserve. But they could cut you after one game because they could get access to somebody else. You know what I'm saying? Longevity was not a term used very often there in the Eastern League."

Chaney remembered other ways players had to earn their pay, including one system that was based on tickets sold. He laughed about how his teammate Howie Landa "would go off to look at the cars in the lot. If . . . the lot was filled up, Howie would be jumping up and down, 'John! We going to make a lot of money.'"

Chaney also claimed that a team in Lancaster, Pennsylvania, was "hanging on" financially and came up with a creative idea for paying the players. "Lancaster, where the meat markets were, they paid them . . . with meat! With meat! We thought we was big shots because we were being paid $35, $40, or whatever, depending on the crowd at the time. . . . Those guys, we used to tease them about getting paid with a roll of bologna!"

Former Belmont Abbey College star Danny Doyle, who had his proverbial "cup of coffee" playing four games for the Detroit Pistons in 1962 before joining the Trenton Colonials, told Peter Vecsey of the *New York Post* in 2009 about a rather unusual cash payment. "One night after a win, the owner told me and Alan [Seiden] all he had was quarters so we'd have to wait until next week to get paid the two games he owed us,"[2] Doyle said. "I was getting $125 per and Alan was getting $175. Alan said, 'The hell with that, we'll take the change.' We proceeded to count out $600 in quarters."

But money wasn't always the main object. As Jim Boeheim explained, "You had to be a basketball junkie, because in the beginning I was making $50 a game. So it wasn't like you're doing it for the money. . . . So you just loved to play, that's all. You just wanted to play."

As Novak told Harvey Araton of the *New York Times* in 2001, "In the days before there were turnpikes, we'd drive through tiny towns, one after another, with a church on one corner and a bar on the other. And the weather was so bad."[3] Novak then spoke of one player who had to take two buses from Philadelphia into south Jersey to then make a three-hour drive with him to Eastern League games. "John Chaney, the Temple coach," Novak said. "That kid would've done anything to play."

Some players saved money on local lodging on weekends by staying with other Eastern Leaguers or fans turned friends. "I found different places, and I stayed with a truck driver many nights. He was a good guy," Boeheim said. According to Scranton's team owner Art Pachter, "Boeheim . . . never wanted to stay in a hotel. . . . He was always on my couch in my house."

Eastern League players also were always happy to be invited by teammates for a good free meal before or after games.

Banks recalled that when he was a Wilkes-Barre teammate of Stan Pawlak, "his mom was one of the best cooks that I've ever been around. When we'd go to the Philly area, to Jersey or something, we'd all go and he'd invite us to dinner at his folks' house."

Pawlak also used to host his teammate John Postley at his house for pregame dinners before they would pick up their coach Stan Novak and drive to games together.

And Miners guard Lalli, the Scranton native, recalled that at home games "I would have Boeheim over to the house where my mother and father, of course, lived, and my mother would feed us, either a pregame or a postgame meal."

Sharing life on the road and their mutual passion for basketball helped to forge bonds between players who traveled together. That some of these friendships formed notwithstanding race seems notable in an era when pioneering black athletes in other professional sports often felt isolated from their white teammates.

In Sunbury, Chaney reunited with fellow Philadelphian Landa, whom he had first seen play when they were both city high school stars. They forged a lifelong friendship on the road, as Chaney would ride with Landa and his wife, and sometimes Novak, to get to the various gyms around the league.

In separate interviews more than 50 years after their playing days, Chaney and Landa gave remarkably similar summaries of their life together in the Eastern League.

"When I went to Sunbury we played together," Chaney said. "We were just quite a tough backcourt together. I mean just tough. Nobody could handle us. And we became great friends."

Said Landa: "John and I were bad together. . . . I roomed with Chaney. Chaney and I were very close . . . and we drove together and everything."

Chaney and Landa's teamwork sometimes occurred off-court as well, as when they and their teammates thought Novak was undercounting the attendance and not paying them adequately.

"So Chaney sent [Bob] Gainey on one side of the court to count how many people were in the damn stadium, I swear to G-d to you," Landa said. "And I eventually had to go to Novak and say, 'Listen, I'm the captain, and they came to me and complained that you were holding back on money.' So Novak gave them four more dollars extra . . . and then traded my ass to Wilkes-Barre."

Landa recalled how tightly he and Chaney had to budget themselves, especially when they shared a hotel room on the road. "We paid $5 for the hotel. If it snowed, we were really in trouble," he said, because the weather cut into attendance. "I remember one time it snowed . . . and I think we made $8 the night of the game and it cost $5 for the motel and gas and all that other stuff. So we never made any money that night."

A similar friendship formed in one of the New York City carpools between 6'4" guard Carl Green, a former Harlem Globetrotter noted for his toughness, and 5'10" Alan (Allie) Seiden, a smart but scrappy playmaker and scorer with his own short fuse. Their relationship began as fellow New York City high school stars and solidified in the Eastern League, where both played for nine years.

After Green left the Trotters during the 1959/60 season and looked at the NBA, he sensed that the owners tried to keep the different minorities in the league segregated from each other as a way to keep them marginalized. Green instead joined the Williamsport Billies of the Eastern League, where he played for five years, and became especially close to Seiden.

"He was good and smart," Green said. "That was one of my best friends in life. . . . I'm looking at his picture, man, right now. His father and mother . . . his brother, and my mother. . . . That was me and him. We just loved each other

. . . because we was just people. We didn't care about Jewish or the religion, all that stuff."

After Seiden's death in 2008 at the age of 71, Peter Vecsey of the *New York Post*, who said it took "over seven months to write about the death of someone I idolized for so long,"[4] included this about the Seiden-Green relationship: "When I quit," said Green, Alan's Eastern League protector, driving partner, and Dora Seiden's "adopted" third son, "he was right there asking if I needed something. He told me, 'You got family, I got money.' His friendship was all I wanted and we had it for 48 years."

And Steve Kelley, a former *Seattle Times* sportswriter whose father was a part owner of the Wilmington Blue Bombers in the early 1960s, described in a 2011 column how the game of basketball and his friendship with the black players on the team influenced his life. "The players of the Blue Bombers, almost all of them African-American, also became family friends,"[5] he wrote. "My father invited many of them to the house for dinner. They shot hoops with me in my backyard. Some of them came to my junior high school games. . . . We'd meet them for breakfast on Sundays, and often the players would be the only black people in the restaurants."

Kelley said he was fortunate that Swish McKinney, who played briefly for his dad's Wilmington team, "spent hours helping me—unsuccessfully—with my jumper," and offered some life lessons. "He also told me about his days in the Army and the names he used to be called. He told me he was a shooter, not a fighter, and he would try as hard as he could to ignore the taunts. Playing basketball always was a way to escape for him."

Kelly concluded his column by saying, "Basketball broke down barriers. . . . It freed me from my white-bread world. . . . It taught me that there were no differences between black and white."

Ultimately, what most Eastern Leaguers seemed to recall from their days in the league was how much fun it was. The sacrifices, it seemed, were worth it.

"I loved it. It was a tremendous experience," Boeheim said of his time in the league. "Working five days a week and going to college grad school [at Syracuse] and then driving down there Saturday and playing Saturday and Sunday night. I usually got back around two in the morning or three or four in the morning and then started working again at seven o'clock at school. And going to grad school and then coaching. I was coaching the freshman team and working with the varsity, so I worked until about nine o'clock at night every day of the week, and then took off on Saturday and Sunday. . . . I'm not sure how I got through that now that I look back on it."

"I remember standing at center court for my first appearance at Madison Square Garden,"[6] Dick Bavetta was quoted as saying in the *Eastern Basketball Association 1977–1978 Official Guide*. "There must have been close to twenty thousand people there to see the Knicks and the Celtics. It was an intense game and I had to be prepared. I never thought I'd catch myself saying, 'Thank you Eastern League and your fans and your snowy January nights,' but I had to."

9

THE TOWNS, THE GYMS, THE FANS

Big-Time Basketball on a Small Scale

For two hours on wintry Saturday and Sunday nights the Eastern League brought some of the best basketball players in the world to small, blue-collar towns to play before enthusiastic and appreciative fans in tiny high school gyms and a few oversized arenas and armories. A typical Eastern League crowd was predominantly male, and certainly in the first decade or so of the league many of them were dressed up in jackets and ties and wore proper hats for the night out. They were knowledgeable basketball fans, rabid boosters of their hometowns, and highly vocal, especially to referees and opponents.

And this being the era before the surgeon general's warnings, many of the fans smoked. Hazleton sports personality Ron Marchetti recalled when management "used to turn all the lights out" except for "the lights [that] would be on the floor . . . and you could see all the smoke, you could see them smoking."

Sports fans in the Eastern League's rugged towns packed those often smoky gyms, especially in the '50s and '60s, because they knew they were experiencing something unique: tough, fast-paced, high-scoring action and the chance to see top-notch professional athletes in person, and often up close. In the years with maybe one NBA game on television each week and no cable TV, the Eastern League offered an extraordinary opportunity for locals to see or even meet pro players, many of whom they had only read about before.

"People would read about those guys, and now they're seeing them in the league," said John Chaney. "Seeing them right before their eyes . . . Many of those towns looked at us from the standpoint of their heroes in their city, their towns, because that was the only pro basketball that they could see [in person]."

As Marchetti put it from the fans' perspective: "That was the big thing when I was a kid—Eastern League. . . . I mean, jeez, you get to see these guys and some of the guys were great, great players. Sherman White, Tom Hemans, [former Duquesne star] Fletcher Johnson . . . They were so entertaining. . . . Back then, nobody had seen many NBA games. It was all Eastern League."

As a result, home fans and owners were supportive, boisterous, and sometimes scary. As former Scranton player Jim Boeheim said, "Small, little, tiny bandbox places and fans right on top of you . . . I've never been intimidated by any gym after playing in that league. . . . You couldn't run too close to the sidelines; they'd trip you." Boeheim's home court—the smoky Catholic Youth Center—was typical, with team owner Arthur Pachter standing or sitting aside the team bench, often with a cigar in his mouth and harassing refs and opposing players.

Perhaps this rabid, hometown atmosphere is why former players like Charley Rosen recalled that "home teams almost always won," and Chaney said that "everybody figured you were being cheated when you played away from home." As former referees Dick Bavetta and Joe Crawford describe in chapter 13, the hometown crowds could be frightening, to the point of making leaving the gym occasionally adventurous.

That home team advantage also produced a strange kind of parity. In the 1957/58 season, six teams finished within one game of each other in the regular season. Wilkes-Barre, Hazleton, and Easton-Phillipsburg tied for first with 18–10 records. Sunbury, Scranton, and Williamsport were second at 17–11.

Almost anytime players, coaches, and fans reminisced about the Eastern League, the characteristics and oddities of the league's various venues were likely to enter into the discussion. But one gym in one small town stood out—Sunbury High School in Sunbury, Pennsylvania, population 15,000 when the Mercuries joined the Eastern League in its second season (1947/48), smack in the middle of the state and nearby the Susquehanna River, or as some might say, the middle of nowhere.

As former Eastern League player and University of Connecticut coach George Blaney said, "The Eastern League was filled with . . . high school gyms, a lot of auditoriums that were turned into gyms. But Sunbury was pretty unique."

What was so special about the Mercs' quirks at Sunbury High?

The gym had a wall so close to one of the baskets that players had to "go in for a layup vertically,"[1] said Eddie Mast, a former New York Knick who played for Allentown, in a 1971 article in *Sports Illustrated*.

Veteran guard Richie Cornwall had similar memories: "If you scored on a layup, you were probably going to hit the wall because the end lines were right up against the edge of the wall." He added, "You could barely fit between the wall and the line to throw the ball in bounds."

At the other end of the court in Sunbury was another obstacle—a stage that the players would sit on during the game. As Walker Banks said, "You couldn't even run out of bounds. You had maybe two feet, three feet out of bounds because they had a stage. The stage was at the end of the basketball court. You had to run on an angle."

Cornwall also questioned the position of the half-court and three-point lines. "The backcourt line was at three-quarter court. The three-point line was 28 feet. . . . I don't think anybody was really measuring it."

As if those eccentricities weren't enough, the school still used half-moon backboards, much to the dislike of visiting players. "They didn't have the regular backboards," said Howie Landa. "It had the fan-shaped thing, you know. So your shooting was different, too."

Added George Bruns, "[I] only went to Sunbury once, and they had . . . the half-moon backboards. I said, 'Holy shit.'"

Despite being the smallest town in the league, Sunbury fans were particularly loyal. "The team regularly attracted crowds of nearly 900 fans and the 'Let's Go Mercs' chant thundered in the gym,"[2] wrote Cindy Inkrote, the director of the Northumberland County Historical Society, in a 2009 retrospective published in the *Daily Item* newspaper in Sunbury. "Kids' Nights attracted the younger crowd and their families and often the preliminary game offered young YMCA teams the chance to show their stuff before the Mercs took over."

The hometown folks in Sunbury also pulled together in the 1948/49 season when the Mercuries were in danger of being expelled from the league for missing a road game and forfeiting their $500 performance bond. According to basketball historian Chuck Miller writing in the *Albany (NY) Times Union* in 2010, "Within a week, the citizens of Sunbury raised over $500 out of their own pockets to repay the performance bond."[3]

Even though Sunbury won just one Eastern League championship, in the 1950/51 season, the team competed for 24 straight years and consistently fielded solid teams against clubs with much bigger fan bases, like Baltimore, Wilmington, and Hartford.

The Sunbury gym wasn't the only venue players found peculiar.

Regarding the cavernous and ancient Kingston Armory in Wilkes-Barre, which used a portable court, John Chaney recalled, "That was the biggest court I've ever played in. . . . I remember dribbling the ball going from one end to the other, and I thought I reached it, but when I looked up, [I] still had a long ways to dribble." He also observed that "it was hard to keep the heat in there because it was so damn big."

Opposing players who were new to the Kingston Armory often were stunned to learn that there was only one shower in one shower room for both teams. According to Scranton Miners guard Joe Lalli, "Ideally you would stand in line. Jones would shower, he'd get out of there, and Smith would shower, but you could have a long line. . . . I would stand off to the side, at 5'8", and catch the water as it cascaded off the shoulders of the 6'8" players who were taking up all the space near the shower head."

Recalled Wilkes-Barre star Stan Pawlak, "It was more important for guys at the end of the game to be the first guy in that shower than it was maybe to win the game."

At the Scranton CYC, Bruns said, fans in the first row of an upstairs section directly above the players' benches "poured water on you, yelled shit down at you, spit at you, things like that. . . . There was wild-ass stuff."

Some Eastern League teams also would occasionally play home games on multiple courts, and that could be confusing. Hall of Fame NBA referee Dick Bavetta, who like several other NBA officials got his start in the Eastern League, recalled arriving at the King's College gym in Wilkes-Barre and being surprised by a full parking lot and the sound of screaming patrons.

Figuring he was mistakenly late for the game, Bavetta sped to a nearby parking spot and introduced himself as one of the night's officials. As reported in the *Eastern Basketball Association 1977–1978 Official Guide*: "In the course of striking up an innocent conversation with an usher on the way to the main arena, Bavetta discovered that the large turnout that night was for a pro wrestling show, and the sight of a ring at midcourt soon confirmed it. Unbeknownst to him, the Wilkes-Barre Barons' basketball contest had been moved to another gym across town, where a crowd of sixty diehards was waiting for the referee to appear."[4]

The occasional exhibition games with NBA teams (and teams from other major professional leagues during the early years) brought even more opportunities for Eastern League fans to see some of the world's best players. While the NBA temporarily suspended exhibition games with the Eastern League as punishment for accepting players involved in the 1951 college basketball gambling scandal, the big league agreed to resume those contests in 1956.

Examples of memorable exhibition games: Before 2,000 fans at the Kingston Armory in 1956, the Barons, led by Danny Finn's 26 points, held the high-scoring Dolph Schayes to six points (13 below his NBA average) and defeated the Syracuse Nationals, 78–67. And in 1961, two weeks after leading Boston to the NBA title, Bill Russell brought teammates Bill Sharman, K. C. Jones, Sam Jones, and Satch Sanders to Pennsylvania under the name of the Bill Russell All-Stars and beat the Allentown Jets, 120–106.

"I remember I played against the Celtics . . . and it was the biggest thrill of my life, to play against Satch Sanders, and Russell, and Sam Jones," said Ray Scott, a Jet before a long NBA career.

Towns with Eastern League teams also benefited in other ways. According to Whitey Von Nieda, the league's scoring leader in its first season, some towns wanted teams as a way "to improve the economy of the area. I think Hazleton was one of them. It was primarily to help the economy. The coal areas, they had lost a lot of the attraction when coal started to go bad. So I think that's part of it."

Von Nieda also said that towns "were looking for some of the stronger areas to help and create rivalries" similar to the old coal-town baseball teams of the early 20th century. Indeed, rivalry games—like Wilkes-Barre vs. Scranton in the '50s and '60s—drew huge crowds at the Kingston Armory and the new 4,800-seat Scranton Catholic Youth Center, which opened in 1950.

Eddie White, one of the league's organizers and an owner/coach of the Wilkes-Barre Barons, promoted the fierce rivalry with Scranton when both teams were in the American Basketball League. Along with the owner of Scranton's ABL team, Joseph "Speed" Maloney, the rivalry carried over when both teams were in the Eastern League. Maloney's grandson Brian recalled how White and Maloney—who were actually good friends and shameless showmen—staged it.

"You had a tremendous rivalry between Scranton and Wilkes-Barre because prior to that the rivalries were the baseball teams of the coal companies," explained Brian Maloney. "But the coal companies [were] tanking . . . so . . . that's not getting the same rivalry. Now all of a sudden you get this basketball league, these people, they're going nuts about it. They're absolutely crazy about it. . . .

"So my grandfather and Eddie White, they'd get on the court screaming and yelling, throwing their jackets at one another. Then they'd go out and have dinner. They knew what they were doing, and that sold seats. And . . . if a player ended up leaving the Barons and came and played for the Miners, oh my G-d, that was sacrilegious. That went on for years."

Unfortunately, real fights occasionally broke out in the stands, and dealing with rabid fans was an occupational hazard for the players.

Bruns remembered winning a playoff game on the road and a local fan tried to enter the visiting locker room carrying a gun. "He was going to come after somebody," he said. "But somehow or other he got intercepted and we all got the hell out of there."

For black players juggling family, careers, low pay, and difficult travel conditions, occasional incidents of off-court discrimination brought an additional challenge.

"I know that the people looked at us as heroes," said Chaney, but he also noted that "there was always . . . somebody in the town that looked for trouble and would try to make things hard for you. In fact, I remember one of our [Sunbury] players. . . . One of the black guys on my team, was seeing a white girl up there" and found a note at their Sunbury hotel saying, "Do not go out tonight."

Chaney said, "They put [the note] up with this guy's name on it because they wanted to make sure that, you know, we stayed in the hotel and make sure that you didn't find yourself going out and mixing with the white girls. Yeah, I remember that situation."

Chaney added, with a laugh, "The local fans knew that we would come and go. I mean, we weren't going to stay around. So they only had to put up with us for two days, on Saturday and Sunday, babe. Drive in and drive out, man."

Some black players also remembered being denied food service in Eastern League towns. "There were restaurants in Allentown that we were not welcome in," recalled former Jets star Ray Scott. "We were not welcome. . . . The door closed in a lot of those towns."

Scott also remembered an incident when he was in Baltimore for a game against the Bullets during their years in the Eastern League. "I was 20 years old and I was refused service in a White Castle," Scott said. "I'm a kid from Philadelphia. I don't know anything about that type of attitude. And they said, 'No, we're just not going to serve you. . . .' And this is in Baltimore, Maryland."

That hurt stuck with Scott for years. After being traded by the Detroit Pistons to the Baltimore Bullets of the NBA [today's Washington Wizards] in 1967, he promised that "I would never, ever, as long as I was in Baltimore, eat in that White Castle, and I never did. I never did."

When scoring and rebounding great Tommy Hemans was asked about the dynamics of mostly black players and mostly white fans in small, blue-collar Eastern League towns, he simply replied: "Fans just came to see excellent basketball. . . . The fans enjoyed the opportunity to see outstanding players play the game at the highest level, and they knew that a majority of the star players, black or white, should/could have been playing in the NBA."

But Hemans also recounted the time he, Sherman White, and three other black players walked into a bar outside of Hazleton. The bartender at first refused to serve "coloreds," but after a stare-down grudgingly poured them drinks. "At some point during our conversation the bartender . . . joined the conversation after he apparently realized that we were 'basketball stars' from the EBL. From that point on our drinks were on the house."

Hemans continued, "Before we left, the bartender apologized to us for his remarks and asked us to promise that we would stop at his place after our game the following Sunday. We said yes. The following Sunday when we arrived . . . the parking lot was packed with cars. When we entered the tavern, it was filled with customers. The bartender came from around the bar and greeted us with handshakes and introduced us to the customers like we were his best friends in the whole world! . . . During that particular season we continued to stop at this place whenever we got the chance. The place was always crowded, and the drinks were always on the house. And we always left a very large tip!"

Waite Bellamy, who became one of the league's all-time top scorers with the Wilmington Blue Bombers, recounted coming with his wife to Scranton in 1963 after being cut by the St. Louis Hawks, getting a tip from Scranton owner Art Pachter about an apartment for rent, and being turned away when the landlord said, "We don't rent to coloreds."

Pachter remembered that Bellamy came back to his office "crying. . . . I immediately called Wilmington and just gave him to them." Bellamy ended up playing eight years with the Blue Bombers and became one of the league's top players.

Bellamy also faced discrimination in Wilmington when the Blue Bombers organization sent him to various businesses to apply for jobs. He said he discovered "they just wouldn't hire you for one reason or another. One guy sent me to a shoe store and I was going to be a salesman selling shoes, but he was afraid, you know, that I would be touching the white women's feet. . . . He said, 'We can't have you do that.' I went to a bank one time to be a teller, and the guy said, 'No . . . You can be a janitor.' . . . One guy sent me to a clothing store to be a salesman and he said, 'Well, you know, I got to train you how to sell clothes, and you got to be touching people.'"

Even while on the road, black and white teammates traveling together couldn't avoid racial stereotyping. Richie Cornwall recalled an incident when driving with his wife in the front seat and three tall black teammates in the back. "The five of us were trying to get from Boston to Scranton to play, and I'm flying . . . and we get pulled over," he said. "So the cop comes up to the car and he sees these giant guys sitting in the back of my car, and [the policeman] thought we were hijacked. So after about 20 minutes of trying to explain to him, he says, 'Whatever, just get outta here.'"

But most players interviewed for this book indicated that racial incidents were more of an exception than the rule in the Eastern League's small towns.

When Swish McKinney was living and working in Scranton, he was so popular that he had his own sports radio show there in the late 1960s.

John Chaney said, "You know, it's extraordinary. In those various towns, there weren't that many black people living in those towns that I can remember. But there was a certain kind of respect they had for players, for the athletes. We would eat in those towns. Williamsport was another one that I can remember. We never had any problems, because I coached and played in Williamsport in my waning days in the Eastern League."

Chaney, whose nickname was "Chick," noted that he and other players would "stop and eat in Harrisburg on the way to Sunbury and every time there would be somebody coming over [and saying] . . . 'Chick! Hey Chick!' The kids would come over, man. Oh, you felt so important. . . . You look forward to going into a place where people idolize you. . . . It was made possible by the Eastern League for so many of our players, and we were happy."

Speaking of food, in December of 1975, the Eastern League's Long Island Sounds got lucky on the first road trip of their one and only season when the team stopped outside a small Pennsylvania factory town at a fast-food place with a "Grand Opening" sign.

As told by Paul Montgomery of the *New York Times* in 1976, "The owner, seeing so many tall men overflow his new booths, rushed up to ask what team they were with. 'The Knicks,' said Bernard Hardin, a skinny forward from Brooklyn, who is playing for $35 a weekend on the remote hope that a big league scout will see him and sign him. Hardin introduced himself as Earl Monroe and his teammates under appropriate pseudonyms. The owner, overwhelmed, passed around a menu and offered the players hamburgers in exchange for their signatures. The Sounds dutifully complied. Some, it is said, signed twice, once with each hand."[5]

A perpetual issue for many franchises was low attendance, especially after the American Basketball Association (ABA) formed in 1967 and took many of the Eastern League's top players, and the rise of cable television made more professional games available for fans to watch on TV.

Pachter said he remembered sellouts in Scranton, one being when ex–Philadelphia Warriors star Paul Arizin joined the Camden Bullets, and big crowds for Scranton/Wilkes-Barre rivalry games, but he noted that "you only had a couple of those games a year." Otherwise, he said, attendance at the CYC was "terrible. Most of the time in Scranton you drew 700, 900."

Pachter mostly blamed the local media, which he said covered home games but otherwise "did nothing for us . . . nothing to whet your appetite to make you want to go to a game. You didn't have media that covered a team. . . . We got zero press that got into anything that created . . . an interest by the sports fan."

That's also why Pachter tried other ways to boost publicity and put fans in the CYC seats. For a time, he said, he paid local reporters to write articles for the city's two newspapers. "If you didn't have somebody at the *Scranton Tribune* writing some kind of an article for you once a week, and they got their check, you didn't get anything from the *Scranton Tribune*," he said. "If you didn't have somebody at the *Scranton Times* getting a check for writing an article, you got nothing in the *Scranton Times*."

He also said the Scranton newspapers wouldn't send staff to away games— not even to Wilkes-Barre, 20 miles down the road—so to keep the team in the news, he volunteered to phone in a game summary, a box score, and an attendance number for the local papers to put in their next editions.

Pachter loves to tell a story about a home-and-home series against the Harrisburg Patriots when only a few hundred fans showed up at the massive Harrisburg Farm Show Complex for the Saturday night game. When Pachter called in the stats to the Scranton papers after the game, he decided to make the contest appear "more interesting" by reporting "a crowd of over 9,000. When [the Harrisburg] players came here the next day and saw the paper, they were laughing."

Every so often the Scranton management would earn extra income by raffling off a pony, which almost always meant Pachter or someone else from management would help the winning ticket owner "sell" the pony back to the farmer who brought it to the CYC. Usually, Pachter said, "everybody was happy. But there were a couple of times where we got stuck and the farmer didn't come back and they couldn't negotiate . . . and the pony wound up in my front yard. . . . What the hell am I going to do with a pony at midnight?" But, he added, "it worked out."

Although more than 40 years have passed since the Eastern League folded in 1978, many fans are still eager to share their memories of favorite teams, games, and players.

One of the best examples is Bob Ryan, a renowned sportswriter at the *Boston Globe* since 1968 (he recently retired as a longtime columnist but still contributes to the Sports section) and a regular on ESPN's Sunday morning TV show *The Sports Reporters*. Growing up in Trenton, New Jersey, he faithfully followed the Colonials from their start in the 1961/62 season, and he hasn't let go of the memories . . . or the stats.

"First season in Trenton. The first game was at Notre Dame High School— that was their home court in those days—and they played the Williamsport Billies and they beat them 121–103 and Wally [Choice] went for 10–20–40 [10 field goals, 20 free throws made, 40 points]," Ryan said. "I loved Wally and I got his autograph in my little red autograph book, which I still have."

Ryan also recalled listening to Trenton away games on WBUD 1260 and trying to imagine what the "notorious gym" in Sunbury and the Wilmington Blue Bombers' Salesianum High School gym looked like. "Who could forget that? Who could forget that? Salesianum," he said.

"Obviously, I just fell in love with the whole [Eastern League] thing," Ryan added. Even his high school yearbook quote was about the league: "What do you mean, study. The Colonials played last night." (Read more from Bob Ryan in the foreword for this book.)

And when Brian Maloney was in high school in the 1960s, he could claim he briefly played with the pros. Well, sort of. While Eastern League teams typically had just one official practice before their games on Saturday night, players who lived in or near their team's town would try to stay in shape by recruiting other athletes, including high school players like Maloney, for pickup games.

"We [his high school team] practiced at the CYC and usually on Thursdays. If we were practicing, the Miners would come in and work out, too," said Maloney. "There was Swish McKinney, there was Jimmy Huggard, there was Boeheim, there was Spivey. And all these guys would come in, and they'd actually . . . work out with us. . . . When they were taking you to the hoop, they were gonna grind you. The one guy I remember because I had to guard him a couple times, Jimmy Huggard, he was only like five foot eight. He was like a tank, though. Jesus Christ, he was tough. He'd elbow you and push you. Oh, he was brutal."

After all these years, former Eastern Leaguers still love to be picked out of a crowd and thanked by fans. They said it happens more than you think.

"I still run into some people from Scranton who saw me play when I [was] down there," said Jim Boeheim. "It's a great, great thing."

Stan Pawlak, who became a medical device salesperson whose territory included towns like Wilkes-Barre and Scranton, said that "people remembered me all the time just by hearing the name, which was fun. It's like 30 years later, people still remembered who you were and they remember the Barons. . . . It's amazing to me, but they do."

Owners and officials of the newly organized Eastern Professional Basketball League meet in August 1946 at the Hotel Altamont in Hazleton, Pennsylvania, to plan the opening season. Seated at left is Wilkes-Barre Barons owner and coach Eddie White, one of the league's founders. Next to him is Hazleton newspaperman William D. Morgan, the league's first president. *Hazleton Standard-Speaker* photo. *Source:* Newspapers.com

1947-48 WILKES-BARRE BARONS - l to R Standing: Carl Franks, John Barr, Coach Eddie White, Bob Dehnert and Chick Craig. Seated: Steve Chanecka, Billy Chanecka, Herk Baltimore, Ted Hanauer and Cas Ostrowski.

Owner and coach Eddie White (standing in center) and his 1947/48 Wilkes-Barre Barons after winning the championship in the Eastern League's 1946/47 opening season then jumping to the American Basketball League. On the Barons were early Eastern League stars, brothers Steve and Bill Chanecka (seated first and second at left) and high-scoring Cas Ostrowski (seated first on the right), and future longtime Eastern League coach Chick Craig (standing at far right). *Source:* Jason Sereyka

The 1952/53 Sunbury Mercuries pose for a team photo. Kneeling from left to right is the close-knit Philadelphia contingent of Jack Ramsay, Jerry Rullo, Jack McCloskey, and player-coach Stan Novak. *Source:* Northumberland County Historical Society

The two best-known players implicated in the 1950s gambling scandals, Sherman White of the Hazleton Hawks (L) and Jack Molinas of the Williamsport Billies (R), pose together in this 1956 photo. *Hazleton Standard-Speaker* photo. *Source:* Newspapers.com

Former Harlem Globetrotter and rugged Allentown Jet pivotman Roman "Big Doc" Turmon. *Source:* Jason Sereyka

Hal "King" Lear, the sublime scoring machine for the Easton Madisons, Camden Bullets, and other Eastern League teams. *Source:* Jason Sereyka

Fierce and powerful Richie "Dick" Gaines, who played for several Eastern League teams including Easton, Camden, and Scranton. *Source:* Jason Sereyka

All-around player Andy Johnson starred for many years for the Allentown Jets after playing for the Harlem Globetrotters and in the NBA. *Source:* Jason Sereyka

Talented but temperamental Allie Seiden (22) of the Scranton Miners dishes to a teammate in a game against the short-lived Johnstown CJ's. *Source:* Arthur Pachter

All-time Eastern League scoring leader Julius McCoy of the Sunbury Mercuries, who former Eastern Leaguers describe in reverent terms. *Source:* Bill Mitchell

Multitalented Cleo Hill played for four Eastern League teams in six years after one season with the NBA's St. Louis Hawks, whose veteran stars were unhappy that Hill's scoring cut into theirs. *Source:* Jason Sereyka

Seven-footer Walter Dukes played for the Harlem Globetrotters and for seven years in the NBA before bringing his rebounding skills to the Eastern League. *Source:* Jason Sereyka

Bill Spivey of the Scranton Miners shoots over Allentown Jet Hank Whitney (11) before a full house at the Scranton Catholic Youth Center. Jets Bob Mantz (10) and Andy Johnson (8) look on. *Source:* Arthur Pachter

Tough inside player Hank Whitney starred with the Allentown Jets for five seasons before a four-year ABA career. *Source:* Jason Sereyka

Longtime Eastern League star Tom Hemans receives a television set from Scranton owner Arthur Pachter after being voted Most Popular Miner by fans. *Source:* Arthur Pachter

Rugged post player Bill Green was a first-round draft choice of the Boston Celtics but left the NBA because of a fear of flying and played eight seasons in the Eastern League, mostly with Wilkes-Barre and Scranton. *Source:* Jason Sereyka

Bobby McNeill was a perennial Eastern League All-Star guard with Camden, Trenton, and Allentown after a two-year NBA career. *Source:* Jason Sereyka

George Blaney played one season with the Knicks, then five in the Eastern League with Trenton, Camden, and Allentown and was one of the league's first three-point marksmen. *Source:* Jason Sereyka

Shooting guard Waite Bellamy played all eight of his seasons in the Eastern League in Wilmington and is the Blue Bombers' all-time leading scorer. *Source:* Jason Sereyka

Scranton Miner Willie Murrell goes inside against Sunbury's John Richter in the cozy confines of Sunbury High School, as Scranton's Tom Hemans and the Mercuries' Walt Mangham look on. *Source:* Arthur Pachter

Stan Pawlak was one of the league's top shooters and fifth all-time scorer after a 10-year career, mostly in Wilkes-Barre. *Source:* Jason Sereyka

In his six seasons in the Eastern League, Swish McKinney was a prolific scorer—he holds the league record for most points scored in a season—and was a fan favorite. *Source:* Jason Sereyka

John Postley of the Wilkes-Barre Barons was one of the most intimidating players in the league, both for his chiseled physique and his reputation that he killed a man in prison. *Source:* nasljerseys.com and Keith Olbermann

Chick Craig, seen here coaching the Scranton Miners, played for nine seasons in the league, including its opening one, and coached seven different Eastern League teams.
Source: Arthur Pachter

Jim Boeheim spent six seasons with the Scranton Miners and Apollos while going to grad school and serving as an assistant coach at his alma mater, Syracuse University. He was often described as "professorial" because he was one of the few players to wear eyeglasses.
Source: Jay Rosenstein

Ken Wilburn was a ferocious rebounder and scorer for the Trenton Colonials and Allentown Jets and a two-time league MVP. He also played in the NBA and ABA. *Source:* Jason Sereyka

Stocky Willie Somerset of the Scranton Miners drives to the hoop at the Scranton Catholic Youth Center while teammate Swish McKinney slides in from the wing. *Source:* Jason Sereyka

Scranton Apollo Richie Cornwall is surrounded by a trio of Hartford Capitols—Tony Koski (10), Craig Mayberry (3, in mismatched shorts), and Claude English (16). *Source:* Arthur Pachter

Coach Tony Upson, who played three seasons in the league, coaches up Hamden Bics players (left to right) Dave Scholz, Johnny Mathis, Bob Keller, and Bruce Spraggins. *Source:* Jason Sereyka

Happy Scranton Miners Willie Somerset and Bill Spivey dunk owner Art Pachter in the showers to celebrate a 1966/67 regular season division title. They lost to Wilmington in the championship finals. *Source:* Arthur Pachter

Guard George Bruns, who played nine seasons and coached in the Eastern League, also had a brief fling in the ABA. *Source:* George Bruns

Hartford Capitols' Willis "Spider" Bennett elevates for a short jumper as teammate Tony Koski (10) positions for a rebound. Robert Naboicheck photo. *Source:* Jason Sereyka

Free-spirited Eddie Mast played 12 seasons in the Eastern League and Continental Basketball Association and also had three seasons in the NBA. *Source:* Jason Sereyka

10

THE IMPACT
OF THE ABA AND
THE BEGINNING
OF THE END

The Eastern League was at its peak in the mid-1960s, deep with talented players and teams.

In 1965/66, the Wilmington Blue Bombers—with a backcourt of Freddie Crawford and Bob Weiss (both future NBAers), Maurice McHartley, and Waite Bellamy, and frontcourt stars Tom Hoover, former Minneapolis Laker Boo Ellis, John Savage, and Frank Corace—won the best-of-three championship playoffs. They beat the Wilkes-Barre Barons and their dynamic backcourt of former Philadelphia 76er Larry Jones and Levern Tart, Bill Green and Bob Keller inside, and aging but still-capable reserves Dick Gaines, Alan Seiden, and former 76er Larry Costello.

The Blue Bombers repeated the following season, besting Scranton in the now five-game finals, despite losing Crawford to the New York Knicks during the season. Leading Scranton were sensational second-year player and league MVP Willie Murrell, an explosive backcourt featuring Swish McKinney and Willie Somerset, still-productive veteran frontcourt players Bill Spivey and Tom Hemans, and rookie swingman Jim Boeheim.

Scranton had to get past its archrival Wilkes-Barre in the best-of-three first round of the playoffs. The combined firepower of the teams was such that the Barons won the second playoff game by a 160–151 score, while Scranton came back to take the final, 141–130.

"Levern Tart, Larry Jones, that was a pro backcourt," recalled Jim Boeheim from his 1966/67 rookie season with the Scranton Miners and their showdowns with the Barons. "That was like an NBA backcourt. They were really good."

Wilmington, Scranton, and Wilkes-Barre weren't the only talent-laden teams. In 1965/66, the league adopted a two-division structure for the first time in 14 years, and the Trenton Colonials tied the Blue Bombers for best in the East Division with 20–8 regular season records. Leading Trenton was Rookie of the Year Bob "Butterbean" Love, who the following season joined the Cincinnati Royals to begin a productive 11-year NBA career. Teaming with Love on the Colonials (coached by the ubiquitous Chick Craig) were Stacey Arceneaux, George Lehmann, Bruce Spraggins, and four-year NBA veteran Al Butler. Former NBAer Walter Dukes provided rebounding.

The always tough Sunbury Mercuries and Allentown Jets made the playoffs in both '66 and '67. Julius and Jim McCoy, Walt Mangham, John Richter, and Big Jim Davis led the Mercs, while the Jets had four former NBA players in Andy Johnson, Tom Stith, Brendan McCann, and Bobby McNeill, as well as Walt Simon, Hank Whitney, Carl Green, Johnny Jones, and Frank Card. Other top players in the league included Harrisburg's three-year NBA veteran Charlie Hardnett, Frankie Keitt of New Haven, and Hartford's Art Heyman, who led the league in scoring in 1966/67, his only season in the league.

At the close of the 1966/67 season, the all-league team consisted of Murrell, Weiss, Julius McCoy, Heyman, and Tart on the first team and Somerset, Simon, Spraggins, McHartley, and Lehmann on the second team.

By early in the 1967/68 season, however, all but the venerable Sunbury scoring machine, McCoy, were gone. Weiss had made the NBA to stay with the Seattle Supersonics, while Lehmann's golden shooting touch had taken him to the St. Louis Hawks. The rest—all seven of them—left the Eastern League to join the new upstart professional league, the American Basketball Association (ABA).

The ABA was the brainchild of a loose collection of entrepreneurs and sports promoters whose goal was to compete with and ultimately force a merger with the NBA. But they needed players—good players. As author Terry Pluto described in his colorful book *Loose Balls*, when the ABA prepared to launch its first season, it was desperate to find talent.

"Our biggest job was to find players,"[1] Pluto quoted former Dallas Chaparrals general manager and coach Max Williams as saying. "I got a lot of letters and calls. . . . We had an open tryout and drew about 100 guys. That was just a zoo, people killing each other, but we didn't find anyone of significance."

In addition to tryouts, ABA teams tried raiding NBA rosters, but with little initial success. They searched the American Athletic Union (AAU) basketball teams, which were still around, though in decline. They checked NBA rosters from previous seasons to find former players who were no longer active. They sought out college players and former draft choices.

And they raided the Eastern League.

"I'll bet the 30 top players in the league left," said Syracuse coach and former Scranton Miner and Apollo Jim Boeheim. "Walt Simon, Hank Whitney, Levern Tart, Willie Somerset, Willie Murrell, they all left."

Maurice McHartley and his toothpick left Wilmington. Larry Jones left Wilkes-Barre, which, with Tart's departure, depleted their backcourt. Art Heyman, his scoring, and his tempestuousness left. Bruce Spraggins, Tom Hoover, Wilbert Frazier, Howie Montgomery, George Sutor, Jim Caldwell, John Austin, Willie Porter, and Leroy Wright were also among those who left the Eastern League for the ABA's first season, while Spider Bennett, Tom Stith, Don Carlos, and Frank Card were gone the following year. Ken Wilburn, George Lehmann, and Johnny Jones spent time in the NBA in 1967/68 but the following year joined the ABA. John Barnhill, who played seven years in the NBA, would play for the Miners in 1968/69 and then leave for the ABA.

As Pluto described, the ABA was a seat-of-the-pants operation in its initial years. Recalled McHartley: "I got a call from Cliff Hagan, he was the coach, and I go to Dallas, the Chaparrals, not knowing anything about Dallas. . . . But when I got there, I think we had one practice and we went to New Orleans the next day to play. . . . I'm thinking, well OK, I'm going to go and sit around and watch to see what happens. He inducted me immediately into the game, and from that time on I was their starting point guard."

McHartley played four seasons in the ABA for four teams and ended up getting traded back to Dallas in his final year. He averaged 12.4 PPG. He also acquired a reputation as one of the ABA's first fashion plates.

"He was ahead of everybody when it came to fashion," Pluto quoted former San Antonio Spurs announcer Terry Stembridge as saying, "because he was the first guy on the team wearing bell-bottoms and stuff like that."[2]

Larry Jones reportedly contacted every ABA team when the league was created. The Denver Rockets were the only one to answer. A great jump shooter, Jones became one of the league's first stars, averaging 21.2 PPG, making first team all-ABA in the league's first three seasons, and becoming the first player in the league to score 5,000 points. He ended his career in the NBA in 1973/74 with the 76ers.

Jones's former backcourt mate in Wilkes-Barre, Tart, was also one of the ABA's early stars. He held the league's scoring record of 49 points in a game that first season, only to have Jones break it later in the year with 52. He played for six teams in four years in the ABA and averaged 19.4 PPG, and 24.3 in the playoffs.

Former Allentown Jets Hank Whitney and Walt Simon also had productive ABA careers, as did former Scranton stars Willie Murrell and Willie Somerset. Over three seasons Whitney scored 9.2 PPG and collected 7.6 rebounds. Simon lasted seven seasons and averaged 11.9 PPG. Murrell averaged 13.1 PPG and 7.3 rebounds over three seasons, while Somerset averaged almost 22 PPG in two ABA seasons before returning to the Miners in 1969.

The Eastern Leaguers gave the ABA what Somerset called a "jump start" in its inaugural years, enabling it to launch with credible professional basketball players. As former Eastern Leaguer and NBA coach Bob Weiss observed: "When the ABA came in and made very good basketball teams out of a lot of guys that come up from the Eastern League," they showed how good the players were.

"For these people to just go in and start for these teams in the ABA, that should indicate how talented they were at the time," said Hall of Fame NBA referee Dick Bavetta, who got his start officiating professional games in the Eastern League.

The Eastern Leaguers were grateful for the chance to perform at a higher level.

"There was only so much room," in the NBA, McHartley said. "Fortunately, the ABA helped with that, too. Gave guys other opportunities to play."

That was especially so for players who "didn't finish graduating from school" and those who "didn't go to a white school," said former Globetrotter and Eastern Leaguer Bobby Hunter.

Indeed, as discussed in chapter 4, the formation of the ABA essentially ended whatever vestiges may have remained of the NBA's unwritten quota system. As Ray Scott noted, the ABA was a product of the late '60s and early '70s social era and not stuck in outdated notions about race. Plus, they had rosters to fill.

"I think they were looking for the best players. Period," said George Bruns, who played and coached in the Eastern League during that period and played part of a season with the ABA's New York Nets.

Some of the players who left the Eastern League for the ABA actually did so after the season had started. Scranton owner Art Pachter recalled that the Miners started their 1967/68 season winning eight in a row. But then "[everybody] went to the ABA. We lost Willie Somerset, Willie Murrell . . . we lost them all."

The Scranton coach, former NBA player and coach Fuzzy Levane, told Pachter to fire him. "He said, 'You're wasting your money paying me. We don't have the players.' I said, 'Don't be silly.' Then we lost two, we lost two more. He said, 'I'm taking your money and I don't need your money.'"

So Pachter fired Levane and coached the team himself.

Some Eastern League teams brought legal actions against the ABA, but the cases dragged on and got costly. Pachter went to court over Willie Murrell's contract. "They stole him off of me. After $90,000 worth of legal expense we agreed to forget the whole thing on both parts. Just couldn't keep going on. The league wouldn't get involved and I got nothing."

Players weren't the only asset the ABA lifted from the Eastern League. The wide-open, high-flying, high-scoring style of play that had characterized the Eastern League quickly became the signature of the ABA, especially as the new league featured many players from historically black small colleges who previously had found homes in the EPBL. The ABA even adopted the three-point shot that the Eastern League itself had taken from the short-lived ABL a few years earlier.

Back in the Eastern League, however, the departure of so much talent at one time made a difference.

"There were so many good players in the league [in his rookie season, 1966/67]," recalled Boeheim. "It was a battle every night." He said he "was an OK, average player or below average player in the league, not even in the top 25 probably [that season]," and "caught a break" in making the team. "Paul Seymour, who had coached in the NBA, was named the Scranton head coach and he lived here in Syracuse, so he wanted me to ride with him and drive some of the time. And so, I mean, I probably would have made the team, but it would have been close, because the first year it was loaded. I mean I ended up being the sixth man, but there was some really good players cut. . . . I was known as Paul Seymour's driver."

The following year, however, after so many of the top players left for the NBA or the ABA, Boeheim said the league was "watered down." "I was like in the top five or 10 because those . . . guys left." Boeheim averaged 11.4 PPG as an Eastern League rookie, but in his second year led the Miners in scoring averaging 20.9 PPG. "I went from making 100 bucks a night to making 200 bucks," he said. "It was like I was rich!"

"It just seemed to take the luster out of the [Eastern League]," said Richie Cornwall, a Syracuse teammate of Boeheim's who broke into the league in 1968 (and whose high school coach had been former Eastern League star Howie Landa). "Obviously when you take that type of talent out of the situation, it has to dilute it a little bit."

As Boeheim put it: "It just changed, you know, with all those guys going to the ABA."

What changed was the overall depth and stature of the Eastern League. The league still had many good players, but not as many as it had before the ABA. Instead of being perceived as the second-best professional basketball league in the country, it was now third behind the ABA, and much further behind the NBA than it had been in its heyday.

The NBA, meanwhile, had expanded to 10 teams in 1966/67, to 12 and 14 the following two seasons, and to 17 in 1970, while the ABA started with 11 teams and maintained at least 10 for most of its history until it merged with the NBA in 1976. Moreover, European basketball teams were starting to lure talented American players overseas with the promise of decent pay, housing, and opportunities to travel through the major cities of Europe, and not through Pennsylvania coal country.

Thus, the number of full-time, professional jobs for basketball players more than tripled in a decade, leaving the Eastern League with a substantially diluted talent pool. This gave at least some players who might not have cracked the Eastern League in earlier years a chance to make it and perhaps even to become stars.

Bruns, who had been out of college for three years before he made the Eastern League, recalled that in 1966, "I went to Allentown and tried out my first year out of college and got cut. I had no chance of making that team. But a couple of years later I was better, and I think the ABA started so the league was not as strong as it had been in the mid-'60s."

Still, the ABA didn't kill the Eastern League. Many top players remained, like Julius and Jim McCoy, Swish McKinney, Waite Bellamy, Stan Pawlak, Rich Cornwall, Bill Green, Bobby McNeill, John Richter, Bob Keller, and Frank Corace.

"There's a heck of a lot of good ballplayers out there," said Cornwall. "I think the talent was still at a really high level. . . . I don't think people realize how very good the basketball was."

"I don't think the [Eastern] league diminished as much as people want to believe it did," said Pawlak, who in 1968/69 led the Barons to a 26–2 record, best in league history, and the postseason championship. "There were a lot of guys that played in that league afterwards that were really good players," he said, "and when things didn't work out for them in the ABA, they came back and played in the Eastern League."

Bruce Spraggins, Willie Somerset, Ken Wilburn, Levern Tart, and George Lehmann were among the Eastern Leaguers who had gone to the ABA and eventually returned.

"Some of these guys went to the ABA and played a few years," recalled Bavetta, "and for whatever reason . . . came back to the Eastern League. Obviously, they were older; their talent levels had somewhat diminished. And of course they remembered me when they first were in the league and went to the ABA, and when they came back, they also thought that my talent level had diminished as a referee," he said, laughing.

For many of the top players who remained, especially those with families, the temptation to jump to the ABA or NBA wasn't enough to risk their outside careers, especially with most ABA players getting contracts for around $10,000 with no guarantees, and NBA players not doing much better. Said Pawlak:

> You didn't want to go to be just another guy at camp. You wanted them to make some sort of commitment to you, and they wouldn't do it. . . . And if you had a family, you just can't uproot yourself for a chance like that, because the money wasn't that good.
>
> Pittsburgh called me and that's exactly what I did. . . . I said, "Look, just give me an $18,000 contract but give me three of it up front. That's all you got to do for me to sign." I didn't even ask for no-cut. They wouldn't even do that. That was after I was MVP in the Eastern League. . . . I wanted to try but . . .

Pawlak, who by then was married, had a child, and had begun a teaching career, added: "We had jobs and families. How many times in September when they had training camp could you go to your boss and say 'Hey, I'm just going to go try out again.' You couldn't do that all the time. I did it like three times."

Recalled McKinney, ABA Nets coach Lou Carnesecca "called me up and he said, 'We'll sign you for $12,000.' And I said, 'I just got married and I got a good thing here' [in Binghamton, New York, where he had started a job with IBM]. I didn't want to go."

McKinney said Binghamton team owner Tom Mineo told him, "My G-d, Swish, you're crazy. You got to go. You got to go."

"I said, 'I love it right here,'" McKinney said. "'I don't want to go to the city. I love it, want to make a family here.'"

McKinney also got a call from the ABA's Oakland Oaks, in his hometown, for whom his boyhood friend, Jim Hadnot, played. He said they offered him a place to live, told him to bring his family, and even asked him how much money he wanted.

"Just give me a no-trade contract," he said he told them. The Oaks refused, and eventually stopped calling. McKinney stayed in the Eastern League.

"I had an offer to go to Pittsburgh," recalled Waite Bellamy. "They called me in and they wanted me, but they wanted me for cheap. I was teaching and everything and I had a family, I had two small kids. They wanted me too cheaply. They didn't want to pay me enough to move from Wilmington, Delaware, to Pittsburgh and uproot."

Bellamy also got inquiries from Cleveland, but "they wanted to pick up players as cheap as they could get them at the time," so he turned them down and stayed in Wilmington.

As described in chapter 5, Jim Boeheim had a chance to go to the NBA when Paul Seymour, his coach in Scranton, asked Boeheim to join him in Detroit when Seymour became head coach of the Pistons. "But . . . I just wanted to stay in coaching and keep doing what I was doing," Boeheim said, "and it was the right decision. I would have been a very marginal NBA player at best, so I figured I was in the right place. And it turned out to be a really good decision," he said with a laugh.

Bruns agreed that it made sense for fringe players not to leave a good job for a chance at the NBA or ABA. But, he said, "there's nobody who wouldn't have played in the bigs if they could have made it. I'm going to tell you that right now. I don't give a shit what they were making and weren't making. . . . All these guys, we all aspired or dreamed of playing for a pro team."

For the players who stayed and newcomers to the league, the Eastern League remained tough and competitive, if somewhat short of the star power it had once enjoyed.

"It was a step up" from college competition for most players, said Bruns.

Recalled Pawlak: "Guys and everybody respected each other in that league. Because we all knew it wasn't the easiest task. And there were some bad guys, and were some incidents. But in all the years I played in it, I thought we had great rivalries."

Above all, it remained physical. Very physical.

"I mean I saw some things—violence, violent stuff in the late '60s," said Bruns. "And you know the problem was, like they play in the [NBA] now . . . nobody wants to hurt anybody. Everybody's making a good living [now], and I always felt those days nobody gave a shit about anything. You came down the middle one time too many you're going to get leveled and carried out, and I saw that happen. So you'd better know how to pull up and take your jump shot."

Richie Cornwall recalled his first game in Sunbury, playing in their tiny gym against the McCoy brothers. "Jim McCoy was playing me, and I remember it like vividly. . . . I passed, and I started to cut through, and he gave me like a forearm shot to the chest, and then said, 'Welcome to the league.' . . . It wasn't like dirty or anything like that. It was just like, you got to earn your respect here. So that was pretty neat."

A 1971 *Sports Illustrated* article described Allentown Jets center Wayne Cruse as "a gentle, soft-spoken soul." But "on weekends he sets picks, blocks shots and crashes boards with a ferocity that belies his weekday manner. 'You have to play rough,' he says. 'This is a rough league. I broke my right hand and fractured my left one year, but I played. I had no choice. In the EBA no play means no pay.'"[3]

Pawlak recalled playing against his friend and sometime driving buddy John Richter. "I was friendly with John. . . . Good rebounder, good defender. Would get six fouls every game, would make sure he got his six. If you came in the lane, no matter how friendly you were, you were going to get hit in the head. That was just the way it was. He was going to use up those fouls."

"I mean, you would have riots, fights," said former NBA referee Joe Crawford, who started officiating professional games in the Eastern League. "Some nights . . . all of a sudden there would be . . . this huge fistfight. . . . You'd be jumping in the middle of it. It was amazing! It was a circus. And I didn't know anything different. I had no idea."

"You didn't mess in the league," Boeheim said. "It was a physical, tough league. I stayed 25 feet, 20 feet from the basket most of the time [laughing]. That was no place to go in there. . . . There was a lot of fights, a lot of physical play. I didn't get involved in them. I stayed as far away as I could. But Joe Lalli used to get in fights. A kid from Scranton . . . He got into some battles in that league."

At 5′8″ and from nearby Dunmore, Lalli was a local favorite, one of the top athletes produced by the Scranton area at that time and a graduate of George Washington University. Despite his size, he was never afraid to drive inside and was noted for his tight, harassing, pesky style of defense. One night, he was guarding Allentown's Bobby McNeill.

"And Bobby and I had some battles," Lalli said. McNeill was driving downcourt for a layup, and Lalli "was just trying to go up and block the shot or whatever, and we might have tumbled out of bounds." But one of the Jets' big men "thought I had undercut Bobby McNeil on a fast break. And I didn't."

But in retaliation, "I was blindsided, on purpose, by a big 6′8″ center who fractured my cheekbone with the hit. I felt if I could not protect myself from a blow from behind then it was time to move on."

That was Lalli's last game in the league.

Though attendance was declining by this time, fans who continued to attend games remained as fervent as ever, particularly for rivalry games like Scranton vs. Wilkes-Barre.

"I remember when the host Wilkes-Barre Barons would play the Scranton Miners at King's College,"[4] posted fan Matt Engel on an Eastern League fans

Facebook page, recalling the abuse the Barons' fans would direct at Scranton owner Pachter.

With top-tier players less plentiful, the Eastern League redoubled its efforts to develop a working arrangement with the NBA. In 1970, the league rebranded itself as the Eastern Basketball Association (EBA). "The purpose of this action," according to a league history that appeared in the Scranton game programs that year, "was to establish a similarity in name with the major basketball associations."[5]

Also in the league that year, the Scranton Miners changed their name to the Scranton Apollos in recognition of the 1969 moon landing.[6] And, of greater significance to the league, the aging Harry Rudolph, the league's president since 1954, resigned (with some urging by the owners) and was replaced by Bill Montzman, longtime general manager of the Allentown Jets, which had established a reputation as a well-run organization.

"The reason I think the Jets were so successful . . . was that they had top business and basketball minds in charge,"[7] wrote Jean-Pierre Caravan in an email. Caravan grew up as a Jets fan in Allentown in the 1960s and worked for the Jets as a ball boy, an assistant trainer, then trainer, and finally director of public relations.

Caravan explained that the Jets developed a working relationship with the NBA's Knicks through Frank Wagner, a Jets team official who replaced Montzman as Allentown's GM. Fuzzy Levane had coached Allentown in 1961/62 and was a friend of Red Holzman, who became the head coach of the Knicks and got to know Wagner through Levane. Because of this connection, the Jets became a conduit for players whom the Knicks wanted to farm out. Roman Turmon, Brendan McCann, and Tom Stith were former Knicks who went to Allentown in the early 1960s.

"We had nothing in writing; it was all a gentleman's agreement,"[8] Wagner was quoted as saying in a 1998 newspaper article. "If [Holzman] had players he felt were not quite ready, he wanted a place to send them to make sure they would play."

Mike Riordan was another such player. The Knicks selected Riordan from Providence College in the 12th round of the 1967 NBA draft. He spent the 1967/68 season with the Jets before going on to a nine-year NBA career with the Knicks and the Baltimore (eventually Washington) Bullets.

"Mike Riordan was a guy who was a personal friend who only spent one year (in the Eastern League)," said Bruns. "He spent the year in Allentown and was honing his skills, then made the Knicks the next year as the 12th man."

In 1969 the Knicks drafted Eddie Mast out of Temple University and sent him to the Jets. He averaged 19.7 PPG for the Jets and 13.1 rebounds (fourth in the EPBL), and teamed with Wilburn and Johnny Jones to lead the Jets to the championship. The following season he joined the Knicks for two seasons and then the Atlanta Hawks for one. He rejoined Allentown in 1973 and would play the next 10 years in the Eastern League and Continental Basketball Association, with a brief stint in the ABA.

Harthorne Wingo was a raw, athletic 6′6″ forward who played at Friendship Junior College in Rock Hill, South Carolina, and burst upon the Eastern League with the Jets in 1970. His sensational leaping and the way he bounded down the floor dazzled fans, and as a rookie he finished second in the league in rebounding. The following year he was the league's MVP, averaging 22.6 PPG and 14 rebounds, and teaming with Wilburn, Bruns, and Jay Neary to lead the Jets to another championship. Halfway through the 1972/73 season he was signed by the Knicks, where he became a huge fan favorite and played for four seasons.

Tom Riker, a 6′10″ center from the University of South Carolina, was the Knicks' first-round pick in 1972, and after 14 games was sent down to the Jets. The following year and in 1974/75 he would be a spot player for the Knicks.

The Jets' arrangement with the Knicks became a model that other Eastern League teams followed. Eastern League teams didn't receive the financial support from NBA clubs that they hoped they would get, but at least they had a stream of players to work with and offered prospects the hope of someday playing in the NBA.

"I think Scranton was a farm team for Philadelphia, and Allentown was for the Knicks, and also Hartford was for the Celtics," Bavetta recalled. "I was a fledgling official in those days, just trying to hone my craft, and I would do a Hartford Capitols game and I look in the stands and I see Red Auerbach and I see Tom Heinsohn. . . . It became a shuttle . . . between the parent team in the NBA and the farm team in the EBA."

Perhaps the best known of the Eastern League alumni of the '70s was Charlie Criss. The 5′8″ dynamo played in the league for five years and was its dominant star, winning the MVP Award in 1976 and 1977 with Scranton. In 1977 the Atlanta Hawks brought him to the NBA, launching an eight-year NBA career in which he averaged 8.5 points and 3.2 assists per game.

Two other Eastern Leaguers who enjoyed NBA careers of note were M. L. Carr and Major Jones. Carr was a 6′6″ forward from Guilford College in North Carolina who bounced between the Eastern League and the ABA from 1972 to 1976, before enjoying a nine-year NBA career as a key player for the Pistons and

Boston Celtics. He later became the Celtics' coach and general manager. And Major Jones was a Portland draft pick who played for the Jets from 1976 to 1978 before a six-year NBA career with the Houston Rockets and Detroit Pistons.

"I suspect if you were really comparing that league with what they have now it's very similar to the G League [the NBA's minor league], where they would bring guys in for 10-day contracts or send them up there to see how" they perform, said Tony Upson.

"The opportunity was there for these guys to either go to the ABA or NBA," Bavetta said. "I always looked at the Eastern League as a league to hone your craft, be lucky enough to be observed on a good night, and be brought up to the parent team at some point in time."

Walker Banks got drafted by the Knicks out of Western Kentucky University but also got a call from the ABA's Pittsburgh Condors. He went to Pittsburgh's camp and made the team, playing 16 games. But then when teammate and bad boy John Brisker got into a scrape with Banks, the team decided to send Banks to the Eastern League to keep peace. Said Banks: "[A] majority of the guys had aspirations to play in the NBA. So all of us knew that the pro scouts, the NBA scouts, were looking to the Eastern League as a minor league of sorts. So that's the inspiration we had to try to work out, try to be in shape, try to play hard, to be seen."

For Scranton owner Art Pachter, one of the saddest stories of former NBA prospects consigned to the Eastern League was that of Cyril Baptiste. "Cyril Baptiste can possibly be the best athlete" he ever saw, Pachter said. Baptiste was drafted by the Golden State Warriors in the 1971 NBA Hardship draft. "The trivia question with him is he was the first guy picked as compensation for the ABA stealing an NBA player. The ABA stole Rick Barry, and in return the first pick in the draft went to [Golden State], and [they] picked Cyril."

Pachter got a phone call one day from an agent he had met on a trip to Florida several months earlier. The agent told Pachter that Baptiste had used up the large signing bonus he had received, had been released by Golden State, and "was all drugged out." The agent asked Pachter if he was interested, and Pachter told him to fly Baptiste to Scranton. Baptiste would play for the Apollos the next three seasons as a part-time player.

"He was some athlete," said Pachter. "He was great." But "he got hurt. We were in the playoffs. And he got tripped by Ken Wilburn accidentally . . . and I remember after the game going to the hospital and they had his leg up. He was finished. Yep, that was it. His career was over that night."

With the Eastern League's prestige in decline, so too was its attendance. The 1970s recession hit the league's small factory and coal towns hard. Discretionary dollars for entertainment were becoming scarcer in the receding economies of the Rust Belt. Populations were decreasing, too. Young people, always the core of the Eastern League's fan base, moved away from the small, blue-collar towns and didn't come back. Cable television brought professional basketball to homes almost every night of the week.

"They started carrying more games on TV," said Bruns, "so all those folks who lived in those little towns could turn on their TV and watch stuff rather than have to come to the CYC . . . or down in Rockne Hall in Allentown or places like that."

The 1971 *Sports Illustrated* article, "Toughing It Out around the Purgatory League," captured both the status of basketball players suspended between the minor and the major leagues and the sense of decline cloaking the once-thriving Eastern League, which it referred to as pro basketball's "nether regions."[9]

On the night that was the subject of the article, Andy Johnson had returned to Allentown for the first time since his final season with the Jets in 1969. This time, however, he was the coach of the visiting Camden Bullets. Only 931 paying fans turned out at Rockne Hall, whose 3,500 seats used to be filled with fans chanting, "Let's go Jets!"

On that night, the article said, "The place bristled with indifference."[10]

Declining attendance was a problem league-wide. One longtime Scranton fan recalled that the Miners used to draw 4,000 or more to the Scranton CYC but by the late 1960s only a fraction of that. Teams were struggling, cutting costs by lowering salaries and releasing highly paid players, and moving to new towns or folding altogether.

Pawlak recalled that he "was disappointed . . . we had such a nice [Wilkes-Barre] team that won [the championship] in '69, and they just broke the team up, basically." That 1969 team had a regular season record of 26-2, an all-time league record with a winning percentage of .929. But the following season Bill Green and Bob Keller went to Hamden, "so the team, the next two or three years, wasn't the same," Pawlak said. "The recession took a toll on the league."

"It was difficult for these franchises to exist," Rich Cornwall recalled. "Then there was a lot of flip-flopping towns and changing. . . . You just had so many different teams playing each year that I think it just became hard for the people to grasp one of them, to really stay with them. . . . It was difficult to survive, it really was."

"Hamden basically disbanded after we got to the semis" in 1970/71, Bruns said. "The . . . owners wanted to use the team as sort of a barometer to maybe buy an ABA team, and they weren't getting the cooperation that they wanted from the city and access to the arena there, and they folded the team up."

The league, which had peaked with 10 franchises for three straight seasons from 1965 to 1967 and again in 1968/69, was down to six teams in 1971/72. In 1974/75 it had only four—Hazleton, Allentown, Scranton, and Cherry Hill, New Jersey.

The end, it seemed, was near.

STARS OF THE ABA ERA AND THE EASTERN LEAGUE'S FINAL YEARS (1967–1978)

Even though the ABA poached most of the Eastern League's top players in the first two years after the new league was formed, a nucleus of good players remained. When the Continental Basketball Association (CBA) announced its all-time basketball teams in 1996 in commemoration of the Eastern League's 50th anniversary, the star players from the 1967–1978 era who made the team were Stan Pawlak, Charlie Criss, and Ken Wilburn. Waite Bellamy, Jim Boeheim, George Bruns, Rich Cornwall, and Mack Daughtry received honorable mention.[1]

Here's a look at players who are often mentioned by former Eastern Leaguers and fans when discussing the top players of the years from the ABA to the CBA. Note that several began their Eastern League careers before 1967. However, some were just beginning to emerge as stars when they left for the ABA in 1967 or 1968, and then returned to the Eastern League. Others stayed in the league and were its dominant players in the seasons following the formation of the ABA. Players are listed roughly in the order of when they began playing in the Eastern League.

WAITE BELLAMY

Waite Bellamy's Eastern League career almost ended before it began.

After a prospective landlord turned Bellamy and his wife away in Scranton because they were black, the former St. Louis Hawks' fourth-round draft pick from Florida A&M University (FAMU) got discouraged.

"I called my mom and I said, 'I'm coming home,'" Bellamy recalled.

But Miners owner Arthur Pachter told Bellamy that a new team had just started in Wilmington, Delaware, and they were looking for players.

"So I went and . . . I practiced with them," Bellamy recalled. "Soon as I ran up and down the court a couple times and hit a couple shots out of the corner, they signed me up."

Bellamy would stay with the Blue Bombers for the life of the franchise, from 1963 to 1971, and was its all-time leading scorer, a league MVP, three-time all-league selection, and two-time Eastern League champion. On three occasions he scored 50 or more points in a game.

"Waite Bellamy was a tremendous player," said Jim Boeheim. "He was really, really difficult to guard down low. He could score, he could get to the basket, he was one of the really good players left in the league [after the ABA started up]."

"He's as good as they got," recalled Stan Pawlak. "He was just tough."

Bellamy and Pawlak squared off many times, most notably in the 1969 championship finals, which the Barons won, three games to two.

"We had battles, Waite and I," Pawlak said with a mix of admiration and pride.

Bellamy was an excellent outside shooter. But at a solidly built 6'4", Bellamy—who had the choice of playing either football or basketball at FAMU—liked to use his size and strength to gather offensive rebounds and score on putbacks.

"He was such a tough rebounder for a guard, my goodness," said Pawlak. "He took a shot, you had to block him out every time. If you forgot, he was going to score."

"You know," said George Bruns, "[Bellamy] was a guy that I thought—you wondered why he wasn't playing for the Philadelphia team in the NBA. . . . He could really play."

Bellamy had tryouts with three NBA teams—including one training camp with the New York Knicks when he roomed with rookie Phil Jackson (who later coached the Chicago Bulls and Los Angeles Lakers to 11 NBA championships). Bellamy said he was there just to provide a body in camp. He could have left for the ABA in 1967 when his backcourt mate Maurice McHartley and other Eastern Leaguers departed, but as described in chapter 10, he didn't get what he thought was a fair offer.

"I was a schoolteacher at the time," said Bellamy, who was teaching physical education in the Wilmington elementary schools. "I had my degree, and I had an apartment, and I had a wife and two kids. . . . So I said, 'You've got the wrong person, I'm not your man.'"

SWISH MCKINNEY

Maybe it was the nickname—"Swish"—that first got your attention.

It was presumptuous, a name that demanded someone who had it to back it up, especially in the tough, ultracompetitive worlds of professional and playground basketball. As George Blaney said: "Well, nobody goes through life with the name Swish if you can't shoot."

And that was the thing about McKinney. "I mean, he could really shoot," Blaney said. "The ball didn't touch anything. It just touched the nets. That's all. He was 6'2". He was quick. He was strong. And he could get the jump shot off against anybody."

"Swish was the best shooter from 15 feet that I've ever seen in my life," said Joe Lalli, who played with and against McKinney. "He didn't go under too often. . . . But he'd pull up at 15 feet and there was a reason he was nicknamed Swish, I guarantee you."

Sonny Hill, when asked in an interview with the JockBio website who the best player was in the Eastern League that nobody's heard of, said: "There was a tremendous player that I played against and I played with. His name was 'Swish' McKinney out of Oakland, California. If you mention that name today, very few people would know who he is. He was a tremendous offensive player, great shooter."[2]

As McKinney himself put it, "Every time I shot it was boom, boom, boom, boom, boom."

Swish, of course, wasn't his given name. His real first name was Cleveland. He completed McClymonds High School in Oakland—the same school as Bill Russell, Frank Robinson, Vada Pinson, and Curt Flood, among others—at age 16 when he was told that he had finished the academic requirements for all the grades and the school didn't have any more courses for him.

He eventually entered the army and, to his good fortune, was assigned to Panama and put in charge of the athletic program, where he spent hours in the gym, day after day, for almost three years, playing pickup, shooting, and sharpening his skills. At some point he acquired the nickname "Swish" and made the all-Army team (whose coaches included Bobby Knight).

McKinney eventually made the U.S. team for the 1963 Pan American Games, which also included future NBA stars Willis Reed and Lucious Jackson, and won the gold medal. After the team returned, the St. Louis Hawks invited McKinney to their preseason camp.

"I don't know why I didn't make the team," McKinney said. "They couldn't stop me. They couldn't do anything."

But the Hawks sent McKinney to Wilmington, where he was the Eastern League's Rookie of the Year in 1965, finishing fourth in the league in scoring with a 24.3 average. He played for five more teams in the league, with his best years coming in Scranton and Binghamton.

In 1967/68 McKinney set the league record for most points scored in a season with 1,206. But in a statistical quirk, he finished second in scoring average that season with 34.5 PPG to Julius McCoy's 34.9, because McKinney played three additional games as a result of a midseason trade from Scranton to Binghamton. He scored 50 or more points seven times in his career, second only to King Lear's 10.

McKinney was a fan favorite everywhere he played. He was demonstrative, liked to talk on both ends of the court, interacted with fans and in the community, and was fun to watch. In Scranton he had his own weekly call-in radio program, which he ended with: "Remember Swish's ABCs: Always be cool."

"He was fun," said Blaney. "He was really a fun guy. Everybody liked him. . . . He was a handful to guard, but always very competitive and very good."

"Swish had this thing," said Tony Upson, "this dribble where if you played him real tight, he'd dribble between your legs. He'd throw the ball between your legs and he'd grab it and shoot it. He did me like that one day. Man, I was so mad I wanted to kill this guy."

BRUCE SPRAGGINS

Bruce Spraggins was a solid, complementary player early in his Eastern League career, who didn't emerge as a star until late in the 1960s.

Spraggins started his professional career in the short-lived ABL and came to the Eastern League in 1962/63 when the former league folded. He began with the Trenton Colonials and was the team's third leading scorer as a rookie with 13.6 PPG behind Wally Choice and George Blaney. For the next three seasons he played in Trenton with a revolving cast of accomplished scorers, including Eastern League veterans Stacey Arceneaux, Frank Keitt, Cleo Hill, George Lehmann, Blaney, and short-timers Bob Love (on his way up to the NBA) and Jim Hadnot (in between stints in the NBA and the ABA).

In 1966/67, Spraggins finally had a breakthrough season, finishing fourth in the league in scoring with 30.1 PPG for the New Haven Elms. The 6'6" Spraggins left the following year for the ABA, averaging 12.2 PPG with the New Jersey Americans, then returned to the Eastern League for four more years with New Haven and Hamden. He was a three-time all-league pick and is the league's 16th all-time career scorer.

"Bruce was a good player, good scorer," said Waite Bellamy of the 6'6" swingman. "He was a kind of thin guy; he was wiry and quick."

"He . . . preferred to take it to the basket," said Upson, his coach in Hamden. "However, he could also hit from 12–15 feet. . . . He was an 80–85 percent free throw shooter . . . a good defender, and a good rebounder."

STAN PAWLAK

Stan Pawlak is the first to say he wasn't ready for the Eastern League when he broke in with the short-lived Harrisburg Patriots in 1966 as an all-Ivy and honorable mention All-American from the University of Pennsylvania.

"I was a rookie. I played like a rookie, too," recalled the 6'3" Pawlak. "I hadn't played that much guard, but it was a proving ground for me." He said the league's top guards like Hal Lear, Bob Weiss, Swish McKinney, Levern Tart, and Maurice McHartley took advantage of him.

"Those guys, they taught me a lot of lessons my first year. . . . I got my ass handed to me by all those guys, because I was not ready to be a guard to the level that they were."

But Pawlak, a native of Camden, New Jersey, across the river from Philly, went back home and played guard in the summer Baker League against top pro and college players. The following season, after Harrisburg folded, Wilkes-Barre Barons coach Stan Novak (a fellow Penn alum) "brought me up to Wilkes-Barre, and basically that's when I started to be a pretty good player in the league."

Indeed. By 1967/68, Pawlak would average 25.0 PPG, finish among the leaders in scoring, and establish himself as one of the league's top guards. By the time his 10-year career ended—eight of them with Wilkes-Barre—Pawlak was a five-time all-league selection, led the league in scoring twice and in assists three times, and won MVP in 1969. He is fifth on the all-time Eastern League scoring list with 5,729 points, behind only fellow all-time Eastern League team members Julius McCoy, Stacey Arceneaux, Tom Hemans, and Hal Lear.

Pretty heady company for a player who, by his own admission, "didn't look like the most athletic guy."

"Stan Pawlak was a really good player," said Jim Boeheim. "Physical, tough guard . . . Could get to the lane and could shoot it . . . He was one of the best scorers in the league. We went head up a lot, because Scranton/Wilkes-Barre was a big rivalry."

"Unbelievable shooter," said Rich Cornwall, another former Scranton back-court player. "He wasn't the quickest guy that was on the court, but he knew how to move without the ball and all he needed was a split second to get his shot off. He was real smart and, again, knew exactly what he needed to do to get a shot that he wanted."

"Stan was an awesome, awesome shooter," said his former Barons team-mate Walker Banks. "Stan Pawlak could have played with a[n NBA] team that needed a shooter."

Pawlak played forward in college and "used my strength" to create shots. But watching fellow South Jersey native George Lehmann hit three-point shots changed Pawlak's game.

"Playing against George is what incentivized me. Soon as I saw that three-point line, I said, 'Well this is going to make my life a lot easier if I can do this,'" Pawlak recalled.

Pawlak would lead the league in three-point goals six times—five of them consecutively starting in 1968/69. His highest single season total was 49 in 1969/70, despite taking relatively few attempts compared to today's standards.

Though most of his scoring came from outside, Pawlak still could and would use his strength to take smaller players inside.

"Stan would take me in the bucket as a guard and I couldn't handle him," said Joe Lalli, who at 5′8″ was one of the shortest players in the league. "I could play him outside, guard outside and play at the top of the circle, et cetera. But he would take me inside and I would soon have to come out of the game. . . . I really had an impossible task, to guard Stan Pawlak."

"Hard-nosed player, good shooter, good scorer," recalled Waite Bellamy, another big shooting guard who battled Pawlak for many years on the court and for the league scoring title.

Pawlak had tryouts with several NBA teams, was the last player cut at a Chicago Bulls training camp, and among the last with the Philadelphia 76ers. But he does not seem to regret not playing in the NBA.

"I know by what I did in the Baker League and stuff like that that I could play anywhere," Pawlak said of the Philly summer league where he competed against top pro players.

WILLIE SOMERSET

Not many pro basketball players who stand 5'8" are known for their toughness and strength.

Willie Somerset was.

A stocky, muscular, fireplug of a man, Somerset was quick and a terrific outside shooter. But it was his remarkable strength that people talk about first.

"Willie was so strong," said his former teammate Jim Boeheim. "I mean, he was a strong kid. He was maybe 5'10" . . . but he was big. He could get to the basket against anybody and he could shoot it. He was really, really a good player."

"Very strong for his size," Waite Bellamy remembered. "Little stout-built little guy."

Somerset starred in basketball and football at western Pennsylvania sports powerhouse Farrell High School and went on to become a basketball All-American at Duquesne University. His playing style was a throwback to his old-school roots, right down to shooting free throws underhand, just as his high school coach insisted.

The Baltimore Bullets drafted him in 1965, and he played eight games for them before landing in the Eastern League with Johnstown, an expansion team that folded after a 3–25 season.

The following season Somerset played in Scranton, teaming with Swish McKinney to give the Miners a potent backcourt. They won their division and made it to the championship finals, where they lost in five games to the Blue Bombers. Somerset averaged 27.2 PPG and made second team all-league.

In 1967/68 he jumped to the Houston Mavericks of the ABA and became one of the new league's early stars and leaders in scoring and foul shooting. He was an ABA All-Star in 1968/69, splitting the season with Houston and the New York Nets, and ranked fifth in the league in points per game, eighth in assists, and third in free throw percentage. In two ABA seasons, Somerset averaged 22.8 PPG.

Then Somerset, a pharmacist by profession, decided to retire from the ABA and pursue his career, so "I came back to the Eastern League and I played with Art Pachter again."

Pachter and Scranton fans were glad he did. In 1970/71 he was the league's leading scorer with 26.3 PPG, the MVP, and led the newly named Apollos to their first championship since 1957. The following season he finished fourth in scoring at 23.4, but the Apollos couldn't repeat. He retired after that season and is the league's 28th all-time leading scorer.

"The best guard that I played against, without question," said Stan Pawlak, "not counting [my] early days in the league [when he played against Lear and others]. He could do everything—could shoot, he played hard. . . . Until Charlie Criss, he was the toughest. In our league, he was as good as it got."

KEN WILBURN

Ken Wilburn was the kind of player who opposing players and fans loved to hate.

A wiry 6'6" forward who weighed less than 200 pounds, he made up for his lack of size with a nonstop motor and aggressive play—some might say overly aggressive. But his relentlessness paid off. By the time his career (which included two seasons in the CBA) ended, he was one of the Eastern League's most decorated players ever with two MVP Awards, Rookie of the Year, five all-league selections, league record holder for most rebounds in a game (38 in 1966) and in a season (668 in 1967/68), and three league championships.

"Kenny Wilburn was a really good player," recalled Boeheim. "I got matched up against him a little bit because I played a little forward when I was first there, and he was tough, he was tough to play against. He was physical."

Wilburn, a two-time small-college All-American at tiny Wilberforce College in Ohio (now known as Central State University), broke into the EPBL with Trenton in 1966/67. Former Trenton teammate Tony Upson remembered him as a "small . . . wiry, thin guy," which belied his ferocity on the boards and as an inside scorer.

As a rookie he was runner-up in rebounding to Willie Murrell with a 19.8 average and scored 22.1 PPG. The next season he was the league's leading rebounder (20.9) and fourth leading scorer (27.7) and won his first MVP. He copped his second MVP in 1972 (20.5 PPG, 10.7 rebounds)—the league's first two-time MVP since Jack McCloskey in 1953 and '54—teaming with Harthorne Wingo to give Allentown a dominant front line and a championship.

Wilburn had some chances to move up. Philadelphia drafted him in the fourth round in 1966, but he didn't make the cut. In 1967/68 and early the next season he played in a handful of games with the Chicago Bulls. When the Bulls released him, he moved to the ABA and played with three teams in 1968/69. The following season he returned to the Eastern League with the Allentown Jets, for whom he would play for six seasons.

Wilburn's game had one glaring weakness: he was a terrible foul shooter, and was often fouled by opposing teams late in close games. As he was quoted in a 1971 *Sports Illustrated* article: "When it comes to foul shooting . . . I'm a regular Wilt Chamberlain."[3]

GEORGE BRUNS

Like most of the guys who played in the Eastern League, George Bruns was a gym rat.

"I loved to play," said the New York City native, who went to high school in the same Brooklyn neighborhood as another Eastern Leaguer, referee Dick Bavetta. "I used to play all over. . . . I've been in every gym you could imagine."

A 6'0" guard from Manhattan College, Bruns said he "was a pretty good player in college. I had only played a couple of seasons. I had no scholarships to college. I was one of these kind of guys, sort of in the shadows. . . . I used to play in all sorts of leagues."

His play in one of those leagues led to an introduction to York Larese, the former Eastern League and NBA player who was coaching the Hartford Capitols.

"So I went out and tried out and made the team" in 1968, and that's how Bruns started his nine-year career in the Eastern League. He would play one season each with Hartford and Hamden. But it was in his seven seasons with the Allentown Jets that he became one of the league's top point guards.

Once again, it was Larese who gave Bruns his chance. Larese had coached the ABA's Nets for a season, then came back to the league as coach of Allentown. When Hamden folded, he picked Bruns in the dispersal draft.

"[Larese] liked me," Bruns said. "I could distribute the ball and score a little bit. . . . I was always a little undersized for that level . . . [but] I continued to improve."

That season, 1971/72, Harthorne Wingo joined the Jets and with Wilburn and Bruns led them to the championship. The Jets were champs again in 1974/75 and 1975/76 (absent Wingo, who by then was in the NBA) with Bruns the floor general, scoring around 20 per game and among the league leaders in assists. He was named to four first team all-league teams and is 18th on the all-time scoring list. In his final season, 1976/77, he was the Jets' player-coach.

"George was one of the better guards in the league," said Pawlak. "He was like a true point guard. You knew when you played George you were always going to have a tough time, because he was really smart. . . . What I thought was the quintessential, all-around point guard. . . . He did everything well."

The New York Nets brought Bruns to the ABA at the end of the 1972/73 season. He played in 13 games, averaging 6.6 PPG and almost three assists as a backup, but didn't make it out of training camp the following season.

"I got on the Nets and . . . played well almost instantly," Bruns said. "Louis Dampier [a Naismith Memorial Basketball Hall of Fame guard who played in the ABA for the Kentucky Colonels] said to me, 'Where you been? Where you been playing?' So you know, I was good enough to play."

RICH CORNWALL

At first glance, Richie Cornwall—at barely 6'0" and with a boyish face—didn't look like a pro basketball player.

Tony Upson thought of Cornwall as a "guy [who] looked like you wouldn't pick him up if you were out on the playground," but "hey, he could play."

Cornwall compensated for his lack of size with smarts, dogged competitiveness, and a great outside shot.

"Richie was a thorn in my side," said his longtime rival Stan Pawlak, "and he would work so hard all the time to guard me. . . . I always knew I had to work about three times harder than I did with anybody else."

Waite Bellamy described Cornwall as one "of those kind of guys . . . [who would] get up under your arms. . . . Kind of annoyed you a little bit."

Cornwall's exposure to the EPBL actually began in high school outside of Philadelphia, where his coach was Eastern League veteran and coach Howie Landa. He used to accompany Landa to Trenton to watch him coach the Colonials.

"I remember a lot of these guys, like Wally Choice, a lot of the guys that were in the league, so it was a great experience," Cornwall said.

Cornwall went to Syracuse University, two years behind fellow Eastern Leaguer Jim Boeheim, and "was drafted by the Knicks, but it was such a late round and it wasn't even a possibility." He could have stayed at Syracuse as a graduate assistant coach but was married, had a child, and "I still wanted to play. It was still in my blood." He taught school, became Landa's assistant at Trenton Junior College, and joined the new Eastern League team in Binghamton in 1968/69.

Cornwall entered the league as a playmaker and led the league in assists his first two seasons, averaging 6.7 and 5.8 per game, and again in 1973/74 with 5.4. He was Rookie of the Year in 1969. But he developed a deadly outside shot and within a few years added a scoring punch to complement his floor game and tough defense.

"He didn't score as much in the beginning," recalled Pawlak, "and then he became more of a three-point shooter and a scorer as time went on. . . . I can't say enough about him. Other than myself, he was one of the better three-point shooters in the league."

Indeed, when Pawlak led the league in three-point shooting for six out of seven years, Cornwall was the guy who interrupted the streak in 1973/74. After Pawlak retired, Cornwall would lead the league in three-pointers in its final three seasons, including a league-record 83 in 1977/78, and holds the record for most treys in a game with nine. He was also a top free throw shooter, leading the league three times, and holds the two highest free throw shooting percentages in Eastern League history—.936 in 1976/77 and .930 in 1973/74.

Cornwall played nine seasons in the Eastern League—six of them with the Scranton Apollos. He also spent the 1974/75 season playing in Holland, had a tryout with Pittsburgh in the ABA, and continued playing in the CBA. He was named to all-league teams twice and is the 13th all-time leading scorer in Eastern League history with 4,454 points.

MACK DAUGHTRY

Mack Daughtry may be one of the most well-liked players of the Eastern League's last decade. Just listen to what former teammates said about him.

"I had the pleasure of playing against Mack and playing with him," Rich Cornwall said. "What a really nice man . . . Mack is a real good guy, and a really good player."

"Mack Daughtry was one of my favorite players of all time in the Eastern League," said Walker Banks, who played with him for many years in Wilkes-Barre and Scranton.

"It was a love affair between me and Mack," said his longtime backcourt mate Pawlak. "He was unselfish. . . . Mack was a pleasure to play with."

Daughtry joined the Barons in 1968 as a rookie out of Albany State University in Georgia. A 6'3" guard, Daughtry was a complete player. He could do everything well.

"He had the total game," said Cornwall. "He could play defense, he could pass, he wasn't a great shooter but he could score."

"Mack Daughtry could play," George Bruns said. "Just smart, tall enough, and good enough."

"Tremendous all-around player," Banks said. "Offense good. Excellent defensive player."

In his rookie season, he found his niche as a point guard whose primary role was to play tough defense and feed Pawlak and the Barons' big guys, Bill Green and Bob Keller, during their league-record 26–2 regular season and postseason championship. Daughtry and Pawlak would win another title in 1972/73 with the Barons—this time with Walt Szczerbiak (a 6'6" sharp-shooter, former ABA player, and father of former NBA player Wally Szczerbiak) and Banks up front.

Daughtry could also score, usually in double figures, and hit 19.9 PPG with Scranton in 1974/75. His speed and tenacity also made him a solid defender.

Daughtry would win one more championship with the Barons in 1977/78 and continued to play three more seasons with Wilkes-Barre in the CBA. Three ABA teams gave him brief looks in 1970/71, but otherwise he played 13 seasons in the Eastern League and its successor, all but one of those seasons in either Wilkes-Barre or Scranton.

BILLY DEANGELIS

Like many of the other players on this list, Billy DeAngelis was a hardworking overachiever.

"I've known Billy [DeAngelis] from the time that he was a kid," said Pawlak, who was a couple of years ahead of DeAngelis in the south Jersey school and playground leagues and played at Penn in Philadelphia's Big Five while DeAngelis was at St. Joseph's. "Got better after college. . . . He basically forced himself on the Eastern League and became a force."

The 6'1" guard was an accomplished playmaker. In his second season, 1969/70, he would finish third in the league in assists, averaging 3.9. In 1974/75 he led the league with 5.8 per game, and had four more seasons in the top three. But it would take a couple more years before he would emerge as a scorer. In 1971/72 playing with Hazleton, he finished third in scoring with 24.1 PPG, and was fourth the following year with 23.8.

"George Bruns and Billy DeAngelis," said Rich Cornwall, another top point guard from that era who made himself into a scorer, "I would clone those two guys. Both offensively really intelligent guys, very capable scorers, I mean solid games. We were probably all around the same size. Bruns may have been a little bigger than Billy D and I. They were solid players."

DeAngelis made second team all-league four seasons in a row from 1972/75. He had an eight-game fling with the Nets in 1970/71 but otherwise had a 10-year Eastern League career plus one in the CBA playing for six different teams.

Said Pawlak: "I followed him and he just got better, and better, and better, and better."

JOHNNY MATHIS

Jokes about sharing a name with the famous singer aside, Johnny Mathis was a smooth, tough forward who played five years in the league—three with Allentown—and upheld the Jets' tradition of solid professional players.

While some players of that era started in the Eastern League, moved up to the NBA or ABA, and then ended their professional careers in the emerging European market, Mathis did the opposite. He graduated from Savannah State in 1965, played a couple of years in Spain, and returned to the U.S. when the ABA formed. He played for the New Jersey Americans in the ABA's opening season, then went to the Eastern League.

At 6'6", Mathis could play guard or forward and played both well.

"Tough player around the basket," recalled Waite Bellamy. "Tough player, tough player."

George Bruns, who played with Mathis in Hamden, said "he could really play . . . 6'6" forward, good pass, good screen. He couldn't shoot that well, but he really understood the game."

Mathis's coach at Hamden, Tony Upson, described him as "the prototype of the guard that they were looking for at that time—6'5", 6'6" who could handle the ball . . . like [Ben] Simmons is doing now with Philadelphia."

Mathis was a three-time all-league selection, and in 1969/70 finished in the top 10 in scoring (22 PPG) and top five in rebounding (12.6) and assists (3.8).

"You knew he was going to have a good night almost all the time," Pawlak said.

EDDIE MAST

Eddie Mast was a fun-loving guy who loved to play basketball.

"He was the kind of guy that just everybody liked," said his friend, author and former Eastern Leaguer Charley Rosen. "He was ready to do anything."

Mast entered the Eastern League through the New York Knicks–Allentown Jets pipeline. The Knicks drafted him in the third round in 1969 and sent him to Allentown. As a rookie, he averaged 19.7 PPG and 13.1 rebounds for the Jets, helped take them to the league title, and won Rookie of the Year.

He went back to the Knicks the following season, but in two years with New York and one with Atlanta he got little playing time and averaged only 2.0, 2.6, and 2.8 PPG, respectively. So he returned to the Jets and remained in the Eastern League and its successor CBA to stay. Mast again helped the Jets to the finals in 1974 and then to championships in '75 and '76. He was a steady 20-plus a game scorer for the Jets and was named all-league in 1976 and '77.

"I remember Eddie very well," said Stan Pawlak. "Eddie was around south Jersey a lot playing basketball. . . . He loved playing basketball. When he played with Bruns in Allentown, they were tough. Eddie was really tough. Blocked shots, he was like a 'stretch four'—a big guy that could shoot it, that could move, a big guy that played a couple of positions. . . . He was just terrific."

"He didn't really develop until after he played in the NBA, when he had a chance to play," said Rosen, who got to know Mast through their mutual friend and Mast's roommate with the Knicks, Phil Jackson. "Eddie developed into a really good shooter . . . very accurate. He could drive both ways; he had a great left hand. And hook shots with his right hand . . . But he could score, he could rebound. He was really smart; he knew the game. If he had got [another] shot at the NBA after maybe two or three years in the Eastern League, he could have been an NBA player."

CHARLIE CRISS

Charlie Criss was what one might call single minded.

"All I wanted to do was play ball," Criss said. "And I'd do anything I could just to play ball. That's what I wanted to do. That's what I did. Basketball was my thing."

But listed at 5′8″ and undrafted out of New Mexico State when he graduated in 1970, making it to the NBA was a long shot.

So Criss went back to his native New York City area and kept playing in various leagues. He got his break when another player in those leagues, Eastern Leaguer Eddie Johnson, went back to Hartford and told his coach, Pete Monska, about Criss.

Criss got a tryout, and Monska kept him for four games in 1972/73 as Hartford won the regular season title but lost to Wilkes-Barre in the finals. The following year he made Criss the starter, and Hartford won the league championship with Criss averaging 20.5 PPG.

Notwithstanding their championship, Hartford folded the following season and Criss went to Cherry Hill, an expansion franchise. He had a breakthrough year, scoring 30.6 PPG to lead the league.

But again his team folded, "and . . . I was in a dispersal draft," Criss recalled. The Hazleton Bullets had first pick, and many people expected their coach, Sonny Hill—a former Eastern Leaguer who, like Criss was a speedy, undersized guard—to draft Criss.

But "[Sonny] doesn't draft me," Criss said, "and everybody couldn't understand it why he didn't draft me." Criss got drafted by Scranton. "So the night we played them and Stan Novak was my coach at Scranton, Stan said to me . . . 'I want you to score tonight.'"

At first, Criss didn't understand what Novak meant. He was averaging over 30 a game (including a 63-point performance a month earlier). But Novak told Criss to turn it up a little more, and he did. That night, January 25, 1976, Criss scored 72 points on 27 field goals and 18 free throws—and no three-pointers as Criss likes to point out—in a double overtime win over Hazleton, breaking Wally Choice's 14-year-old single-game record of 69.

"That's the reason," said Criss about his motivation for his scoring outburst that night. "That's the league record. It's still there."

Criss would win the scoring title that season averaging 38.5 PPG and was selected MVP. The following year he won the scoring crown for the third straight season and was again MVP—the only player to win the award in back-to-back seasons other than Jack McCloskey in 1953 and '54—and led the Apollos to the 1977 championship.

"I played against him and I also played with him," recalled Rich Cornwall. "Playing against him wasn't a lot of fun. He was a very, very difficult assignment. He had the whole package. He could shoot, he was quick, he was strong. He wasn't big, but he was strong."

Despite his success in the Eastern League, Criss wasn't content. He still wanted to play in the NBA. He'd had tryouts but didn't stick. Enter former Eastern Leaguer Hubie Brown, coach of the Atlanta Hawks, a team that had cut its payroll and was looking for fast, aggressive players who could press, share playing time, and play up-tempo all game.

Brown contacted Criss, "and he said, 'No, I'm going to try out for the Knicks.' I said, 'Yes, but you've been cut from the Knicks like four or five summers in a row. . . . I'm guaranteeing you now that we'll keep you and play you eight exhibition games. Then it will be up to you whether you make the team or not.' So he agreed to that. And he came down, and that was the best thing that happened for him, and best thing for us. . . . He was outstanding."

12

THE COACHES

Just as players and teams moved from town to town from season to season in the Eastern League, so, too, did coaches.

Some longtime Eastern League coaches, it seemed, worked with just about every team in the league at one point or another, and some teams had two or three coaches in a single season. Stories abound about many of the league's coaches, who collectively were a colorful group. As longtime Scranton owner Arthur Pachter put it: "There's a million stories. . . . I've had a million coaches."

Wilkes-Barre's Eddie White was one of the league's founders and early coaching giants. He was the Barons' owner and coach during the EBL's 1946/47 opening season, as he had been for many years when they played in regional semipro leagues. White moved the Barons to the ABL the following season, then back to the Eastern League in 1954 when the ABL folded. His Barons won Eastern League championships in 1955, '56, '58, and '59, with star players such as Danny Finn, Larry Hennessey, and Bill Spivey. The only team to break that streak was Scranton in '57, as the two teams—and the two cities—built on their rivalry.

White sold the Barons and left coaching in the early 1960s, but in 1965 he apparently got the itch to coach again and ended up back in the league—incredibly—as coach of Scranton.

Said grandson Eddie White III: "I can remember when I was real little people saying, oh my G-d, it would be like someone from the Red Sox going to play for the Yankees or vice versa. It was like how does Mr. Wilkes-Barre Baron go coach Scranton? But my grandfather wanted to coach, and he did it."

The Miners went 13–15 (that was the season in which, as described in chapter 7, Allie Seiden, Carl Green, and other players threatened a revolt over White's coaching), and White was out. A decade later, in 1975/76, he returned one last time, as head coach of the Wilkes-Barre Barons.

White is fifth in career victories among Eastern League coaches with 113 and finished with a winning percentage of .536.

As the Eastern League's stature increased in the 1950s, it attracted big-name coaches—well-known former professional and college players and coaches. One of the first was Hank Rosenstein, a New York City product from Brooklyn and CCNY. He was a member of the New York Knicks of the Basketball Association of American (BAA), the predecessor to the NBA, and played in what is considered the first NBA game in November 1946. The following season Rosenstein joined the Scranton Miners of the NBA's rival American Basketball League (ABL), where he starred for the next five seasons.

After his playing days ended, Rosenstein returned to Scranton in 1956/57 to coach the Miners in the Eastern League. The Miners won the title in Rosenstein's first season led by Ed Roman, one of the star players implicated in the 1951 point-shaving scandal and banned from the NBA. Rosenstein coached in the league until 1968, for Scranton (twice), Williamsport, Wilkes-Barre, and Asbury Park; compiled a 152–114 record; and is the league's fourth winningest coach.

"Hank Rosenstein—he was a brilliant mind," said Pachter, who fired Rosenstein as coach in 1960 then rehired him two years later. "And he was big. He played basketball . . . people knew him, and he knew . . . all these guys. He knew [Red] Sarachek [legendary coach of Yeshiva University], [Lou] Carnesecca [longtime coach of St. John's University]. So he had this in into a lot of those places."

Another former Williamsport coach was Bobby Sand, the brilliant young assistant coach and recruiter at CCNY whom some observers credited for a large part of the school's basketball success in the early 1950s. Sand was never implicated in the point-shaving scandals, but his association with the tainted program appeared to have prevented him from climbing the coaching ladder. He compiled a 36–33 record in three seasons in the Eastern League ending in 1960.

When the Baltimore Bullets entered the league in 1958, their choice for coach was obvious: Buddy Jeannette. He was considered the best backcourt player in pro basketball in the years preceding the NBA when he starred in the National Basketball League (NBL) with Sheboygan and Fort Wayne. In 1946/47 he moved to the ABL, becoming player-coach of the Baltimore Bullets and leading them to the championship. When the Bullets moved to the BAA the following year, Jeannette continued as player-coach and again won the title.

Harvey Kasoff, who was part of Baltimore's ownership group, recalled how Jeannette quickly built the Bullets into one of the league's top teams. "Buddy had connections, and he got together a lot of guys who had NBA connections and everything," said Kasoff. "And he had a real good team."

At various times in the Bullets' three years in the Eastern League, players included Bill Spivey, Sherman White, Ralph Beard, and Roman. In 1959/60, with Spivey leading the league in scoring, the Bullets lost in the finals to Easton. The following season, the Bullets beat Allentown for the championship.

Neil Johnston of the Philadelphia Warriors was the top center in the NBA during the early 1950s. He played in six All-Star Games and was first or second team all-NBA six times. After he retired in 1958/59 because of a knee injury, Johnston became coach of the Warriors for two seasons, and then an assistant at Wake Forest under former Eastern Leaguer Jack McCloskey.

So when the Wilmington Blue Bombers needed a coach in 1964/65, their second season in the Eastern League, Johnston was an obvious pick. In his two years coaching the Blue Bombers, Johnston won a league championship and established a reputation as a good teacher and players' coach, the kind who could win and make good players better.

Bob Weiss recalled that he had lost his confidence when the Philadelphia 76ers cut him and sent him to Wilmington. He wasn't playing much and feared that he might get cut. So he talked with Johnston:

> And Neil Johnston said to me he said, "Well, when you're a guard and you go in a game something has to happen, whether it's good or bad. You are out there playing not to make mistakes and nothing's happening."
>
> So I said to him, "OK, I'll just cut it loose." And it was like . . . he saved my career, because I was on the borderline of being cut. And he told me that, and it was like a light switch going on in a room. I said, "OK, I'll make things happen." And I went out there with a different attitude, and by the end of the year I was starting and we won the championship.

The following year, Weiss was in the NBA to stay, and has enjoyed a long post-playing career as a head coach and assistant coach.

Art Pachter recalled how early in his ownership of the Miners he hired Elmer Ripley, a legendary college coach who, in a career that began in 1922, had coached at Wagner, Georgetown (in three separate stints), Yale, Columbia, Notre Dame, John Carroll, and Army.

Unfortunately, after all those years of coaching, Ripley was, in Pachter's words, "an elderly man. . . . He was really old."

Charley Rosen, who was in his brief tenure with the Miners, recalled the first game of that season with Ripley as coach:

First game was in Wilkes-Barre. As I looked down, Elmer Ripley was asleep on the bench. No shit . . . And he was like this old shaky guy . . . and we were all afraid that this guy was going to have a heart attack. I don't know how old he was but he really looked ancient.

So every time a call went against us that was blatantly wrong, he'd get up like he was going to start screaming at the referee, and we would say like, "No, no, no, no coach, it was the right call. Take it easy, why don't you sit down. It was the right call—whatever it was."

Scranton owner Pachter didn't find quite as much humor as Rosen did in Ripley's drowsiness. "As I was sitting in the stands, watching closely the players," said the owner, "I noticed that Elmer fell asleep. He was sleeping on the bench. Needless to say he only lasted part of the season."

Pachter's next attempt to hire a big-name coach was much more successful. He brought former NBA player and coach Paul Seymour to the Eastern League to coach the Miners in 1966.

Seymour was basketball royalty. He played for 12 seasons in the NBA, all but one with the Syracuse Nationals, and was a three-time All-Star and two-time all-NBA player. For four of those years with Syracuse, he was their player-coach.

In 1962, as coach of the St. Louis Hawks, Seymour was involved in the Cleo Hill story (described in chapter 4) when Hawks owner Ben Kerner fired Seymour for refusing to bench Hill. Seymour returned to Syracuse, where he owned a liquor store and a hotel, and was out of basketball for a couple of seasons.

Jim Boeheim, who had recently graduated from Syracuse University, was a Scranton rookie under Seymour. Boeheim said he made the team, at least in part, because Seymour wanted someone to share the driving from Syracuse. An article on the Syracuse.com website said, "For Boeheim, the car rides were a graduate course in basketball with Seymour as the professor."[1]

Seymour took Scranton, led by Willie Murrell and Willie Somerset, to the division title and the championship finals, where they lost to Wilmington. The following season, 1967/68, Seymour left to coach the Detroit Pistons. But he did leave Pachter a parting gift.

"He got me Fuzzy Levane for coach," Pachter said.

Andrew "Fuzzy" Levane was a New York City basketball fixture. He starred at St. John's in the 1940s and was a player and player-coach for several teams in the NBL, BAA, NBA, and ABL. In 1956, Levane became an assistant coach for the New York Knicks, and two years later head coach for one season and part of the next.

Ironically, Levane was the guy that Ben Kerner hired to coach St. Louis in 1961 after he fired Seymour. Levane had started the season coaching the Allentown Jets in the Eastern League before he replaced Seymour in St. Louis. In 1967, Levane replaced Seymour again when Seymour recommended that Pachter hire him to coach Scranton.

Unfortunately for Levane, he became Scranton's coach the same season as the ABA began. As described in chapter 10, the Miners won eight straight games to open the season. But then Murrell, Somerset, and other top players left for the ABA. Levane told Pachter the team couldn't win without them and that Pachter should fire him and coach the team himself, which Pachter did.

"Some of these coaches, it was heartbreaking to fire them," Pachter said. "[Fuzzy] fired himself."

At least one coach kept coaching even after he was fired. Bob Raskin led the Jets to the Eastern League championship in 1970. But after a slow start the next season, the Jets fired him. Raskin, however, "agreed to coach the team for one more game"[2] because the new coach, York Larese, couldn't get there until the next night. "I feel a little like I'm presiding at my own funeral," *Sports Illustrated* quoted Raskin as saying.

The three most successful Eastern League coaches were Stan Novak, Earl "Chick" Craig, and Pete Monska. They, along with Rosenstein and White, comprise the all-time top five in coaching victories and are the only coaches to win 100 or more games in the league.

Craig and Novak were Eastern League "lifers." Craig played during the league's opening weekend in December 1946, left for the ABL with Eddie White and the Wilkes-Barre Barons for the next two season, and thereafter either played or coached in the league throughout its life span, with a couple of brief gaps between coaching gigs in the 1970s. Novak joined the league in 1949 as a player for Sunbury, became its player-coach in 1951, and coached in the league for some 30 years. Monska, though not a lifer, played in the league in 1950/51 and coached for 10 years and into the CBA era.

Between the three of them, they coached 11 different Eastern League teams. They all coached Trenton and Wilkes-Barre, and Novak and Craig also coached Scranton and Allentown. And, of course, at one time or another, they all coached for Pachter.

Novak is by far the winningest coach in league history with 478 wins against 309 losses (.607). He won titles in 1951 with Sunbury, in 1969 with Wilkes-Barre, and in 1971 and 1977 with Scranton. He was named Coach of the Year a record six times and was selected in 1996 as coach of the Eastern League's all-time team. And he did all this while spending most of that time as a teacher, principal, and high school basketball coach in suburban Philly.

Novak's strength as a coach, according to former players, was in his teaching, calm demeanor, and ability to help players play their best.

"Stan was excellent," Somerset said. "Got along good with ballplayers, he communicated well, and he had all the fundamentals of a coach in the NBA. I think he could have been excellent in the NBA."

As a coach, Novak relied more on teaching players to execute rather than on strategy or innovation.

"He had 10 plays," Pawlak said. "No matter where you went, he had the same 10 plays. . . . It wasn't like you ran an offense. You called out one of the 10 plays. . . . There never was a new one, there never was an old one. Same 10 plays. When I played for him in Wilkes-Barre, [then when] I went to Scranton, the same damn 10 plays. Four years later. It was funny."

Pawlak also recalled another quality of Novak's. "Stan always liked to have a couple guys on his team that he could ride with to save money. I'm not kidding you about that, either."

One could trace the lineage of Novak's Philadelphia-area carpools, from Sunbury teammates Jerry Rullo, Jack Ramsay, and Jack McCloskey; to Howie Landa and John Chaney through the late '50s; to Pawlak, John Postley, and Hubie White with Wilkes-Barre for a few years in the '60s; to Richie Cornwall with Scranton in the '70s and Pawlak during his one year with the Apollos in 1974/75.

Said Pawlak: "The all-time Eastern League team has like 20 people on it [including Pawlak] and what makes me . . . proudest of it is Stan Novak is the coach of that team—he was picked the coach—and my college coach, going way back Eastern League, is another guard on that team, Jack McCloskey."

Craig is second to Novak in career wins with a record of 267–262 (.505). He is tied with Novak with four Eastern League championships: In the 1959/60 season as part owner and coach of the Easton Madisons led by Lear, Gaines, and Choice; in 1972/73 coaching the Wilkes-Barre Barons; and in 1974/75 and 1975/76 as coach of the Allentown Jets. He was named Coach of the Year twice.

Craig played for four teams in his eight seasons in the Eastern League. But he was even more nomadic as a coach, heading seven different teams over 10 different tenures, including three turns as Trenton's coach, two as Wilkes-Barre's, and one each for Easton, Scranton, Binghamton, Allentown, and Providence.

Craig was a dapper, personable character who over his long career made numerous contacts throughout college and professional basketball and enjoyed a reputation as a sharp talent scout. He could always find players. He began working as a part-time NBA scout during his coaching days in the Eastern League.

"That guy knew everybody," said Pachter. "He knew everybody. He was with every club. . . . He worked for a couple different clubs in the NBA as a scout. So he knew ballplayers. He was able to come up with ballplayers. . . . He scouted all the time, so he knew ballplayers coming out of the ears."

Monska was another Philadelphia area product. A graduate of West Chester State Teachers' College, he played seven games for the Lancaster Rockets in the Eastern League in 1950/51, and then played and coached the Washington Generals and Philadelphia Sphas—two of the traveling opponents for the Harlem Globetrotters.

He began coaching in the Eastern League in 1962/63 with Camden, where he was named Coach of the Year for bringing the Bullets into a regular season tie for first place (the addition of Paul Arizin that season did not hurt). He went to Allentown the following year and altogether would coach six teams—Trenton, Hartford, Cherry Hill, and Wilkes-Barre in addition to Camden and Allentown—and continued coaching in the CBA. He won championships in 1973/74 with Hartford and in 1977/78 with Wilkes-Barre and was Coach of the Year three times.

Pete Monska may not have won as many games as Novak and Craig, but to hear Pachter tell it, he had more outlandish stories than both of the other coaches combined. "The best storyteller of all the coaches was Pete Monska," who coached the Barons in the league's final season after Pachter moved the Apollos franchise from Scranton to Wilkes-Barre. "Every story he told you, one was weirder than the other. One was more unbelievable. You would think they're lies, every one of them. And every one you checked out, [and] none of them were ever lies."

One of Monska's favorites was challenging Pachter to find somebody else named Monska in any telephone book in any city. "Every airport we went to, the thing was he had to go to the phones in the middle of the airport and look up Monska," said Pachter. "There's none in any phone book anywhere. We were in Chicago. We were in Denver. We were in San Francisco. Every town we ever went to he couldn't find a Monska. Unbelievable."

Many Eastern Leaguers became coaches in the professional, college, and high school ranks.

Stan Novak's buddies, Ramsay and McCloskey, of course, would have distinguished careers as college and professional coaches. McCloskey became the general manager who assembled the Detroit Pistons' NBA champion "Bad Boys" teams of 1989 and 1990. Hubie Brown coached for 17 seasons (15 as a head coach) in the NBA and ABA and was a two-time Coach of the Year. Ray Scott coached the Detroit Pistons for three and a half years from 1972 to 1976 and won a Coach of the Year Award.

Other Eastern Leaguers who became NBA or ABA head coaches were Bob Weiss, M. L. Carr, York Larese, and Larry Costello.

John Chaney, Jim Boeheim, and George Raveling went on to Hall of Fame careers as college coaches. Former Eastern League players Floyd Layne, George Blaney, Fran Dunphy, Fran O'Hanlon, and Tom Penders also became college coaches, Howie Landa became one of the most successful junior college coaches of all time at Mercer County (NJ) Community College and served as interim head coach at University of Nevada–Las Vegas, and George Bruns coached a women's community college team.

Boeheim had the benefit of learning from both Seymour and Novak during his years in the Eastern League, and said both influenced his coaching.

Too many Eastern Leaguers to count became high school coaches, but among them were Julius McCoy, Stan Pawlak, Waite Bellamy, and Rich Cornwall. Cornwall continued to follow his mentor, Landa, working as Landa's assistant at the junior college before becoming a high school coach.

"With Howie we started one of the first girls' basketball camps in the country," Cornwall said. "I mean Howie was like a father to me. We did so much."

Bruns is still coaching high school. So is Johnny Mathis, a legendary high school coach in the Bronx.

Tommy Hemans became director of New York City's Public School Athletic League. He said: "During my EBL career five of the best professional coaches in my opinion [in no particular order] were Bobby Sand, Stan Novak, Hank Rosenstein, Paul Seymour and Chick Craig. Without question, any one of them would have been excellent coaches in the NBA."

13

THE REFS

Just as the Eastern League was a stepping-stone for many players to the NBA, several well-known NBA referees began their professional careers in the EBL.

Hall of Fame referee Mendy Rudolph was the son of Harry Rudolph, the league's longest-serving and most influential president. Harry Rudolph began his service to the league as a referee in its opening season in 1946 and soon began bringing 20-year-old Mendy with him to officiate games. The father-and-son Rudolph team worked more than 125 games together and regularly officiated the league's playoff and championship games.

In 1953 Mendy Rudolph officiated in his first NBA game and would go on to become perhaps the greatest NBA referee of all time. He served as the NBA's head official for many years and was widely admired for his colorful style, his judgment, and his knowledge of the game.

Other Eastern League referees who made it to the NBA were Hall of Fame officials Earl Strom and Dick Bavetta, as well as Joe Crawford and Ed Rush.

Jim Boeheim recalled that Bavetta and Rush were the referees for his first game in the Eastern League in 1966. "They were both in their 20s," Boeheim said in an interview on Syracuse.com, just as Boeheim was that night.[1]

Another familiar sports figure who spent a brief time as an Eastern League ref was Tommy Lasorda, the longtime Los Angeles Dodgers manager. As described in a 1990 article in *Sports Illustrated*,[2] Lasorda was working his way up the Dodgers' organization as a scout in Pennsylvania in the early 1960s and needed off-season work. So even though he had no basketball officiating experience, he got into the Eastern League's referee rotation for the 1961/62 season.

Calling Eastern League games was not without its hazards, however. As reported in the *SI* article: "After ejecting Bill Spivey, the seven-foot star for the Wilkes-Barre (Pa.) Barons, five minutes into a home game one night, Lasorda had to leave town on bruised shins, courtesy of a high-heeled octogenarian at courtside."[3]

Lasorda's future, of course, was in professional baseball, but he kept at least some Eastern League ties. He remained longtime friends with another former Eastern League referee, Ray Saul, who succeeded Harry Rudolph as commissioner of officials and was the league's secretary and public relations director for almost two decades.

Rudolph and Saul set high standards for league referees, and the officiating was generally considered good. When asked what surprised him most about the Eastern League, Tom Hemans included on his list, "The overall high quality of coaching and officiating. Even though it was known that officials 'leaned' towards the home teams."

And perhaps not all referees met those standards every night.

Pachter recalled two referees who he believed were biased against Scranton.

"Anytime you saw those two guys at one of our games, we were in trouble," Pachter said, recalling one particular night in Camden.

We got to the arena and the [parking lot attendant] said . . . "You wanna buy insurance?" And I said, "What the heck is insurance?" He says . . . "You have tires when you come out." I said, "How much is it?" The guy said, "A dollar." And I gave the guy $5. I said, "I'd like my four tires and my spare, so I want my insurance on everything." And he parked my car.

We went into the game. And we never won in Camden. They always had wonderful teams, the best teams. And we went in. And after it we lost. . . . We're almost ready to go. And I get a knock on the window. It's [the ref], who had just murdered us. The game was like—it was only a difference of two points or something, he just killed us at the end. Real home job on his part. Knocking on my window and, "Arthur, Arthur, I'm in trouble!" "What's the matter?" He said, "Somebody give me four flats!" "Right," I said, "Jeez, you know what they did to you? I guess that's what you did to me that last five minutes. Have fun." Left. I put up my window and left him there.

He sent in a thing to the league saying that I wouldn't help him, right? But hey, it came to a league meeting. They brought it up. I said, "No, I didn't help him. . . . What do you want me to do? He didn't buy insurance."

Eddie White also sensed that a particular team of officials had it in for him. As told by his grandson:

> He had the Wilkes-Barre police help him out, and he literally bugged [the refs'] locker room. And it was something like, he had the guy with the headset listening, and right before the game . . . the policeman comes running out and he says, "Hey, we were listening, and yes, they said that they're going to get you. They're going to call some quick fouls on Spivey."
>
> And my grandfather said, "OK, thanks." So the game's about to start and the referees come out and they're shaking hands, and my grandfather . . . says, "So you guys are going to try to get Spivey out of there early tonight, huh?" And they're like, "Wait a minute, how did he know what we were thinking?" . . . And he said, "Hey, I got it on tape." And the . . . thing is, I don't think they called a foul on Bill Spivey the whole game.

Crawford and Bavetta said the Eastern League was a great training ground for aspiring NBA referees because it gave them a chance to call professional games at the next-best level to the NBA. "I was a kid, 22, 23 years old, but I always knew I wanted to be a pro basketball referee," said Crawford, a Philadelphian whose father was famed baseball umpire Shag Crawford. "I got a little bit of exposure in the Baker League in Philly, and I knew that the Eastern League was the only place at that time" where he could get experience calling games under NBA rules.

Crawford credited veteran ref John Thompson with mentoring him and teaching him how to officiate a game. "You really got a lot of experience. And . . . Johnny Thompson was a veteran ref, and . . . he was awesome. The guy just took me and said, 'This is what we're doing,' and I said 'OK.' And he would teach me . . . but it was hard."

What Crawford recalled most about the league was how wild it was—both on the court and in the stands.

"The play was good," he said, but "I mean, you would have riots, fights. That basketball was hard, and then you'd go in and Art Pachter was nuts in Scranton. He was crazy. He'd be screaming at you. And going nuts on the sideline . . . But again, I would have reffed the Eastern League every day of the week. . . . It was pro basketball, and it was awesome. It was just awesome. If I had a game in the Eastern League, I was so excited. I couldn't wait to get to the gym. It was tremendous."

"Crawford was the same guy [in the Eastern League] as he was in the NBA," said Stan Pawlak. "Hard-minded ref who you didn't want to give any trouble. Just a good referee."

"All business" was how Rich Cornwall described Crawford. "He reffed the game as a competitor. He focused entirely on the game."

Bavetta got his start in the league with an assist from his older brother, Joe, who was a league ref for several years before going to the ABA. "Because my brother preceded me, he was able to speak up directly to Harry Rudolph . . . on my behalf and say, 'He can referee and can work with me.' So he got me in the league and got me into a professional league. Now, what I liked about that is . . . I was actually refereeing professional rules—three-point field goals, backcourt foul. . . . So I was as prepared as anyone could be to make the adjustment to professional basketball."

Like Crawford, Bavetta also spent time officiating in the big-city summer leagues, where he called games played by pros from the NBA and the ABA, in addition to players he knew from the Eastern League.

"In those days, the hub of basketball was New York, Philadelphia, Boston," Bavetta said. "Every player went to the Rucker League, the Harlem pro league in Harlem. Great players were there. So when someone asked me, 'When you worked your first game in the NBA in December of 1975 were you nervous?' I said no, not at all, because all of these players I had experienced in the Eastern League on their way up and in the Rucker League in the summer and stuff like that. Between the Eastern League, which became the CBA, and the Rucker League and all these other leagues, I honed my craft and became prepared."

"Bavetta," said Cornwall, "great, great man, great guy. Very personable, talks to you all the time, but don't give him any shit. You couldn't take advantage of him because he was going to be nice to you."

"Dick Bavetta was my favorite," agreed Walker Banks. "And he was one of the nicest officials that you could ever be on the court with. . . . He used to laugh at me because I'd be silly sometimes. . . . He'd call a foul, and I'd say, 'Dick, I didn't mean it! I didn't mean it, Dick! It was just a little foul.' And he actually started laughing. It never worked, it never worked. My humor never worked with him, but it was always a lot of fun."

In the Eastern League's final years, no two referees were held in higher esteem than Crawford and Bavetta. Recalled Steve Kauffman, the Eastern League's commissioner from 1975 to 1978:

We had a playoff game in Scranton. I had to assign Crawford and Bavetta. They were the only guys who could officiate in my opinion at a high level, and it was a tense, close game in a high school gym and the bathroom [that the refs used] was the same bathroom the public used at halftime.

So we're [in the men's room] at halftime and the fans started harassing Joey and Dick. And then it started: "Look at that guy, he's the commissioner or something." And they were like giving us such a hard time. And I'm a pretty strong person, I'm not afraid of this kind of stuff, but I'd never been in that and I'm thinking, are they gonna kill us? What's going on here? And I don't know if it was Joey or Dick or both of them, they said, "Oh, don't worry about it. Another day at the office."[4]

Jim Drucker, the commissioner from 1978 to 1986 and son of former NBA referee Norm Drucker, recalled Mendy Rudolph reminiscing with the elder Drucker about the tough crowds in the Eastern League. "It was Uncle Mendy talking about the old Eastern League," Drucker said. "If it was a tough crowd, I remember once Mendy saying to my father, 'Normy, this is nothing. You should have worked in the Eastern League.'"[5]

Bavetta recalled one night in Sunbury:

I was lucky to get to the locker room. Most of these locker rooms are in the home team's area and at that point I was just . . . forget the shower, I just wanted to throw my overcoat on and get my bag and get out of there. The people were banging down this locker room door to get in. I said I'm never going to be able to get out, so I go over and I see a window, a basement window, which is where we were. And I put a couple of milk boxes on top of each other and threw my bag out the window, climbed up, went out the window, got the bag. I have a hat on. I have my overcoat. Still have my referee outfit on.

And I get to my car in the parking lot and start driving out of the parking lot and there's police with the flashlights, directing traffic, and everybody is in the front of the building waiting for me to come out from the players' entrance. I start driving and this police officer is there and he says, "Oh, wait a second." I said, "Uh, oh, I'm in trouble now." I just said to the guy, "Officer, what's all this commotion? What going on here?" And he said, "I'm just stopping you because your lights are out . . . so put your lights back on." And when I put the lights back on, the lights come on in the car a little bit and then he looks and he sees a New York plate and he goes, "Wait a second. Here's the referee!" They start running after me and I made my way through the crowd and I made my way out of there.

And, of course, Eastern League referees had to negotiate other challenges that their peers in the NBA and ABA did not—like getting paid after the game by the home team, especially after a tough loss.

Pachter described a night in which he was especially angry at Bavetta's officiating. "I thought we got hosed. And when the check's in . . . I said [Bavetta] really, really owes us. I took the checks. And when I did, I had two envelopes—the other guy's check and his. I handed the check to the other guy, and [Bavetta's], I lit it on fire."

Which might further explain why the home team almost always won.

Just as former players remember the Eastern League as a fun, unpredictable rite of passage, so do the referees. Said Crawford:

> It was a circus. And I didn't know anything different. I had no idea. And then . . . you would get done the game. You'd go down. Hopefully they had a shower for you. You'd get a shower. You'd go out. I remember every place seemed like it was like two degrees out. You know, you're freezing, and you'd have this little, stinkin' Toyota you were getting into. And you were driving down the Turnpike going back to Philly. It was wild, it was wild.
>
> I was happy. The rides were a pain in the tush. But if I could have, like I said, I would have reffed every night of the week in the Eastern League if they played every night.

Bavetta recalled thinking, "When the weather is so bad and I can't even find the highway, I hope I make the NBA real soon so I don't have to keep doing this stuff anymore."

THE CBA AND
THE END OF THE
EASTERN LEAGUE

It was 1975. Steve Kauffman was a bright young Philadelphia lawyer with a newly earned CPA, a huge love of sports, and a father-in-law who loved to brag about him.

"My father-in-law used to talk me up to the point where it was embarrassing," Kauffman said.

One place where Kauffman's father-in-law would do some of his bragging was at his regular breakfast spot in the suburbs outside Philly, where he would eat every morning, often with fellow regulars. One guy who also frequented that spot was veteran Eastern League coach Stan Novak. Knowing Kauffman's love of sports, his father-in-law struck up a conversation with Novak. Kauffman remembered:

> He said, "You know, my son-in-law would like to get involved . . . in your league in some way." He says that to Stan and gets Stan to agree to have lunch with me.
>
> And we're talking and I swear, I'm not making this up. I just wanted to be involved in sports even if it's not a career, I just loved it so much. . . . I said [to Novak], "Is there anything?" . . . I was thinking about could I keep score, could I keep the time clock, you know, anything?
>
> And so he says to me, looks in my eyes and says, "How would you like to be commissioner?" And I don't know how to react to this. I recall that I tried not to react too much one way or the other because I thought he was nuts.

Novak told Kauffman that the commissionership was "just a part-time job, you know, 10 hours a week, and said the league would hire a marketing director and an assistant commissioner." Kauffman, who up until that conversation with Novak knew very little about the Eastern League, continued:

> And then at the end of the lunch . . . I honestly said, "Well let me think about that," because I was bewildered. I was bewildered, I was stunned. And he said, "Well, OK, that's fine, I didn't expect you to make up your mind on the spot." . . .
>
> So I left that night and I never remember doing this in my life, but about three, four o'clock in the morning I just kind of shot up out of bed and I said, "Wait a second . . . how can I not do this? I mean, I don't know where this is going to lead. How can I not do this?"
>
> And I call Stan and I say, "OK, I'm interested." And he said, "OK, great. The election is in Allentown" or whatever he called it, such and such a date, and I said, "What do you mean, 'the election'?"

Apparently the league owners—after several years of Bill Montzman serving as president and league secretary Ray Saul handling most of the administrative work—had decided that they needed a more active commissioner to help rebuild the league.

Two other people, both young attorneys like Kauffman, had already applied for the league commissioner's job, and at least one of them had some experience working for one of the teams. Kauffman expressed concerns to Novak.

But Novak told Kauffman, "You're a Philadelphia lawyer, that's pretty much all you need. And you can BS well about basketball. That'll be it. You talk well."

It also helped that Scranton owner Art Pachter was impressed with Kauffman. "I remember being an instigator at the time in getting [Kauffman]," Pachter said.

"So I go to the vote," Kauffman said. "My recollection isn't clear, but I win the thing like 4–2 or 5–2 . . . and that's how I became commissioner."

What Kauffman stepped into was a league that seemed to be on its last legs.

"In the '74–'75 season, before I took over, there were four teams—Allentown, Scranton, Hazleton, and the Cherry Hill Rookies," Kauffman recalled. "They were maybe going to not operate. And I can't honestly tell you how we got the other three [teams] in . . . we had seven [in 1975/76] . . . and I don't think I had a lot to do with it."

Kauffman also soon found that not only was the league struggling, but it didn't have much structure, nor were there many sources for him to turn to for guidance.

"When I took over in that first year and I figured what do we do, and then I asked somebody . . . 'Well, where are our articles of incorporation and our bylaws?'" Kauffman knew that some businesses and organizations did not keep timely documentation, "but I figured we had something, articles of incorporation or whatever. There was nothing. Nothing was ever filed in any way, shape, or form. No corporation notice or form, no 501(c)(3) . . . but nothing."

So Kauffman started making decisions—about schedules, about hiring referees, about disputes between teams.

"It was the seat of my pants," he said. "I mean, no one had a book on how to be a commissioner."

The league opened the 1975/76 season with eight teams, though one folded during the season. The following year it opened with seven, but two teams moved during the season and another folded.

A 1976 *New York Times* article, "Mill-Town Basketball, or Life in the Minors," portrayed a sense of futility permeating what it called "the hardscrabble league,"[1] its players, and many of the economically declining communities in which it played. "For all but a handful of players" in the league, the article said, "the National Basketball Association and the American Basketball Association are tantalizing visions, forever receding an inch beyond their grasp."

It described Eddie Mast, then with Allentown, as a player who "cannot quite accept the idea that there is no job waiting for every good player." It said Mast, "who played two years as a reserve for the Knicks and a year for Atlanta, has tried out with six teams in the last two years and been cut by each. He works during the week in Sea Isle, N.J., teaching emotionally disturbed children, but reserves his weekends for basketball."[2]

"It's the best run I've got," the article quoted Mast. "I might as well keep playing as long as I enjoy it."[3]

The *Times* also mentioned George Bruns, then 30 and playing with Allentown, whose "one chance came in 1973, when the New York Nets needed a guard and he played 13 games for them. He was cut in the next training camp." The article continued: "Bruns has seen players arrive and depart in his seven years in the league," and quoted Bruns: "Some of the people have been great players in different places, and now they're kind of playing out the string. . . . Nothing's ever going to happen for them again. It's a sad thing to watch sometimes."[4]

One night, it reported, the Connecticut Gold Coast Stars drew only 120 fans to a game. That team soon folded. Another team, the Long Island Sounds, reportedly went from 500 fans its first home game, to 250, to 140. They, too, would leave the league at the end of the season.

The article also focused on Allentown's James "Fly" Williams, a legendary New York City high school and street ball player who had been one of the nation's top collegiate scorers and an All-American at Austin Peay State University before leaving to play one season in the ABA. "I don't figure to stay here too long," said the confident Fly. "I'm eligible for the N.B.A. draft in the spring. I don't care what round I go in, I'm not coming back home this time."[5]

After the season, the Philadelphia 76ers drafted Williams in the ninth round but did not sign him. He did not play professionally in the U.S. again.

Perhaps the most significant event in the league in 1976 occurred after the season ended, during the summer, when the U.S. Olympic basketball team still consisted entirely of collegians and toured the country playing tune-up games. One of those tune-ups was against the Allentown Jets, who had won the Eastern League championship the previous two seasons, and the other was against a hastily assembled group of Eastern Leaguers in a game played in Wilkes-Barre.

"We [the Jets] got together for one night of practice or two nights in order to play them," recalled Bruns, who by then was the Jets' player-coach. "And they had a good team."

Indeed. That Olympic team had Notre Dame's Adrian Dantley, Indiana's Scott May and Quinn Buckner, and North Carolina's Mitch Kupchak and Phil Ford. UNC's legendary Dean Smith was coaching the team, assisted by his friend, Georgetown's John Thompson.

More than 3,800 fans watched the Olympians take on the Jets on July 10, 1976, at Liberty High School in Bethlehem, Pennsylvania, according to writer Evan Burian in an article in the *Allentown Morning Call*.[6] The Jets hung tough in the first quarter, but the Olympians ran away from them in the second and cruised to a 122–103 victory.

"They owned us," Bruns said wryly.

Smith arranged the second exhibition with a collection of Eastern League players through another friend in the coaching community, King's College basketball coach Ed Donohue.

As reported in Wilkes-Barre's *Citizens' Voice* newspaper,[7] Donohue compiled a team of Eastern Leaguers, including Mack Daughtry and some local Wilkes-Barre players. King's College had a new gymnasium at the time, and the game attracted some 2,500 people.

"It was a real nice crowd," Donohue told the *Citizens' Voice* in an interview many years later after Smith's death. "They got a chance to see some great basketball players."[8]

The Eastern Leaguers were just a few points behind at halftime. But, Donohue said, "at halftime, John Thompson came in our locker room and told me Coach Smith wanted to know if we could play a zone in the second half. I told him that I wasn't sure if any of these kids could have *spelled* zone."[9]

But Donohue obliged, and the Olympians ran away with the game, 101–83, and soon left for Montreal where they won the gold medal.

The league remained in flux during the 1976/77 season, as a new cast of teams joined longtime franchises Allentown, Scranton, and Lancaster. Still, Kauffman was optimistic that the league was rebounding. At least, so he told another bright young Philadelphia attorney, Jim Drucker, whom he met late that season at a 76ers game.

Drucker said Kauffman told him that the Eastern League "was starting to recover" from the effects of losing so many good players to the ABA. With the NBA/ABA merger in 1976, several former ABA teams disbanded, causing what author and former Eastern Leaguer Charley Rosen called "a return migration of high-quality players back into the Eastern League."[10]

Drucker started working for the league, writing new bylaws and revising the player personnel system. "Everyone was arguing over players, so we straightened all those problems out and put some structure in the league and some rules of how to run the team."

That off-season of 1977, fate struck the Eastern League from all the way across the continent.

As Kauffman remembered, "I get this call from a guy named Rick Smith in Anchorage and telling me how much he loves basketball and I'm wondering, 'Why is this guy calling from Anchorage?' And he said, 'We'd like to join your league.' And I said something to the effect of 'You're in Anchorage.' And he didn't do it in a bragging way, he said, 'We love basketball, and we have the money.' And it turned out they had oil money and everything else and were very wealthy as an ownership group."

The Anchorage group was so eager to bring professional basketball to Alaska that they offered to pay the cost of flying teams out for games, put up hotel expenses, and pay the other teams to play in Anchorage. Kauffman presented the proposal to the league's owners. There was pushback from some, especially small-market owners who sensed that the geographic expansion of the league could put them out of business.

"The league thought I was nuts," Kauffman said. "But it turned out to be really good, and I just remember when our owners were looking at it—especially Art, [saying] 'Are you fucking crazy? What are you talking about? We're the Eastern League, and that's way out there.'"

But Kauffman thought expanding to Alaska would bring favorable publicity, and ultimately, the owners voted to admit Anchorage, as well as new franchises in Long Island; Quincy, Massachusetts; Providence, Rhode Island; Washington, DC; and a reincarnated team in Brooklyn.

That season also found a familiar face in a new place. Scranton won the championship in 1976/77; then Pachter moved the team to Wilkes-Barre.

"We weren't drawing anybody in Scranton . . . there was [no team] in Wilkes-Barre, so we went there," he said.

If that move had been made several years earlier, people around the league would not have believed that the owner of Scranton would dare to bring his team to the home of his archrival. But by then, the old coal-town rivalries had died. Wilkes-Barre fans who remained interested in the league had been coming to Scranton to see games. They were glad to have an Eastern League team back in their town, especially when they won the league championship.

Pachter and his Barons were scheduled to open the 1977/78 season by playing the very first Eastern League games in Anchorage. Anchorage geared up for the debut as if it were its version of the Super Bowl.

"I'm in Anchorage a couple days early to promote this thing—it was sort of a big thing there—all of the local TV stations, everything," Kauffman said.

"We were the first professional team to play" in Anchorage, Pachter recalled. "And they had press, they had everybody. It was like going to a major political thing."

But Kauffman and Pachter had been feuding. "We were friends," Pachter said. But, "oh, did we have run-ins."

The run-in leading up to the Anchorage game involved a roster move.

"We were flying out on a Friday morning, and one of my players . . . called and said the night before, 'I can't come out. I just got offered a very good job.'"

Pachter wanted to add a player to take to Alaska, but he called Kauffman and the commissioner refused. "He said, 'You can't because the media there already has a list of your team. You cannot substitute and bring another guy.'"

Pachter was furious at Kauffman's decision, and his anger apparently festered on the long flight to Anchorage. The Barons arrived at the Anchorage airport, greeted by fans and media from all over Alaska.

According to Kauffman: "So these guys get off the plane—the players, Art, maybe an equipment guy or a trainer or whatever it was. And I remember I'm standing against the wall talking to a reporter and . . . he comes off the plane, sees me over there, and comes running over to me." Kauffman said he thought Pachter was going to punch him.

Pachter denied going after Kauffman physically but readily admitted to attacking him verbally. He said the media approached him as soon as he got off the plane, and he responded by pointing at Kauffman and yelling, "He's a crook. You know what he did to me?" and bawling Kauffman out before the assembled Alaska media.

"And wow, they used that stuff in the papers," Pachter said. "They were eating this shit up."

"They honestly, literally thought we staged this," Kauffman said. "An article was written like, 'This is wrestling, this is all fake.'. . . I mean they really all thought that. It looked like it was planned."

With "The Fight" getting much of the pregame publicity, the stage was set for the opening game.

"I forget the name of the high school, but it was the biggest high school," said Kauffman, "They had a gym that sat 3,800 or 4,200—so this was a huge, huge thing in Anchorage. So the game sells out, and people wanted to still get in. They were outside the arena for this thing, it was so exciting to them out there."

The players were warming up, and Pachter recalled being approached by Joe Newman, the recently added player whom Pachter had decided to bring to Alaska anyway, notwithstanding Kauffman's decision to the contrary.

"Newman . . . came up to me before the game—didn't even know my name—he said, 'That basket is going to go . . . because it's wobbling, it's not right. It's gonna go.' So I tell [Wilkes-Barre coach Pete] Monska, and Monska goes over and tells Kauffman. And Kauffman says, 'I don't believe a word he says. I'm not interested. . . .' Bingo, minutes before we're supposed to play, the backboard comes down, crashes."

Recalled Kauffman:

I'm just looking, standing there at half-court because I have to make a little tiny speech, a presentation right before the game, and down at one end the guy dunks it and the whole damn thing comes down. I said, "Oh my G-d!" I turned to [Anchorage owner] Rick Smith and I said, "One of us has to do something. Do we have another basket?" And he said, "Yeah, we have one in the back."

So I turn literally to go to the other guys to say we cannot dunk, you know, in the game, we have to decide this but we can't dunk, and literally as I'm saying that—maybe a few seconds after, they haven't heard me or listened to me—some guy breaks that basket! And that one, it so happens, that one came apart and a little piece of glass I still have as a souvenir, it flew over toward me. So we are screwed now.

The Anchorage people scrambled to find another backup backboard, and the game was held up for an hour and a half.

"Long story short, they were able to somehow break into the closest high school gym, basically steal or borrow the basket, so we could play," Kauffman said. He noted that the team offered refunds to fans if they didn't want to wait, but very few people left. "If 20 people wanted a refund and left, there were another 100 ready to come in."

Kauffman was correct that adding Anchorage elevated the league's profile, got it some national publicity, and helped the league financially. The league was organized into two divisions that year, with all 10 teams completing the season. At season's end, Pachter's Wilkes-Barre Barons, behind league MVP Paul McCracken (who had been up and down between the NBA and the EBA) and old reliable Richie Cornwall, won the league championship series.

"It was the championship game of Wilkes-Barre, in Wilkes-Barre, playing Lancaster," said Jim Drucker. "It was a great game, up and back the whole way, and then Wilkes-Barre finally won. . . . I remember it distinctly, because it was the best game I had seen in the Eastern League."

It would also be the last game played in the Eastern League.

That off-season, the owners voted to appoint Drucker as commissioner to replace Kauffman, who by then had started his career as a player agent representing former Eastern Leaguers like Charlie Criss and Jerry Baskerville who had made it to the NBA.

Drucker had plans for expanding the league, making it more professional and profitable, increasing player salaries, and protecting stable franchises from weaker ones. He also wanted a stronger working arrangement with the NBA, including a substantial financial commitment. But he knew that to accomplish all that, he had to do one thing first: persuade the owners to change the league's name.

"My goal was to grow the league and I believed the name 'Eastern' would stifle our growth to other parts of the country," Drucker said. So at the owners meeting that July, "I recommended . . . that we change the league's name," Drucker recalled.

"We discussed several names—United, Federal, Intercontinental, et cetera, but all failed to get the necessary two-thirds majority vote. Many of the old-line Pennsylvania teams didn't believe that the added revenue we would receive from the NBA would offset increased team travel costs, and repeatedly blocked any name change."

Pachter was among the staunchest opponents. Said Drucker:

He was adamant. He knew that [changing the name] would be the end of the small teams because he was smart. And he didn't want that to happen. But I told him that we would protect the teams and were not just going to just cast them aside.

Finally, after about three hours, the meeting was recessed for a bathroom break. In the bathroom, I bumped into Art Pachter. . . . We agreed that spending more time on the name change didn't make sense since we had many more agenda items. Standing side by side at two urinals, I turned my head to Art and said, "Art, we've got to have this name change. There's no way we'll ever get a lot of money from the NBA, get taken seriously by them, because the teams on the West Coast and the central part of the country will say, 'This is an Eastern League.' This is the only way we'll ever break out of that. And if we don't get the votes of the western and central NBA teams, we're never going to get real money. So pick a name. Whatever name you want. It'll be named it."

He said he liked "Intercontinental" but that it was too long a name. "Just drop the Inter," he said. I replied, "OK, Continental it is." We zipped up our flies, returned to the meeting, and Continental received the two-thirds majority vote required. And that's how it became the CBA.

Drucker credited Pachter for breaking the impasse. "He trusted me that somehow I wouldn't screw the old-time guys. And I didn't."

The name change to the Continental Basketball Association for the 1978/79 season did not eliminate the old-line teams outright. Allentown, Jersey Shore, Lancaster, and Wilkes-Barre still remained and would continue to compete in the CBA.

But the character of the old Eastern League was gone. Internally, the league was changing, preparing to modernize, grow, and not look back.

That first year Drucker introduced league rules requiring owners to put up an irrevocable letter of credit from a bank, which meant that if the team stopped playing the league could take $25,000 out of its bank account. He also created a program that allowed a team that finished the season and paid all its bills to sell the franchise back to the league, to protect small-market teams that could not keep up with the rising costs of league operations and give them a chance to get back the value of their teams. The league also rewrote its player contract so that players could not jump leagues, and it enforced that policy. Drucker recalled:

When the NBA signed two of our players in '78–'79, we sued the NBA and the teams. The settlement of that brought in about $115,000 to the league the first year . . . every team got like $15–20,000. . . . I wrote a player contract which I thought was strong enough to withstand a court, and apparently the NBA when they saw it agreed. They thought they were dealing with the old Eastern League in that '78–'79 season. But it turns out we stuck to our guns. Plus, I had a relationship with the NBA people and a young lawyer in their office, David Stern. I had knocked on the door trying to get money from these guys, and I said to him, "Wouldn't it be smarter to have a relationship, so you could take players without a hassle? And if you put in a small pot of money, we'll use it to improve player salaries to attract better players."

The NBA bought the idea and increased its financial commitment to the CBA, as well as started a program with the league to train referees.

With the higher profile, a slicker product, and more money to be made, the league became more attractive for sports entrepreneurs, especially in midsized cities with corporate sponsors and professional-caliber sports arenas instead of the Eastern League's old high schools and armories. Rochester, New York, and Bangor, Maine, joined the CBA in 1978/79. Hawaii had a team in 1979/80. Alberta, Canada, and Billings, Montana, joined the league in 1980/81.

"As the league grew, the little guys got out," said Drucker. "We started flying to some games. . . . Their markets couldn't support the teams. And they didn't have corporate sponsorship capability."

Jersey Shore was gone after the first season of the CBA. Allentown became the Lehigh Valley Jets to try to expand its reach, but it was gone two seasons later. So, too, was Pachter, who moved back to Scranton for one last try in 1980/81 with a new club, the Scranton Aces, but sold the team back to the league when the season ended, taking advantage of the buyback program the league had created to protect its legacy teams.

"It was a very expensive venture having a basketball team for all those years," Pachter said. He decided to get out when Anchorage would no longer pay the visiting team's traveling expenses. "I said at the end of one year, my last one, that I would not [pay] . . . $25,000 to go there—I'm not going to go to Anchorage, Alaska, and pay my own way. No way."

And with his children grown and ready for higher education, "I decided I was going to pay for college instead of for basketball players."

The last old Eastern League town to depart was Lancaster, which dropped out for the 1980/81 season, resurfaced the following season, and remained in the CBA until 1985. As Drucker and Pachter had anticipated would happen to the small-town teams, "the league outgrew them."

The old Eastern League was gone.

15

THE LEGACY OF THE EASTERN LEAGUE

As professional basketball leagues go, the Eastern League had a long run—32 years as the EPBL/EBA, 63 years in all if you include its successor, the CBA. Only the NBA, whose predecessor, the Basketball Association of America, was formed two weeks after the Eastern League, has lasted longer.

But did the league accomplish anything more than provide a place to play for guys not quite good enough for the NBA? Was it notable for more than bringing excitement to small, blue-collar towns on the weekends, and producing some great stories of a tough, gritty, entertaining league? Did it leave anything significant behind? The answer, to the people who played in the league, ran it, officiated it, and watched it, is yes, on many levels.

To the basketball world, it left several innovations that we take for granted today.

For example, the Eastern League had a near fiasco with broken backboards on its 1977 opening night in Alaska. So that may partly explain why, when Darryl Dawkins broke two baskets during the 1979/80 NBA season, the CBA was ready to start testing collapsible rims. It used one during the 1980/81 season, and the NBA followed the next year with a similar design.

The three-point shot didn't start in the Eastern League—it was introduced by Abe Saperstein's American Basketball League of 1961/63—but the Eastern League elevated it. When the ABA formed in 1968, league officials recognized the shot's potential to add excitement and keep games competitive, and they made it part of their game as well. As sportswriter and basketball commentator Bob Ryan observed about the three-pointer: "Abe Saperstein brought it to the

ABL, and then Harry Rudolph adopted it for the EBL, and the ABA took it in, and here we are. We got Steph Curry and Klay Thompson."

"We didn't shoot them like they do today," said Stan Pawlak, who led the Eastern League in three-point shooting a record six seasons. "I wish we did. There were no plays. . . . You didn't look for them because they would have been perceived as a bad shot."

But now, George Blaney explained, "the value of [the three-point shot] has increased over the years and the game has drastically changed. . . . Even big guys are planting behind the line."

"The three-point line was like a new revelation of strategy," said Hubie Brown. "It changed a lot of thinking of percentages. . . . Because all your life— grammar school, high school, college, and the NBA—you were accustomed to two points, but then all of a sudden you're in [the ABA] and you've got the three-ball, and then in the last two minutes it would do mental gymnastics with you because you had to stay on top of the fact that that was a three, not a two."

The three wasn't the only change the Eastern League contributed to the way basketball is played. The wide-open, up-tempo, high-flying style that character- izes the modern game was the norm in the Eastern League a decade or more be- fore it hit the NBA, ABA, and major colleges. Many Eastern Leaguers brought a different skill set to the league than most players in the NBA at the time.

"When you speak of the guys that played basketball from that '50s–'60s era, what you learned to do at that time was you learned to be a basketball player," said Ray Scott. "The bounce pass, the chest pass, the baseball pass, the jump shot, the hook shot, the layup. Now, as time progressed, it became the dunk, it became the three-point shot, it became spread the floor as opposed to getting the ball into Kareem, or Wilt, or Russell, or Bellamy, or Thurmond. That game changed right before our eyes. Well think about where that came from, who perfected that? It was the Eastern League. Because they had those same talented guys. They perfected that."

The ABA recognized the crowd-pleasing nature of that style of play and brought in Eastern Leaguers and others who could play it. The NBA eventually adopted it, too, but it had long been the style in the Eastern League.

The Eastern League also left a racial and cultural legacy. Until the mid-1960s, talented black players had limited opportunities to reach the NBA. Though the Eastern League was racially mixed, in some ways it served a similar role in pro- fessional basketball as the Negro Leagues did in professional baseball—it gave black players unwanted by the NBA a chance to compete at a high professional level. The African American players who starred in the Eastern League helped to make it possible for future African Americans to succeed in the NBA.

As former Globetrotter and Eastern Leaguer Bobby Hunter said: "You know a lot of players coming down the line . . . ended up in the right place, right time, right coach."

Moreover, the Eastern League gave Americans in small, predominantly white communities who had little interaction with African Americans a chance to see and get to know people of color, cheer for them, and admire them.

Said Scott: "The Eastern League, much more so than they're given credit for, broke down a lot of walls, sociologically, in Williamsport, Allentown, and Wilkes-Barre, and Sunbury. Those are all . . . working, small towns, small-town America. And they didn't have African Americans living there."

Tommy Hemans's story of the night that he, Sherman White, and several of their black teammates charmed a bar full of fans near Hazleton; John Chaney's remembrances of fans in the towns around Sunbury delightedly calling his nickname "Chick! Chick!"; Swish McKinney's weekly radio show in Scranton all support Scott's point. The Eastern League helped to break down barriers.

"A funny and maybe not so funny story," Hemans called his recollection of the events at the roadside tavern, "but very revealing about practiced discrimination; on and off the court racial dynamics; the involvement of sports in same; about people really getting to know and respect each other; and the reasons why; and it is a true story."

The Eastern League's legacy, too, is about the players—the really, really good and even great players—whose names and games only other basketball people and Eastern League fans still remember.

"You're doing a great thing," Hubie Brown said. "You're bringing back to life some really great old-time players."

With so few jobs available in the NBA, the Eastern League was a haven for players with top-level talent who would do anything to play against the best competition they could find. They would give up their weekends, drive on snowy mountain roads, endure hostile crowds, and battle other big, tough men in a brutally physical style of play. And they got little or no recognition for it.

"I used to get all the time, 'Well, where did you play professionally?'" said Rich Cornwall. "And I would say, 'In the Eastern Pro League.' And they'd go. 'Oh,' or 'What, was that, a semipro league?' I said, 'No, dude, it was a professional league.' People don't understand. . . . You're either crazy or competitive [to drive several hours every weekend to play in the Eastern League]. We certainly weren't doing it for the money."

"You had to be a basketball junkie," said Jim Boeheim. "You just loved to play, that's all, you just wanted to play, and it was . . . high-level basketball. It was good basketball."

"I remember playing . . . against Walter Dukes [a two-time NBA All-Star] in that league," said Pawlak. "I played against Spivey. I played against, believe it or not, K. C. Jones played one year and was a player-coach one year. . . . King Lear was the best!"

"I played against some just fabulous players," Boeheim said. "And, I mean it was like almost playing in the NBA, really. You had the next-best players in the country all playing. . . . It was literally 110 players in the NBA at that time . . . and we had a hundred players in the Eastern League. It was . . . it was the best players in the world."

Finally, for the men who played in the league, they took away relationships, friendships, and memories of some really fine people—not only other players, but also fans in the towns in which they played.

"I think back that there were so few bad guys," Art Pachter said. "Most of the people were good guys. . . . You can only think of a lot of the ballplayers that were really, really good, good guys."

"The thing is, I think people assumed it's a bunch of unintelligent guys, you know what I mean, and just out there, and it wasn't the case," Pawlak said. "Most of them were, most of the guys were college-educated guys that tried to make a buck on the weekend playing the best basketball that they could. They weren't—I mean there were some shmoes, of course, but they were few and far between."

"The thing I had wished I had kept track of was the people," said Swish McKinney. "I did not keep track of the people, and they was wonderful to me. . . . You see them, you touch them . . . they're gone, they're gone, they're gone, they're gone." He especially recalled Art Pachter and the people in Scranton who were "very, very good to me."

Eddie White III recalled former Eastern League player and later college coach "George Raveling, who grew up back there and played for my grandfather, and he'd always ask about him when I'd see him. I couldn't help but run into people, all these names in basketball, who knew of the Eastern League, knew the Wilkes-Barre Barons, knew my grandfather."

Said Cornwall: "It doesn't happen often, but it has happened more than a couple times where I'll just be out somewhere or whatever, just having dinner, at a show, whatever, and somebody'll come up to me and say, 'Are you Richie Cornwall?' and I would say, 'Yeah,' and they'd go, 'I used to watch you play in Allentown' or some other place. And that's kinda neat, too, when that happens."

"It's funny," said Pawlak, "that the rest of my life, different things brought me to Scranton and Wilkes-Barre. I ended up being a medical device salesperson and I had a nice career doing that, but my territory often included Wilkes-Barre and Scranton. And people . . . remembered me all the time just by hearing the name, which was fun. It's like 30 years later, people still remembered who you were and they remember the Barons all the time. You can go to Wilkes-Barre and they remember the Barons. It's amazing to me but they do. . . .

"They ought to make a place for the Eastern League in the [Basketball] Hall of Fame," said Pawlak. "Not individual players. . . . They had a whole 30 years of really great basketball players. They should just put the league in. . . . If nothing else, the quality of people that played and coached in that league. It deserves some sort of recognition."

Pawlak's idea is worth pursuing. The men who played in the Eastern League should be recognized. The tiny gyms and rabid fans resurrected, at least in pictures. The stories of John Chaney and Howie Landa; Allie Seiden and Carl Green; King Lear, Dick Gaines, and Wally Choice remembered. People should know about the scoring magic of Julius McCoy, the shooting touch of George Lehmann, the enduring frustration of Bill Spivey, the brilliant but tarnished Jack Molinas and Sherman White. They should trace the lineage of Stan Novak's carpools through some 30 years with Jack Ramsay, Jack McCloskey, and Jerry Rullo; John Chaney and Howie Landa; Stan Pawlak and others, and learn what a remarkable collection of basketball men emerged.

In January 1996, the CBA hosted a celebration in Sioux Falls, South Dakota, to commemorate the 50th anniversary of the Eastern League's founding. A few years later, when it appeared that the CBA might fold, *New York Times* sportswriter Harvey Araton wrote a tribute to the league and its predecessor titled "The League of Dreamers Is No More."[1] He went to suburban Philly to interview Novak, who was named the coach of the all-time team for the Eastern League years. Araton wrote:

"Novak rattled off the names of the all-time players: Charlie Criss . . . Hal Lear . . . Bill Chanecka . . . Julius McCoy." Then Novak added: "It was amazing that [the anniversary event] came off because it was a horrible night. . . . An unbelievable blizzard."[2]

Wrote Araton, "As it had to be."[3]

16

EPILOGUE

Life after the Eastern League

When their playing days were over, former Eastern Leaguers went on to lives as teachers, as coaches, and in business. Many stayed connected to the game in one way or another, often crossing paths with each other, staying in contact with former teammates and opponents, and sharing memories of the Eastern League. Here's what became of some of them.

STACEY ARCENEAUX

While playing in the Eastern League, Arceneaux (who was also known as Robert Stacey) worked as a claims adjuster with Empire Mutual Insurance Company in New York, eventually becoming head of claims adjusting for both Empire and Fireman's Fund Insurance Co. "He was truly one of the meanest adjusters you'd ever want to meet," said Marvin Salenger, an attorney who had to negotiate claims with Arceneaux. Salenger and his partner, a former high school teammate of Arceneaux's, were so impressed with his toughness that when Arceneaux retired, they hired him to work at their law firm as a negotiator on personal injury cases. "He was delightful," said Salenger. "He was modest, he was unassuming, and you would never, ever know he was [a] famous, famous basketball player known throughout the five boroughs" of New York as a high school legend. Said Felicita Pitt, an assistant at the law firm, "He was a gentle giant."[1] Arceneaux died in Florida in 2015 at age 79.

PAUL ARIZIN

The NBA great who decided to stay home in Philadelphia, work at IBM, and play in the Eastern League rather than move to San Francisco with the Warriors is still considered among the NBA's first superstars and jump-shot pioneers. He was named to the NBA's Silver Anniversary Team in 1970, was inducted into the Naismith Memorial Basketball Hall of Fame in 1978, and chosen as one of the 50 Greatest Players in NBA history in 1996. All of this for a guy who didn't even make his high school basketball team. Arizin passed away in 2006 at age 78.

WALKER BANKS

Banks played in Europe for a Dutch team along with his friend, Eastern League center Al Henry, for a season. Then he began a career as a sales executive for Xerox and Canon in central Illinois for some 20 years, and later in the telecommunications industry. He also owned a Xerox sales agency. He is retired and lives in Champaign, Illinois. "Since I retired, you know, you start thinking about the old days," Banks said. "And I was looking for some of the guys, where they were and what happened. . . . I even started digging back through some of my scrapbooks and things so I could show the kids and my grandkids now."

DICK BAVETTA

After reffing in the Eastern League from 1968 to 1975, Bavetta was hired by the NBA following the retirement of Mendy Rudolph—whose father, former league president Harry Rudolph, gave Bavetta his start in the EBA. In his 39 years in the NBA, he set ironman records for the most officiated games (2,635) and the most consecutive games (Bavetta never missed an assigned game). He retired in August 2014 and was elected to the Naismith Memorial Basketball Hall of Fame in 2015. Known for his sense of humor, his people skills, and his love of basketball and the Eastern League, Bavetta recalled being in New York to ref a Knicks game and learning that Syracuse coach and former Scranton star Jim Boeheim would be one of several coaches signing autographs at his hotel. "I stood on line like everybody else, because I'm part clown anyway. . . . I put this piece of paper in front of him and I said, 'Could you make that out to my favorite basketball referee of all time, Dick Bavetta?' And he looked up and said, 'Oh, my G-d.' He stood up, we embraced each other and he said, 'I have followed your career, I'm so proud of you and what you've accomplished.' He took the words right out of my mouth. I said, 'I have followed *your* career and I'm so proud of what *you've* accomplished.'"

WAITE BELLAMY

Bellamy retired from the Eastern League when the Blue Bombers folded in 1971 but remained in Wilmington for a few years, teaching physical education at an elementary school and selling cars. In 1975 he returned to his hometown of Bradenton, Florida, where he taught in the Sarasota County school system for 26 years, coached football and basketball, and was an assistant high school principal. He and some of the other Blue Bombers stay in contact. Bellamy recalled seeing Jim Boeheim at a basketball clinic in Florida several years ago, and they reminisced about their Eastern League days. "What would be a good thing," he said, is "if they develop an Eastern League Hall of Fame. I think that would be very interesting."

GEORGE BLANEY

After five years in the Eastern League from 1962 to 1967, "I had a chance to go to the ABA and at the same time I was offered the Stonehill College job as coach and athletic director," Blaney said. "I always wanted to be a coach, so I decided I would start the coaching career." He served as the head coach of Stonehill, Dartmouth College, his alma mater Holy Cross for 22 years, and Seton Hall for three years before spending 12 years on the University of Connecticut men's basketball coaching staff, mostly as the assistant head coach under Jim Calhoun, a former Eastern Leaguer. Overall, Blaney coached college basketball for 43 years before retiring in 2013. A native of Jersey City, New Jersey, Blaney now lives on Cape Cod.

JIM BOEHEIM

After six years in the Eastern League with Scranton and seven years as an assistant at Syracuse, Boeheim became head coach in 1976. His teams have won over 1,000 games, appeared in 34 NCAA tournaments, five Final Fours, three national title games, and won the 2003 national championship. He has won several national Coach of the Year Awards and has served as an assistant coach for several U.S. men's national basketball world championship and Olympic teams. In 2005, Boeheim was inducted into the Naismith Memorial Basketball Hall of Fame. From time to time he renewed ties with Scranton. He recruited Scranton native Gerry McNamara, a star of Syracuse's national championship team and now one of Boeheim's assistant coaches, who brought large contingents of Scranton residents to Syracuse games. And Boeheim has returned to Scranton on occasion to speak at basketball-related charity events. "The fans were unbelievable," Boeheim said. "It was a great experience. I loved it. . . . I still think about it from time to time. . . . I mean really great games, great players. Really. It was a lot of fun."

HUBIE BROWN

After his two years in the Eastern League, Brown worked his way up the coaching ladder as a high school coach, college assistant, and NBA assistant. He was head coach of the ABA's Kentucky Colonels from 1974 to 1976 and coached for 13 seasons in the NBA with the Atlanta Hawks, New York Knicks, and Memphis Grizzlies. He was named NBA Coach of the Year twice. He has also built a successful career as a television and radio basketball analyst. Brown was inducted into the Naismith Memorial Basketball Hall of Fame in 2005.

GEORGE BRUNS

Well respected as a smart playmaker and as a player-coach during his time in the Eastern League, Bruns began a longtime career teaching school and coaching basketball and baseball on Long Island. He also earned a PhD in mathematics. Bruns has been head coach of the Manhasset High School varsity boys' basketball team in Manhasset, New York, for nearly 20 years, including a Long Island championship in 2019. He also served as head coach of women's basketball at Nassau Community College during the 1990s. Bruns and his wife have been running a summer basketball camp for kids in grades 2–10 for more than 40 years.

JOHN CHANEY

Chaney's playing days in the Eastern League ended in 1962 after an auto accident. He took his first coaching job in 1963 at Sayre Junior High School in northern Pennsylvania, about an hour from his old stomping ground in Sunbury. He coached high school ball in Philadelphia for six seasons before becoming coach at Cheyney State, an historically black college near Philadelphia, and won a Division II national title in 1978. In 1982 he became head coach at Temple University, where he stayed for 24 seasons and went to the NCAA tournament 17 times. Chaney won 741 games as a college coach and was a fiery presence on the sideline, and his teams were known for playing ferocious defense. He and Howie Landa continued to team up at various coaching seminars, camps, clinics, and basketball events. In 2001 he was elected to the Naismith Memorial Basketball Hall of Fame and twice was selected as the national Division I Coach of the Year. Chaney retired in 2006.

WALLY CHOICE

Choice became a successful businessman and civic leader in his hometown of Montclair, New Jersey, owning several businesses including a pharmacy. He also served as executive director and president of Montclair Grass Roots, an organization that provides services for youths and seniors, and a community center was named in his honor. He remained especially close friends with his former Easton teammates Dick Gaines, Hal Lear, and Jay Norman. Choice died in 2018 at age 85.

RICH CORNWALL

Cornwall was a teacher during his Eastern League playing days and began his coaching career as an assistant to his former high school coach, Howie Landa, at Trenton Junior College (now Mercer County Community College). He later became a high school basketball coach, and in 1974/75 left the U.S. to play in the Netherlands. (Landa was supposed to be his coach but instead took a better offer to coach in Italy.) When Cornwall returned from Europe, his school district had held his teaching job, but not his coaching job. By then he had become an avid tennis player, often playing with Stan Novak who "was really into it, and once he became my coach, he made me get better at tennis. He always wanted to play." So Cornwall became a tennis coach for the rest of his teaching and coaching career, retiring in 2007 after some 30 years. He still teaches tennis lessons and plays in age-group tournaments. "I'm the kind of guy I need something competitive," he said.

CHICK CRAIG

The lifelong Eastern Leaguer played in the league's opening weekend and coached in its final season, as well as one season in the CBA. He was so popular in Wilkes-Barre that he was honored with "Chick Craig Nights" in 1948 as a player and in 1983 as a coach. Craig scouted for numerous NBA teams during and after his Eastern League coaching days and also worked with the NBA's director of scouting, Marty Blake, who himself got his start in the Eastern League working for Eddie White. Craig died in 2008 at age 85. "That guy knew everybody," said Art Pachter. "He knew everybody."

JOE CRAWFORD

Crawford enjoyed a 19-year career as an NBA referee and worked in 50 NBA Finals games, appearing in the Finals every year between 1986 and 2006. He developed a reputation as one of the league's strictest officials. He retired in 2016 due to a knee injury and continues to live outside of Philadelphia. "I must think of the Eastern League, I swear to G-d, I probably think of it every day," he said.

CHARLIE CRISS

After eight seasons in the NBA, Criss worked as a golf instructor and an Atlanta Hawks television color commentator. He also works for the Hawks as director of their basketball camp and as a motivational speaker. Criss said he doesn't play basketball anymore, but "I just shoot around because I work with some kids on their fundamentals. So I get out there and shoot with them and stuff like that just to show them, because a lot of kids don't believe that I . . . scored 72 points." Throughout the telephone interview, Criss could be heard dribbling a basketball.

JIM DRUCKER

After serving eight years as CBA commissioner and getting the league established, Drucker stepped down and worked on building the audience for the league's television broadcasts on ESPN. For several years he was an on-air legal correspondent for ESPN, then left in 1994 to become commissioner of the new Arena Football League. Six years later he launched NewKadia.com, and it has become the world's largest online comic book retailer. Drucker remains CEO of NewKadia and lives near Philadelphia.

DICK GAINES

One of the Eastern League's legendary tough guys, Gaines harbored some bitterness about not making an NBA team. He told author Ron Thomas in *They Cleared the Lane* that he knew he was "better than guys that were there,"[2] and therefore has gone to very few NBA games. He lives in Montclair, New Jersey, where he was for many years a physical education teacher and became head of the Physical Education Department of the East Orange, New Jersey, educational system. He remained friendly with Wally Choice, who lived nearby, and other former teammates.

CARL GREEN

While playing in the Eastern League, Green worked in the New York City garment district, first tying bundles and then as a fabric inspector. He learned the garment business, made contacts, and eventually became a partner in a business making custom men's suits. His basketball connections brought him customers like Wilt Chamberlain, Freddie Crawford, Jack Molinas, and even Sammy Davis Jr. He remains tough, proud, and a revered figure in New York City basketball circles. "I'm 85 years old," he said in a 2019 interview. "You know, I walk around in Harlem, nothing but respect."

TOM HEMANS

The league's all-time leading rebounder and third leading scorer was a teacher in the New York City Public Schools during his playing days and also served as director of a community center. He continued his career in a number of positions for New York City, including supervisor of Citywide Community Centers; executive director/commissioner of the New York City Youth Board; and executive director of the New York City Public Schools Athletic League. He has been a consultant for Mobil Oil and the New York State Parks and Recreation Authority. Hemans moved to Virginia and is currently executive director of the Lancaster/Northumberland Habitat for Humanity, in Lancaster, Virginia.

ANDY JOHNSON

The former Globetrotter, NBA player, and Allentown Jet was for many years the athletic director at the Eastern State Correctional Institution in Philadelphia, where he oversaw all the sports activities and coached the inmate basketball team. He also formed the Andy Johnson Basketball Academy to teach basketball fundamentals to inner-city students in Philadelphia and southern New Jersey and provide support and encouragement for their academic pursuits. He died in 2002 at age 69.

STEVE KAUFFMAN

After his tenure as the league's commissioner ended, Kauffman built his sports agency that began by representing Charlie Criss and other Eastern Leaguers. He provided accounting and legal services for clients such as Muhammad Ali, Julius Erving, and Charles Barkley, and represented athletes such as Dominique Wilkins and Brian Urlacher. He developed expertise in representing NBA coaches and front office personnel, including Lionel Hollins, Jeff Hornacek, Michael Malone, and New York Knicks president Donnie Walsh. He lives in the Los Angeles area.

JOE LALLI

Lalli taught high school and middle school in Arlington, Virginia, during his two years with the Scranton Miners but then moved back to the Scranton area in 1969. There he primarily taught school, coached high school baseball, and officiated numerous high school and college basketball and football games. He still lives in his hometown of Dunmore, outside of Scranton.

HOWIE LANDA

The scrappy little Philadelphian became one of the most respected basketball teachers in the country. He coached for 26 years at Mercer County Community College near Trenton, New Jersey, winning more than 600 games and two national titles and being named National Junior College Coach of the Year three times. He also coached baseball and men's soccer and was a professor and athletic director at Mercer, where the school's basketball court was named after him. At various times Landa was also an assistant coach for the New York Knicks and the WNBA's Phoenix Mercury and on the staff of University of Nevada–Las Vegas, including as interim head coach in 1994. For many years Landa ran a basketball camp in the Pocono Mountains in Pennsylvania with his former pupil, Rich Cornwall, and NBA Hall of Famer Dave Bing. (Cornwall and Bing were teammates at Syracuse.) Cornwall and Landa also started one of the first girls' basketball camps in the country and took American youth basketball players overseas for camps and tournaments. Landa lived in Las Vegas, where he died in 2020.

HAL LEAR

The gifted scorer did not regret playing only three games as a rookie in the NBA. "Actually it worked out very well for me, very, very well," Lear said in a video interview with Temple University.[3] "The Eastern League afforded me as much money as they wanted to pay me in the NBA. Plus, I built a career." He worked for several years as an executive for the City of Philadelphia and for some 30 years was a senior administrator at Albert Einstein College of Medicine in the Bronx, New York. He died in 2016 at age 81.

GEORGE LEHMANN

The great shooter became a guest instructor at basketball camps and clinics, teaching the art of shooting. He has written articles on shooting, has a series of videos on shooting, and marketed a training aid to help players practice shooting. Lehmann has also worked for basketball shoe companies and owns a mail-order T-shirt business in southern New Jersey.

EDDIE MAST

The former Knick ended his pro career in 1983 with Albany in the CBA, but basketball remained part of his life. He coached a high school team in Allentown, coached Catholic Youth Organization teams in his hometown of Easton, and ran "big man" basketball camps. An accomplished guitar player, he was a salesman for Martin Guitars, then started a lumber company with a friend. He also spent a lot of time with his close friends Phil Jackson (his former roommate on the Knicks) and Charley Rosen (Jackson's assistant coach at Albany). Playing in a pickup game at Lafayette College in Easton in 1994, Mast died of a heart attack. He was 46. "He was the kind of guy that just everybody liked," Rosen said. "He was just so easy to be with."

JULIUS MCCOY

The Eastern League's all-time leading scorer led as distinguished a life off the court as he did on it. Living in the Harrisburg, Pennsylvania, area, McCoy was director of physical education at the Harrisburg YMCA and then became a teacher and basketball coach in the Harrisburg School District. From 1983 to 2004, he was director of the Pennsylvania Department of Transportation's Bureau of Equal Opportunity. His list of community service activities and awards is prolific, and he served on numerous boards for organizations ranging from the Harrisburg YMCA and Boys' Club to the NAACP and United Way. In 1973–1976 he was a member of the United States Olympic Basketball Committee. He remained the most revered athlete to come from Farrell High School, near Pittsburgh, and received the 1998 Distinguished Alumnus Award from Michigan State University. McCoy died in 2008 at age 76. An obituary in the PAHoops.org website said he left "a history of caring and respecting people around him."[4]

MAURICE MCHARTLEY

After his ABA career was over, "Toothpick" returned briefly to his hometown of Detroit, then moved to Atlanta where he has been ever since. McHartley worked for the *Atlanta Journal & Constitution* as a delivery driver and eventually an assistant manager. He played basketball in rec leagues until he was about 50 and now plays tennis. "I had to find something else to do after I quit playing ball. . . . Keeps these old legs moving, and I'm thankful to be able to still get out and do that." He remains in touch with Bellamy and other former Blue Bombers and Eastern League veterans.

SWISH MCKINNEY

While playing in Binghamton, McKinney got a job with IBM and developed a facility for computers. When his playing days were over, McKinney returned home to the Oakland area and worked in several information technology jobs, eventually working at California State University–Hayward where he got his degree in computer science in 1980. He taught in the Oakland Public Schools and at a state college until he retired in 2002. He also worked on a U.S. State Department program coaching youth teams that went to Africa to play basketball. Former Scranton owner Art Pachter remembered how McKinney called him regularly after finding out that Pachter had a stroke several years ago. "He used to call every week," Pachter said. "Nicest guy in the world." McKinney now lives in Las Vegas. People still call him "Swish."

JACK MOLINAS

Molinas, a big-time scorer and gambler, played his last year in the Eastern League in 1961, when he averaged 17.7 PPG in seven games for Wilkes-Barre before retiring in mid-December. By 1963 he was sentenced to 10 to 15 years in prison, later reduced to five years, in New York for masterminding the fixing of at least 30 college games between 1957 and 1961. Molinas, who was also known to have been involved with organized crime, pornography, and loan sharking, moved to Hollywood in 1970 and was mysteriously shot and killed in 1975, at the age of 43, while standing in his backyard late at night.

STAN NOVAK

The Eastern League's all-time winningest coach's last season in the league was 1978/79, with the Allentown Jets during the CBA's first year. In 1980 Novak, who had been a part-time NBA scout during his years in the Eastern League, became director of scouting for the Detroit Pistons under general manager Jack McCloskey, his old University of Pennsylvania and Sunbury Mercuries teammate and lifelong friend. Those Pistons teams won NBA championships in 1988/89 and 1989/90. He was also director of scouting for the Minnesota Timberwolves from 1992 to 1997 and a part-time scout for the Utah Jazz. He died in 2006. "You talk about great people, he really, really was a great man," said his former player and tennis partner, Rich Cornwall.

ART PACHTER

The "Red Auerbach of the Eastern League," as former commissioner Jim Drucker called him, remains an entertaining font of information and stories. He especially enjoys talking about the many friends he made through his almost 20 years owning teams in the Eastern League and CBA, and loves hearing from former players and others associated with the league. "My grandson was at Syracuse," recalled Pachter, "and he sees Boeheim coming out of one of the stores. And he goes up to him and tells him who he was. And he says Boeheim for maybe 10 minutes was so nice, talked so, so nice about me, paid all kind of compliments. . . . He said, 'Your grandfather—the best. I have to tell you he did more for people who played with him, more advice, more everything' . . . Nicest things he could say to a kid in school, my grandson. . . . It means something."

STAN PAWLAK

Pawlak taught and coached for several years at Woodrow Wilson High School in his hometown of Camden, New Jersey, starting as an assistant to his friend and high school teammate, Gary Williams, former head coach at the University of Maryland. Pawlak attempted a return to the Eastern League in 1977 but ruptured his Achilles tendon in his first game back. He coached in Saudi Arabia for two years, directing its national team, and then returned to the U.S. and coached the Atlantic City High Rollers in the CBA for a season and a half until they folded in 1982. By then he had started a career as a medical devices sales rep, which at times brought him back to the Wilkes-Barre and Scranton areas. Pawlak is retired and for the past 20 years has been the radio color analyst for University of Pennsylvania basketball games.

JOHN POSTLEY

The league's most chiseled, physically imposing player played six seasons in the Eastern League sandwiched around one game and two points in the ABA for the Pittsburgh Pipers. In July 1970 he was playing in a Baker League game in Philadelphia with his Wilkes-Barre Barons teammate, Stan Pawlak, as they had done for several years. "He threw the ball inbounds to me," Pawlak said. "I turned around and took a dribble, and turned around and looked at him, and there he was on the ground, never to be revived from that point." His death at age 30 was attributed to cardiac arrest.

CHARLEY ROSEN

Following his brief Eastern League playing career, Rosen taught English at Hofstra University on Long Island. He also served as head coach of the women's basketball team at the State University of New York—New Paltz and as men's coach at Bard College. He returned to the renamed CBA in 1983 as an assistant coach to his close friend Phil Jackson with the Albany Patroons for three seasons and later was head coach of the Patroons and several other CBA teams. Rosen is the author of 16 books on basketball, including *Scandals of '51* about the 1951 point-shaving scandal and *The Wizard of Odds* about Jack Molinas. His book *Have Jump Shot Will Travel* is based loosely on his experiences in the Eastern League. He is also a pro basketball commentator whose articles have been published on various websites.

RAY SCOTT

Scott coached the Detroit Pistons from 1972 to 1976 and was named NBA Coach of the Year in 1974. He also coached Eastern Michigan University from 1976 to 1979. When his coaching days ended, Scott became an account executive with the Colonial Life Insurance Company in Michigan for some 30 years. He still lives in the Detroit area where he is active in community affairs and has worked with the Wellspring Lutheran Services agency for children and families.

ALAN SEIDEN

Seiden remained a basketball junkie well after his Eastern League days, playing in tournaments, leagues, and pickup games around New York City with other former city players, and was as mercurial as he was in his playing days—irascible at times, generous at others. He remained close to his former Eastern League teammate and traveling buddy Carl Green, who called Seiden "one of my best friends in life." He was named to Madison Square Garden's All-Decade college basketball team of 1953/54 through 1962/63 with players who included Bill Russell, Jerry Lucas, Elgin Baylor, Tom Heinsohn, Maurice Stokes, Rick Barry,

Jerry West, and Oscar Robertson. Seiden owned a ticket brokerage and lived in Queens. He died in 2008 at age 71.

WILLIE SOMERSET

Somerset enjoyed a long career as a pharmacist following his playing career. "I knew my future was in pharmacy," he said. "I always knew that I wanted to be a pharmacist. . . . That was more of a priority than the basketball was." He worked in hospital pharmacies, for a pharmaceutical company, and eventually ended up getting his own drugstore in Newark, New Jersey. He lives in Harrisburg, Pennsylvania, where he was friends with Julius and Jim McCoy, all of whom hailed from the town of Farrell in western Pennsylvania.

BILL SPIVEY

A businessman even during his 10 years in the Eastern League (off the court he was perhaps best remembered for homebuilding in Scranton), Spivey moved back to Kentucky where he had starred in college. There he sold insurance, real estate, and building supplies, in addition to owning Bill Spivey's Restaurant & Lounge in Lexington. He also used his famous name to enter politics, where he served as a deputy state insurance commissioner and ran (unsuccessfully) for Kentucky lieutenant governor in 1983. Spivey also suffered from chronic lower back pain after a car accident in Florida, and from the heartbreak of being barred from the NBA because of the scandal, for which he was accused but never found guilty. "He never got over it,"[5] Spivey's former wife, Audrey Spivey, said about the scandal. "Bill could not let that go. He was just devastated." Spivey later moved to Costa Rica and, in 1995, was found dead of natural causes at the age of 66.

ROMAN TURMON

The former Globetrotter left the Eastern League in a dispute over money with the Allentown Jets and went on to own two chicken restaurant franchises in Harlem and Brooklyn. The restaurants reportedly fell on hard times, however, and after a short retirement, Big Doc was employed by the State of New York and the Gateway National Recreation Area, part of the National Park Service in New York and New Jersey, where he remained until his death in 2001.

TONY UPSON

Upson—a well-respected player who won the league's John F. Kennedy Sportsmanship Award in 1970—became a physical education and science teacher in the Washington, DC, schools. He got a master's degree and went into education administration, serving as a high school principal for 17 years. He retired in 1998 and is a mentor and coach for principals in the DC area. He still plays in senior basketball leagues.

WHITEY VON NIEDA

The leading scorer during the Eastern League's inaugural season in 1946/47 spent three seasons in the NBL/NBA then returned home to Lancaster for four seasons as player-coach, also coaching at nearby Elizabethtown College for two of those seasons. He remained in the Lancaster area, selling advertising for the Yellow Pages, coaching youth teams, and in 1985 he coached Lancaster in the CBA. He also worked as a bartender in several local establishments where he was known for his wit and storytelling and wrote a local newspaper column. At age 97, he is the second-oldest living former NBA player. "I've done some things, and played all over the place, and made a lot of nice friends," Von Nieda said.

BOB WEISS

After playing 12 years in the NBA, Weiss began a lengthy NBA coaching career in 1978 as an assistant with the San Diego Clippers. He has been head coach of the San Antonio Spurs (1986–1988), Atlanta Hawks (1990–1993), LA Clippers (1993/94), and Seattle Supersonics (2005/6) and has held several assistant coaching jobs. Most recently he coached professional teams in China and served as an assistant coach with the Denver Nuggets.

EDDIE WHITE

One of the league's original founders and legendary owners, promoters, and coaches, White remained prominent in the Wilkes-Barre community after his Eastern League days were over, serving on the city council. He died in 1988 but continued to be remembered as a larger-than-life figure not only in the Wilkes-Barre area but also in the basketball world. His grandson, Eddie White III, a public relations executive for the NBA's Indiana Pacers, said that throughout his career in college and professional sports, he would inevitably run into someone who recalled his grandfather. While working at Super Bowl XXV during Whitney Houston's rehearsal for her "Star-Spangled Banner," White III fortuitously met Sherman White, who was Houston's uncle. When he told Sherman White that he was Eddie White's grandson, the former star player said: "Let me tell you something about your grandfather. . . . Back in the day, a lot of these teams would not pay the black players what they're paying the white players. Your grandfather paid the black players exactly what he paid the white players." Houston overhead the story and said to Eddie White: "I just want to shake your hand. Your grandfather sounds like a wonderful person." Replied White: "He was, and I'm honored to be named after him."

SHERMAN WHITE

White spent 10 outstanding years as a scorer in the Eastern League, mostly with Hazleton. He retired in 1962/63 after playing two years in Baltimore and one year in Wilkes-Barre. He sold storm windows, insulation, automobiles, and liquor during his Eastern League days, but when he retired, he focused on coaching and mentoring inner-city youngsters in Newark and Orange, New Jersey. "I talk to a lot of kids here,"[6] White told Charley Rosen for his book *Scandals of '51*, originally published in 1978. "Some I can help. I'll tell a kid about my involvement in the scandals if I think it will do him any good." According to his obituary in the Associated Press, his second wife, Ellen White, said his participation in the scandal "was the bane of his existence. It gnawed at him for all of his life, and that's why he tried so hard to work with so many young men."[7] Sherman White died in 2011 at his home in Piscataway, New Jersey, at the age of 82.

NOTES

PREFACE

1. Terry Pluto, *Loose Balls: The Short, Wild Life of the American Basketball Association* (New York: Fireside, 1990), 58–63.

2. Mark Johnson, *Basketball Slave: The Andy Johnson Harlem Globetrotter/NBA Story* (Mantua, NJ: Junior Cam, 2010), 134–38.

3. Ron Thomas, *They Cleared the Lane: The NBA's Black Pioneers* (Lincoln: University of Nebraska Press, 2002), 154–61.

4. Lawrence A. Armour, "Toughing It Out around the Purgatory League," *Sports Illustrated*, March 15, 1971, 70–72.

5. Charles Rosen, *Have Jump Shot Will Travel* (New York: Ballantine Books, 1975).

6. Rosen, *Have Jump Shot*, 7.

7. Harvey Araton, "The League of Dreamers Is No More," *New York Times*, February 22, 2001, 1(D).

8. All quotes from Howie Landa are from interviews with author Syl Sobel, March 9, 2018, and January 30, 2019, unless otherwise noted.

9. All quotes from Rich Cornwall are from interviews with author Syl Sobel, March 1, 2018, and July 16, 2019, unless otherwise noted.

10. All quotes from Joe Crawford are from an interview with author Syl Sobel, January 26, 2018, unless otherwise noted.

11. All quotes from Jim Boeheim are from interviews with author Syl Sobel, May 29, 2018, and July 29, 2019, unless otherwise noted.

CHAPTER 1

1. All quotes from Brian Maloney are from an interview with authors Syl Sobel and Jay Rosenstein, November 4, 2018, unless otherwise noted.

2. "Teams in New Eastern League Boast Many College Stars," *Plain Speaker* (Hazleton, PA), November 30, 1946, 10.

3. All quotes from Eddie White III are from an interview with author Syl Sobel, July 15, 2019, unless otherwise noted.

4. Chuck Miller, "A League of Their Own," *SLAMOnline*, December 14, 2007, last accessed January 30, 2020, https:www.slamonline.com/blogs/history-out-of-bounds.

5. Mark Johnson, *Basketball Slave: The Andy Johnson Harlem Globetrotter/NBA Story* (Mantua, NJ: Junior Cam, 2010), 175.

6. The NBA's unwritten racial quotas are discussed in chapter 4, "Blackballed: Race, the NBA, and the Rise of the Eastern League."

7. All quotes from Waite Bellamy are from interviews with author Syl Sobel, November 20, 2017, December 4, 2017, and July 11, 2019, unless otherwise noted. The story of Bellamy being denied a rental is recounted in chapter 9.

8. All quotes from George Blaney are from an interview with author Jay Rosenstein, January 24, 2019, unless otherwise noted.

9. All quotes from Harvey Kasoff are from an interview with author Jay Rosenstein, March 14, 2018, unless otherwise noted.

10. Lawrence A. Armour, "Toughing It Out around the Purgatory League," *Sports Illustrated*, March 15, 1971, 70.

CHAPTER 2

1. Harvey Araton, "The League of Dreamers Is No More," *New York Times*, February 22, 2001, 1(D).

2. "Teams in New Eastern League Boast Many College Stars," *Plain Speaker* (Hazleton, PA), November 30, 1946, 10.

3. All quotes from Whitey Von Nieda are from an interview with author Syl Sobel, February 20, 2019, unless otherwise noted.

4. "Down State Teams in Eastern Pro Cage Loop to Be Strong," *Plain Speaker* (Hazleton, PA), November 16, 1946, 10.

5. All quotes from Rev. Connell McHugh are from an interview with authors Syl Sobel and Jay Rosenstein, November 3, 2018, unless otherwise noted.

6. All quotes from Arthur Pachter are from interviews with authors Syl Sobel and Jay Rosenstein, February 11, 2018, and November 5, 2018, and an interview with author Syl Sobel, September 20, 2019, unless otherwise noted.

7. All quotes from John Chaney are from interviews with author Syl Sobel, July 25, 2018, and June 3, 2019, unless otherwise noted.

CHAPTER 3

1. Charley Rosen, *Scandals of '51: How the Gamblers Almost Killed College Basketball* (New York: Seven Stories, 1999), 194.

2. Charley Rosen, *The Wizard of Odds: How Jack Molinas Almost Destroyed the Game of Basketball* (New York: Seven Stories, 2001), 140.

3. Rosen, *Wizard of Odds*, 141.

4. Charley Rosen, *Crazy Basketball: A Life In and Out of Bounds* (Lincoln: University of Nebraska Press, 2011), 29.

5. All quotes from Ray Scott are from an interview with author Syl Sobel, January 27, 2018, unless otherwise noted.

6. All quotes from Charley Rosen are from interviews with author Syl Sobel, January 27, 2018, and July 21, 2019, unless otherwise noted.

7. Staff report, "LIU Legend White Dies; Point-Shaving Kept Him from NBA," *New York Post*, August 12, 2011, last accessed March 14, 2020, https://nypost.com/2011/08/12/liu-legend-white-dies-point-shaving-kept-him-from-nba/.

8. Rosen, *Wizard of Odds*.

9. Bill Spivey as told to Larry Boeck, "Spivey Played Stilt Even in Exhi, Wants to Face Him In N.B.A.," *Louisville Courier-Journal*, July 26, 1960, 18.

10. Neil Amdur, "7-Foot Spivey, Barred by N.B.A. during Scandals, Retires at 38," *New York Times*, February 13, 1968, last accessed March 14, 2020, https://www.nytimes.com/1968/02/13/archives/7foot-spivey-barred-by-nba-during-scandals-retires-at-38-exkentucky.html.

CHAPTER 4

1. Mark Johnson, *Basketball Slave: The Andy Johnson Harlem Globetrotter/NBA Story* (Mantua, NJ: Junior Cam, 2010), xiii–xviii.

2. Johnson, *Basketball Slave*, 174–75.

3. Ron Thomas, *They Cleared the Lane: The NBA's Black Pioneers* (Lincoln: University of Nebraska Press, 2002), 133–34.

4. All quotes from Hubie Brown are from interviews with author Syl Sobel, March 28, 2018, June 5, 2019, and July 15, 2019, unless otherwise noted.

5. Thomas, *They Cleared the Lane*, 135.

6. All quotes from Ron Marchetti are from an interview with authors Syl Sobel and Jay Rosenstein, November 3, 2018, unless otherwise noted.

7. All quotes from Bob Ryan are from an interview with author Syl Sobel, October 2–3, 2018, unless otherwise noted.

8. All quotes from Stan Pawlak are from interviews with author Syl Sobel, July 17, 2018, May 6, 2019, and July 9, 2019, unless otherwise noted.

9. Johnson, *Basketball Slave*, 97.

10. All quotes from Tom Hemans are from responses to interview questions submitted to author Jay Rosenstein unless otherwise noted.

11. All quotes from Cleveland "Swish" McKinney are from an interview with authors Syl Sobel and Jay Rosenstein, February 17, 2018, unless otherwise noted.

12. Thomas, *They Cleared the Lane*, 136.

13. Earl Lloyd and Sean Kirst, *Moonfixer: The Basketball Journey of Earl Lloyd* (Syracuse, NY: Syracuse University Press, 2010), 61.

14. Johnson, *Basketball Slave*, 101.

15. Thomas, "Eastern League Provides Haven for NBA Rejects," in *They Cleared the Lane*, 152–61.

16. All quotes from Bobby Hunter are from an interview with author Syl Sobel, July 9, 2018, unless otherwise noted.

17. Thomas, *They Cleared the Lane*, 139.

18. Thomas, *They Cleared the Lane*, 146–51.

19. Thomas, *They Cleared the Lane*, 144.

20. All quotes from Maurice McHartley are from interviews with author Syl Sobel, March 22, 2018, and September 8, 2018, unless otherwise noted.

21. Thomas, *They Cleared the Lane*, 134.

22. All quotes from Willie Somerset are from an interview with authors Syl Sobel and Jay Rosenstein, March 3, 2018, unless otherwise noted.

23. All quotes from Joe Lalli are from an interview with author Jay Rosenstein, October 23, 2018, and emails dated October 22, 2018, and October 25, 2018, unless otherwise noted.

24. Sonny Hill, "In a League of His Own," interview by Zack Burgess, JockBio.com, 2011, last accessed February 5, 2020, https://www.jockbio.com/Classic/S_Hill/S_Hill_bio.html.

CHAPTER 5

1. Robert Bradley, "Re: Roster Size," APBR.org: The APBR Discussion Boards, July 28, 2012, last accessed February 3, 2020, http://www.apbr.org/forum/viewtopic.php?f=27&t=4383.

2. All quotes from Bob Weiss are from an interview with author Syl Sobel, March 11, 2018, unless otherwise noted.

3. Ron Thomas, *They Cleared the Lane: The NBA's Black Pioneers* (Lincoln: University of Nebraska Press, 2002), 155.

4. Thomas, *They Cleared the Lane*, 155.

5. All quotes from Marvin Salenger are from an interview with author Syl Sobel, May 8, 2019, unless otherwise noted.

6. All quotes from Dick Bavetta are from an interview with author Jay Rosenstein, November 18, 2017, unless otherwise noted.

7. Charley Rosen, *Crazy Basketball: A Life In and Out of Bounds* (Lincoln: University of Nebraska Press, 2011), 29.

8. Frank Thierer, Facebook message with author Syl Sobel, February 5, 2020.

9. Steve Kelley, "Basketball Still Has Magical Power to Bring People Together, Regardless of Race," *Seattle Times*, January 22, 2011, last accessed March 11, 2020, https://www.seattletimes.com/sports/basketball-still-has-magical-power-to-bring-peo ple-together-regardless-of-race/.

10. All quotes from George Bruns are from an interview with authors Syl Sobel and Jay Rosenstein, February 24, 2018, unless otherwise noted.

11. Sonny Hill, "In a League of His Own," interview by Zack Burgess, JockBio.com, 2011, last accessed February 5, 2020, https://www.jockbio.com/Classic/S_Hill/S_Hill_ bio.html.

12. All quotes from Carl Green are from an interview with author Syl Sobel, June 4, 2019, unless otherwise noted.

13. All quotes from Tony Upson are from an interview with author Syl Sobel, March 5, 2018, unless otherwise noted.

14. Lawrence A. Armour, "Toughing It Out around the Purgatory League," *Sports Illustrated*, March 15, 1971, 72.

15. Mike Waters, "Story Time with Jim Boeheim: Riding down I-81, Playing Pro Basketball for $100 a Night," Syracuse.com, 2016, updated 2019, last accessed February 4, 2020, https://www.syracuse.com/orangebasketball/2016/11/story_time_with_ jim_boeheim_riding_down_i-81_playing_pro_basketball_for_100_a_ni.html.

CHAPTER 6

1. "50th Anniversary Team," APBR.org, last accessed February 4, 2020, http:// www.apbr.org/cbahist.html.

2. Ron Thomas, *They Cleared the Lane: The NBA's Black Pioneers* (Lincoln: University of Nebraska Press, 2002), 159–60.

3. Confession from author Syl Sobel: The first time I heard Ron Allen say that on a radio broadcast when I was eight or nine years old, I somehow formed the impression that McCoy was Chinese.

4. Charley Rosen, *Crazy Basketball: A Life In and Out of Bounds* (Lincoln: University of Nebraska Press, 2011), 34.

5. "Richard Gaines," *Official Program: Scranton Miners vs. Sunbury Mercuries*, 1963/64, 20.

6. Thomas, *They Cleared the Lane*, 157.

7. Sonny Hill, "In a League of His Own," interview by Zack Burgess, JockBio.com, 2011, last accessed February 5, 2020, https://www.jockbio.com/Classic/S_Hill/S_Hill_ bio.html.

8. "Tom Hemans," *Official Program: Scranton Miners*, 1963/64, 23.

9. "Tom Hemans," *Official Program: Scranton Miners*, 1967/68, 3.

10. Mark Johnson, *Basketball Slave: The Andy Johnson Harlem Globetrotter/NBA Story* (Mantua, NJ: Junior Cam, 2010), 137.

11. Johnson, *Basketball Slave*, 135.

12. "Bob McNeill," SJU Athletics, last accessed February 5, 2020, https://sjuhawks.com/sports/ath/roster/bob-mcneill/2413.

CHAPTER 7

1. All quotes from Walker Banks are from an interview with author Syl Sobel, February 17, 2018, unless otherwise noted.

2. Peter Vecsey, "Combustible Star Battled NBA Legends, Reputation," *New York Post*, January 11, 2009, last accessed March 11, 2020, https://nypost.com/2009/01/11/combustible-star-battled-nba-legends-reputation/.

3. P. Vecsey, "Combustible Star."

4. George Vecsey, "A Fallen Star of the City Game," *New York Times*, May 6, 2008, last accessed February 6, 2020, https://www.nytimes.com/2008/05/06/sports/ncaabasketball/06vecsey.html.

5. P. Vecsey, "Combustible Star."

6. Mike Waters, "Story Time with Jim Boeheim: Riding down I-81, Playing Pro Basketball for $100 a Night," Syracuse.com, 2016, updated 2019, last accessed February 4, 2020, https://www.syracuse.com/orangebasketball/2016/11/story_time_with_jim_boeheim_riding_down_i-81_playing_pro_basketball_for_100_a_ni.html.

7. Steve Kelley, email with author Syl Sobel, August 9, 2018.

8. All quotes from Charlie Criss are from an interview with author Syl Sobel, September 6, 2018, unless otherwise noted.

9. Lawrence A. Armour, "Toughing It Out around the Purgatory League," *Sports Illustrated*, March 15, 1971, 72.

CHAPTER 8

1. Morin Bishop, "When His Hoops Career Didn't Fly, Bill Green Made Education His Game," *Sports Illustrated*, February 10, 1986, last accessed March 11, 2020, https://vault.si.com/vault/1986/02/10/when-his-hoops-career-didnt-fly-bill-green-made-education-his-game.

2. Peter Vecsey, "Combustible Star Battled NBA Legends, Reputation," *New York Post*, January 11, 2009, last accessed March 11, 2020, https://nypost.com/2009/01/11/combustible-star-battled-nba-legends-reputation/.

3. Harvey Araton, "The League of Dreamers Is No More," *New York Times*, February 22, 2001, last accessed March 11, 2020, http://movies2.nytimes.com/2001/02/22/sports/22ARAT.html.

4. Peter Vecsey, "Had Warm Heart Hidden Within," *New York Post*, January 18, 2009, last accessed March 11, 2020, https://nypost.com/2009/01/18/had-warm-heart-hidden-within/.

5. Steve Kelley, "Basketball Still Has Magical Power to Bring People Together, Regardless of Race," *Seattle Times,* January 22, 2011, last accessed March 11, 2020, https://www.seattletimes.com/sports/basketball-still-has-magical-power-to-bring-peo ple-together-regardless-of-race/.

6. Jay Rosenstein, "Dick Bavetta: Supervisor of Officials," in *Eastern Basketball Association 1977–1978 Official Guide*, ed. Howard M. Balzer (1977), 7.

CHAPTER 9

1. Lawrence A. Armour, "Toughing It Out around the Purgatory League," *Sports Illustrated*, March 15, 1971, 72.

2. Cindy Inkrote, "Mercuries Madness Was Hot," *Daily Item* (Sunbury, PA), March 22, 2009, last accessed March 12, 2020, https://www.dailyitem.com/news/mercuries-madness-was-hot/article_2755fb3b-3bee-569b-acc1-3a19f06ffdff.html.

3. Chuck Miller, "Twelve Missing Seasons," *Times Union* (Albany, NY), September 7, 2010, last accessed March 16, 2020, https://blog.timesunion.com/chuckmiller/twelve-missing-seasons/3394/.

4. Jay Rosenstein, "Dick Bavetta: Supervisor of Officials," in *Eastern Basketball Association 1977–1978 Official Guide*, ed. Howard M. Balzer (1977), 6.

5. Paul L. Montgomery, "Mill-Town Basketball, or Life in the Minors," New York Times, January 27, 1976, last accessed March 12, 2020, https://www.nytimes.com/1976/01/27/archives/milltown-basketball-or-life-in-the-minors-life-in-the-minor-league.html.

CHAPTER 10

1. Terry Pluto, *Loose Balls: The Short, Wild Life of the American Basketball Association* (New York: Fireside, 1990), 60.

2. Pluto, *Loose Balls*, 60.

3. Lawrence A. Armour, "Toughing It Out around the Purgatory League," *Sports Illustrated*, March 15, 1971, 72.

4. Matt Engel, post in Eastern Basketball League (EBA/EBL) 1946–1978 Facebook group, 2019, last accessed February 8, 2020, https://www.facebook.com/groups/1518986951756310/.

5. "History of the Eastern Basketball Association," *Official Program: Scranton Apollos*, 1970/71, 3.

6. "Marilee Enterprises, Inc. Officers—Scranton Apollos," *Official Program: Scranton Apollos*, 1970/71, 1.

7. Jean-Pierre Caravan, email with author Syl Sobel, January 28, 2019.

8. Paul Reinhard, "Red Helped Jets with Some Players and His Friendship: He Provided Several Future Knicks and Helped the EBL Franchise as Well," *Morning Call* (Allentown, PA), November 15, 1998, last accessed February 16, 2020, https://www.mcall.com/news/mc-xpm-1998-11-15-3225456-story.html.

9. Armour, "Toughing It Out," 70.

10. Armour, "Toughing It Out," 70.

CHAPTER 11

1. "50th Anniversary Team," APBR.org, last accessed February 4, 2020, http://www.apbr.org/cbahist.html.

2. Sonny Hill, "In a League of His Own," interview by Zack Burgess, JockBio.com, 2011, last accessed February 5, 2020, https://www.jockbio.com/Classic/S_Hill/S_Hill_bio.html.

3. Lawrence A. Armour, "Toughing It Out around the Purgatory League," *Sports Illustrated*, March 15, 1971, 72.

CHAPTER 12

1. Mike Waters, "Story Time with Jim Boeheim: Riding down I-81, Playing Pro Basketball for $100 a Night," Syracuse.com, 2016, updated 2019, last accessed February 4, 2020, https://www.syracuse.com/orangebasketball/2016/11/story_time_with_jim_boeheim_riding_down_i-81_playing_pro_basketball_for_100_a_ni.html.

2. Lawrence A. Armour, "Toughing It Out around the Purgatory League," *Sports Illustrated*, March 15, 1971, 70.

CHAPTER 13

1. Mike Waters, "Story Time with Jim Boeheim: Riding down I-81, Playing Pro Basketball for $100 a Night," Syracuse.com, 2016, updated 2019, last accessed February 4, 2020, https://www.syracuse.com/orangebasketball/2016/11/story_time_with_jim_boeheim_riding_down_i-81_playing_pro_basketball_for_100_a_ni.html.

2. Steve Rushin, "This Zebra Turned Dodger Blue," *Sports Illustrated*, October 22, 1990, 12–14.

3. Rushin, "This Zebra Turned Dodger Blue," 14.

4. All quotes from Steve Kauffman are from an interview with author Syl Sobel, March 13, 2018, unless otherwise noted.

5. All quotes from Jim Drucker are from an interview with author Syl Sobel, September 9, 2019, unless otherwise noted.

CHAPTER 14

1. Paul L. Montgomery, "Mill-Town Basketball, or Life in the Minors," *New York Times*, January 27, 1976, last accessed March 12, 2020, https://www.nytimes.com/1976/01/27/archives/milltown-basketball-or-life-in-the-minors-life-in-the-minor-league.html.

2. Montgomery, "Mill-Town Basketball."

3. Montgomery, "Mill-Town Basketball."

4. Montgomery, "Mill-Town Basketball."

5. Montgomery, "Mill-Town Basketball."

6. Evan Burian, "40 Years Ago, U.S. Olympians Played, Beat the Allentown Jets," *Morning Call* (Allentown, PA), July 5, 2016, last accessed February 13, 2020, https://www.mcall.com/sports/mc-allentown-jets-basketball-burian-20150425-story.html.

7. Steve Bennett, "Dean Smith's Storied Coaching Career Included Wilkes-Barre Stop," *Citizens' Voice* (Wilkes-Barre, PA), February 9, 2015, last accessed February 13, 2020, https://www.citizensvoice.com/sports/dean-smith-s-storied-coaching-career-included-wilkes-barre-stop-1.1829993.

8. Bennett, "Dean Smith's Storied Coaching Career."

9. Bennett, "Dean Smith's Storied Coaching Career."

10. Charley Rosen, *Crazy Basketball: A Life In and Out of Bounds* (Lincoln: University of Nebraska Press, 2011), 60.

CHAPTER 15

1. Harvey Araton, "The League of Dreamers Is No More," *New York Times*, February 22, 2001, 1(D).

2. Araton, "League of Dreamers."

3. Araton, "League of Dreamers."

CHAPTER 16

1. All quotes from Felicita Pitt are from an interview with author Syl Sobel, May 8, 2019, unless otherwise noted.

2. Ron Thomas, *They Cleared the Lane: The NBA's Black Pioneers* (Lincoln: University of Nebraska Press, 2002), 159.

3. "Hal Lear," Temple University, May 12, 2010, YouTube video, 2:30, last accessed February 16, 2020, https://www.youtube.com/watch?v=nWhBETmtTWc.

4. Jim Raykie, "Julius McCoy Gave Life to All That Is Farrell Basketball: An Editor's Notes," PAHoops.org, April 4, 2008, last accessed February 16, 2020, http://pahoops.org/julius_mccoy_gave_life_to_all.htm.

5. Frank Litsky, "Bill Spivey, 66, Kentucky Star Implicated in Scandal of 1950's," *New York Times*, May 10, 1995, last accessed February 29, 2020, http://www.nytimes.com/1995/05/10/obituaries/bill-spivey-66-kentucky-star-implicated-in-scandal-of-1950-s.html.

6. Charley Rosen, *Scandals of '51: How the Gamblers Almost Killed College Basketball* (New York: Seven Stories, 1999), 247.

7. Associated Press, "White, Implicated in 50s Hoop Scandal, Dies at 82," *Washington Times*, August 12, 2011, last accessed February 29, 2020, https://www.washingtontimes.com/news/2011/aug/12/white-implicated-in-50s-hoop-scandal-dies-at-82/.

BIBLIOGRAPHY

Amdur, Neil. "7-Foot Spivey, Barred by N.B.A. during Scandals, Retires at 38." *New York Times,* February 13, 1968. Last accessed March 14, 2020. https://www.nytimes.com/1968/02/13/archives/7foot-spivey-barred-by-nba-during-scandals-retires-at-38-exkentucky.html.

APBR.org. "50th Anniversary Team." Last accessed February 4, 2020. http://www.apbr.org/cbahist.html.

Araton, Harvey. "The League of Dreamers Is No More." *New York Times*, February 22, 2001.

Armour, Lawrence A. "Toughing It Out around the Purgatory League." *Sports Illustrated*, March 15, 1971.

Associated Press. "White, Implicated in 50s Hoop Scandal, Dies at 82." *Washington Times*, August 12, 2011. Last accessed February 29, 2020. https://www.washingtontimes.com/news/2011/aug/12/white-implicated-in-50s-hoop-scandal-dies-at-82/.

Bennett, Steve. "Dean Smith's Storied Coaching Career Included Wilkes-Barre Stop." *Citizens' Voice* (Wilkes-Barre, PA), February 9, 2015. Last accessed February 13, 2020. https://www.citizensvoice.com/sports/dean-smith-s-storied-coaching-career-included-wilkes-barre-stop-1.1829993.

Bishop, Morin. "When His Hoops Career Didn't Fly, Bill Green Made Education His Game." *Sports Illustrated*, February 10, 1986. Last accessed March 11, 2020. https://vault.si.com/vault/1986/02/10/when-his-hoops-career-didnt-fly-bill-green-made-education-his-game.

Black Fives Foundation. Last accessed February 29, 2020. https://www.blackfives.org/.

Boeck, Larry. "Spivey Played Stilt Even in Exhi, Wants to Face Him In N.B.A." *Louisville Courier-Journal*, July 26, 1960, 18.

Bradley, Robert. "Eastern Pennsylvania Basketball League/Eastern Professional Basketball League/Eastern Basketball Association History." APBR.org. Last accessed February 3, 2020. http://www.apbr.org/ebl4678.html.

——. "Re: Roster Size." APBR.org: The APBR Discussion Boards. July 28, 2012. Last accessed February 3, 2020. http://www.apbr.org/forum/viewtopic. php?f=27&t=4383.

Burian, Evan. "40 Years Ago, U.S. Olympians Played, Beat the Allentown Jets." *Morning Call* (Allentown, PA), July 5, 2016. Last accessed February 13, 2020. https:// www.mcall.com/sports/mc-allentown-jets-basketball-burian-20150425-story.html.

Daily Item (Sunbury, PA). "Mercuries Win Pair over Weekend, Jump Record Percentage to .894." March 9, 1953.

Engel, Matt. Post in Eastern Basketball League (EBA/EBL) 1946–1978 Facebook group. 2019. Last accessed February 8, 2020. https://www.facebook.com/ groups/1518986951756310/.

"Hal Lear." Temple University. May 12, 2010. YouTube video, 2:30. Last accessed February 16, 2020. https://www.youtube.com/watch?v=nWhBETmtTWc.

Hareas, John. "Remembering the Rens." *NBA Encyclopedia Playoff Edition*. Last accessed January 31, 2020. archive.nba.com/history/encyclopedia_rens_001214.html.

Hewlett, Jennifer. "UK All-American Carried Lifelong Scar of '50s Scandal." *Lexington (KY) Herald-Leader*, May 9, 1995. Last accessed March 14, 2020. http://www.big bluehistory.net/bb/Statistics/Players/Spivey_Bill.html.

Hill, Sonny. "In a League of His Own." Interview by Zack Burgess. JockBio.com. 2011. Last accessed February 5, 2020. https://www.jockbio.com/Classic/S_Hill/S_Hill_ bio.html.

Johnson, Mark. *Basketball Slave: The Andy Johnson Harlem Globetrotter/NBA Story*. Mantua, NJ: Junior Cam, 2010.

Kelley, Steve. "Basketball Still Has Magical Power to Bring People Together, Regardless of Race." *Seattle Times*, January 22, 2011. Last accessed March 11, 2020. https://www.seattletimes.com/sports/basketball-still-has-magical-power-to-bring-people-together-regardless-of-race/.

Litsky, Frank. "Bill Spivey, 66, Kentucky Star Implicated in Scandal of 1950's." *New York Times*, May 10, 1995. Last accessed February 29, 2020. http://www.nytimes. com/1995/05/10/obituaries/bill-spivey-66-kentucky-star-implicated-in-scandal-of-1950-s.html.

Lloyd, Earl, and Sean Kirst. *Moonfixer: The Basketball Journey of Earl Lloyd*. Syracuse, NY: Syracuse University Press, 2010.

Miller, Chuck. "CBA Overall Guide." Unpublished manuscript. 2009.

——. "A League of Their Own." *SLAMOnline*. December 14, 2007. Last accessed January 30, 2020. https://www.slamonline.com/blogs/history-out-of-bounds.

——. "Twelve Missing Seasons." *Times Union* (Albany, NY), September 7, 2010. Last accessed March 16, 2020. https://blog.timesunion.com/chuckmiller/twelve-missing-seasons/3394/.

Montgomery, Paul L. "Mill-Town Basketball, or Life in the Minors." *New York Times*, January 27, 1976. Last accessed March 12, 2020. https://www.nytimes.

com/1976/01/27/archives/milltown-basketball-or-life-in-the-minors-life-in-the-minor-league.html.

Morrison, Dave. "EBA." nasljerseys.com. Last accessed February 29, 2020. https://www.nasljerseys.com/EBA/EBA.htm.

New York Post. "LIU Legend White Dies; Point-Shaving Kept Him from NBA." August 12, 2011. Last accessed March 14, 2020. https://nypost.com/2011/08/12/liu-legend-white-dies-point-shaving-kept-him-from-nba/.

Plain Speaker (Hazleton, PA), April–December 1946.

Pluto, Terry. *Loose Balls: The Short, Wild Life of the American Basketball Association.* New York: Fireside, 1990.

Pro Basketball Encyclopedia. "A Complete History of Pro Basketball: The Early Years." Last accessed February 29, 2020. https://probasketballencyclopedia.com/.

Raykie, Jim. "Julius McCoy Gave Life to All That Is Farrell Basketball: An Editor's Notes." PAHoops.org. April 4, 2008. Last accessed February 16, 2020. http://pahoops.org/julius_mccoy_gave_life_to_all.htm.

Reinhard, Paul. "Red Helped Jets with Some Players and His Friendship: He Provided Several Future Knicks and Helped the EBL Franchise as Well." *Morning Call* (Allentown, PA), November 15, 1998. Last accessed February 16, 2020. https://www.mcall.com/news/mc-xpm-1998-11-15-3225456-story.html.

Rosen, Charles. *Have Jump Shot Will Travel.* New York: Ballantine Books, 1975.

Rosen, Charley. *Crazy Basketball: A Life In and Out of Bounds.* Lincoln: University of Nebraska Press, 2011.

——. *Scandals of '51: How the Gamblers Almost Killed College Basketball.* New York: Seven Stories, 1999.

——. *The Wizard of Odds: How Jack Molinas Almost Destroyed the Game of Basketball.* New York: Seven Stories, 2001.

Rosenstein, Jay. "Dick Bavetta: Supervisor of Officials." In *Eastern Basketball Association 1977–1978 Official Guide*, edited by Howard M. Balzer, 1977.

Rushin, Steve. "This Zebra Turned Dodger Blue." *Sports Illustrated*, October 22, 1990.

SJU Athletics. "Bob McNeill." Last accessed February 5, 2020. https://sjuhawks.com/sports/ath/roster/bob-mcneill/2413.

Scranton Apollos. *Official Program.* 1970/71.

Scranton Miners. *Official Programs.* 1963–1968.

Thomas, Ron. *They Cleared the Lane: The NBA's Black Pioneers.* Lincoln: University of Nebraska Press, 2002.

Vecsey, George. "A Fallen Star of the City Game." *New York Times*, May 6, 2008. Last accessed February 6, 2020. https://www.nytimes.com/2008/05/06/sports/ncaabasketball/06vecsey.html.

Vecsey, Peter. "Combustible Star Battled NBA Legends, Reputation." *New York Post*, January 11, 2009. Last accessed March 11, 2020. https://nypost.com/2009/01/11/combustible-star-battled-nba-legends-reputation/.

——. "Had Warm Heart Hidden Within." *New York Post*, January 18, 2009. Last accessed March 11, 2020. https://nypost.com/2009/01/18/had-warm-heart-hidden-within/.

Waters, Mike. "Story Time with Jim Boeheim: Riding down I-81, Playing Pro Basketball for $100 a Night." Syracuse.com. 2016. Updated 2019. Last accessed February 4, 2020. https://www.syracuse.com/orangebasketball/2016/11/story_time_with_jim_boeheim_riding_down_i-81_playing_pro_basketball_for_100_a_ni.html.

Wikipedia. S.v. "Scranton Miners." Last modified January 8, 2020. Last accessed February 10, 2020. https://en.wikipedia.org/wiki/Scranton_Miners.

INDEX

Figures in the photospread are noted with italicized letters.

contracts, 108; on Sunbury High
School gym, 93; top scorer, 123
Burian, Evan, 147

Cackovic, Joe "Cacky," 13
Camden Bullets, xii, *C, H, I,* 61
Caravan, Jean-Pierre, 110
Carnesecca, Lou, 107; Hall of Famer, 21
Carr, M. L., 111–12
CBA. *See* Continental Basketball
Association
CCNY. *See* City College of New York
Chamberlain, Wilt "Wilt the Stilt," 22
Chanecka, Bill, *A,* 13, 15
Chanecka, Steve, *A,* 13
Chaney, John "Chick," 19, 58–59, 92,
162; on Clifton, 30; on EPBL gyms,
93; on fans, 91, 97; on Finn, 72, 73;
on Gaines, 68; on Green, B., 69; Hall
of Famer, 58, 137, 163; on Hill, C.,
33; on Johnson, 69; on Landa, 73,
88; on Lear, 53; on McCoy, Julius,
55; on NBA scouting limitations, 38;
on New York players, 43; on pay, 40,
86; on race, 28, 29, 34, 38, 96, 156;
Temple University and, 163; on travel
to games, 85
Chicago Herald American (newspaper),
24
Chicago Zephyrs, 6
Choice, Wally, vii, 31–32, 49, 53–54,
163; single-game record of, 129
Citizens' Voice (newspaper), 147
City College of New York (CCNY),
16–17, 18
Clifton, Nat "Sweetwater," 30
community support, 5, 10, 100; all-black
teams enjoying, 25, 28; for Eastern
League, 91–92; economics of, 95; low
attendance and, 98, 99
Continental Basketball Association
(CBA) (1978–2009), xii, 8, 15, 51,

72, 158; collapsible rims and, 154;
Drucker and, 151, 164; EPBL and,
51, 152, 153; league expansion, 153;
league rules of, 152; origin of, 148
Cornwall, Richie, xv, *N,* 124–25, 156,
157, 163; on ABA raiding, 105;
on Bavetta, 141; on Bruns and
DeAngelis, 126; on Crawford, J., 141;
on Daughtry, 125; on EPBL, 106,
113; on Johnson, E., 129; on Landa,
137; on McCoy, Jim, 108; on McCoy,
Julius, 55; on Novak, 169; on Pawlak,
120; on racism, 97; on Sunbury High
School gym, 92–93
Craig, Earl "Chick," *A, L,* 9, 134, 135–
36, 164
Crawford, Freddie, 44, 48, 49, 101, 165
Crawford, Joe "Joey," 72, 85, 109, 140,
143, 164
Crawford, John, 60
Crawford, Shag, 140
Crazy Basketball (Rosen), 58, 61–62,
68, 69
Criss, Charlie, 78, 85–86, 111, 128–29,
164
Cruse, Wayne, 109
"cup of coffee" salary joke, 86
CYC. *See* Scranton Catholic Youth
Center

Daily Item (newspaper), 93
Dallas Chaparrals, 102
Daughtry, Mack, 125, 126
Dayton Rens, first all-black basketball
team in organized professional
basketball, 25
DeAngelis, Billy, 126, 127
Denver Rockets, 103
Detroit Pistons, 3
discrimination. *See* racial discrimination
Donohue, Ed, 147, 148
"double-dipping," 3

ABOUT THE AUTHORS

Syl Sobel and **Jay Rosenstein**, both originally from Scranton, Pennsylvania, have been close friends for nearly 60 years. They were seven years old when their dads first took them to watch the Scranton Miners of the Eastern Professional Basketball League play in the 1962/63 season, and that led to their lifelong fascination with the league and its players. Syl and Jay continued to follow the same path as they went to college together, became professional writers in Washington, DC, and in 2017 teamed up to coauthor this book.

Syl is an author, attorney, journalist, and former senior government executive. He has written several children's books on U.S. government and history, including titles on the U.S. Constitution, the Bill of Rights, and presidential elections, and has spoken at the National Archives, on C-SPAN and NPR, and at schools, book fairs, bookstores, and libraries. Syl is also an award-winning high school sports reporter for the *Town Courier* in Gaithersburg, Maryland, and has had op-eds published in several newspapers including the *Baltimore Sun*. He is a graduate of Georgetown University and the University of Wisconsin Law School, and is active in alumni programs for both institutions.

Jay is a writer and editor, mostly about banking and consumer finances. He started in 1977 as a reporter for the daily financial newspaper *American Banker* for 12 years, primarily covering Congress, federal agencies, and consumer issues. For more than 30 years, Jay was a senior writer-editor for the Federal Deposit Insurance Corporation (FDIC), where his accomplishments included creating, writing, and editing a financial newsletter for consumers for 25 years. He also is a graduate of Georgetown University.